The CHILD *and* The REPUBLIC

The CHILD *and* The REPUBLIC

THE DAWN OF MODERN AMERICAN CHILD NURTURE

By Bernard Wishy

Philadelphia
UNIVERSITY of PENNSYLVANIA PRESS

Library of Congress Catalogue Card Number: 67-26223

Second Printing, 1968

PRINTED IN THE UNITED STATES OF AMERICA
7543

For Julia

WHO
MAY HAVE
PROFITED FROM IT

Preface

ALMOST two centuries of debate about child nurture have preceded today's preoccupation with child psychology and education. Ever since the Enlightenment in the mid-eighteenth century, philosophers and psychologists have been developing "modern views" on the nature of childhood and child development. Of course, writings about these matters go back to ancient times but it was the Enlightenment that set forth the ideas and intellectual tone that eventually came to be called "modern".[1]

A humane curiosity began to temper moralistic certainty about the child and notions of children's depravity gave way to assumptions of their essential innocence, or at least moral flexibility. The concrete experiences and observable emotional responses of the young were emphasized to the gradual derogation of preaching abstract and intellectualized maxims to them, and practical activity rather than formalistic learning became recommended norms in the child's earliest education. By now such ideas have become accepted canons of child-rearing theory, but they spread slowly at first and came fully into their own only recently.

The names of John Locke (1632-1704) and Jean Jacques Rousseau (1712-78) are pre-eminent among the writers who established this new appreciation of childhood and a workable realism about the child's intellectual and emotional development. Since their time, these goals have been sought both for the child's happiness, and as marks of the parents' liberation from ignorance, superstition, and injustice.

The search has not always been marked by intellectual accuracy, moral wisdom, or freedom from its own dogma and orthodoxy. However, despite error and equivocation, being "modern" about the child has consistently involved two conflicting themes: vindicating the claims of the child against tradition and authority, while at the same time trying to find rational sanctions for limits on his freedom. The conflict between these is still fresh today. It spreads to jungle, desert, and steppe as the hopes and possibilities of the Western Enlightenment reach throughout the world. Today, like yesterday, the debate about the child takes forms so varied and complex that they challenge classification, let alone accurate and literate analysis. But wherever a new

[1] Philippe Ariès, *Centuries of Childhood* (New York, 1952) dates the emergence of the essential theory of the modern family—bound by love rather than authority—at about 1700.

child welfare center or school system is set up in Africa or Asia, the myriad of questions is as familiar—and ideological passion as intense—as ever.

Child nurture has undoubtedly aroused so much debate and enthusiasm because it relates to essential creeds of modern enlightened men: the ability of reason to analyze the world and the power of ideas in creating any desirable mutation of human nature. The child's nurture is one important key to a more controlled and rational future and, presumably, parents with the right kind of ideas will assure him the best possible nurture.

Today's interest in the child is, however, not merely theoretical or ideological, for as the creeds of modernity have spread from the intelligentsia into society at large, they have stirred deep desires. Our world moves very swiftly and immeasurably raises the stakes in the game of life. It nurses both an enormous hunger for power and, at the same time, an extraordinary conscience about doing enough for mankind. Today we are as sick from the burdens of bad conscience as we are from being gorged with power. In no aspect of our lives is this double burden carried more directly and painfully than in respect to our children. We seem to believe that little we do today for the child will be judged right by the world tomorrow; thus emotional investment in the children becomes increasingly expensive. A successful and virtuous child repays us for our own failures and fulfills vicariously our own hopes and ideals. The child who somehow "fails" is the worst judgment on us, but succeed or fail, the child imposes a great weight of guilt and anxiety on the modern, idea-conscious parent. It is a burden that even the most loving parent at times secretly resents and whose effects probably cause more problems with his children than errors in toilet training or sex instruction. However innocent we may be born, we end, in our own eyes, as guilty parents. The modern world has taught us new ways to use the child for our own fulfillment but it has also left us dissatisfied about whatever we have done for him. Together, therefore, parental wishes and prejudices as well as enlightened ideas have made every child a test of the worthiness of our passports as modern human beings.

This sensitivity has nurtured an American conceit that no one has done as much or thought as much about children as we have in this century. Freud's and Dewey's works seem to have convinced the enlightened of how little insight and care was given to child nurture before our time. This has helped obscure a vital earlier part of the history of modern nurture movements which this volume will disclose. Although unremembered, a torrent of popular debate about the child and child nurture preceded, by several generations, John Dewey's *School and Society* (1899) and Freud's *Interpretation of Dreams* (1899). While not denigrating the weighty, even revolutionary, changes in nurture ideas since those classics were published, this study will show how deeply the beliefs in "realism" and "experience" in raising the child had already penetrated before then—but among respectable moralists, rather than heretics such as Freud and Dewey. In fact, the story displays a familiar paradox in intellectual history: how notions adopted originally for certain moral purposes become associated eventually with ideals that would have dismayed the champions of those original purposes.

I ought to say clearly that this is not essentially a history of *expertise* on the child, for, first of all, such *expertise* in any degree only appeared as the nineteenth century ended. The great bulk of the literature that concerns us was written for the intelligent lay public, so we have to deal largely with forgotten popularizers rather than with the ideas of famous professional psychologists and philosophers. I have supplemented my work on both would-be and qualified "experts" with an analysis of well-known children's stories of their time. I have concentrated largely on religious ideals and moral indoctrination rather than on practical details and techniques of daily physical care—a strategy encouraged by the fact that principal interests of the period were moral and religious and because several earlier studies seem to me to have covered adequately the detailed history of feeding, clothing, and cleaning the child.

I want also to indicate the reasons for my deliberate decision to exclude or do little with other possible "approaches" to this work that, legitimate in themselves, would have expanded its scope beyond my interests and sense of possible proportions. I have paid minimal attention to "social and economic background" for two reasons: properly treated, such work has to be far more detailed and precise than we usually find it in the history of ideas. Writers often invoke broad cultural changes such as "industrialization" or "urban growth" as explanations for an individual's ideals without documenting how any general change specifically affected the life and work of the authors cited. To provide "background" properly for the large and varied numbers of writers I have studied would have given the volume a much different design than I had in mind.

The same arguments seem to me to hold for not dealing at any length with the so-called "kinship of reform," or the higher gossip, about the personal and intellectual relations among the writers we study. Grant, again, the possibility of "influence," but how demonstrate it or account for the failure of other equally good friends or relatives to take up the same issues or even to rise at all to any "burning question" of their day?

Another scholarly style whose limited attractiveness for me deserves some explanation is cross-cultural study. There is no doubt that there was an international movement for the reform of child nurture throughout the nineteenth century. I am not claiming uniqueness for the variegated American branch of this movement, although there were unique aspects in it, particularly in the emphasis given to republican virtues and the American forms of evangelical Protestantism. However, that a broad general movement happened almost everywhere does not clarify its particulars or undermine their significance anywhere.

In sum, this work does not do everything that might be done or cover questions that might interest others. Nevertheless, it is, I believe, a needed contribution to the study of the iconography of the American child, at home, in school, and at prayer, in a period which we have too long mistakenly assumed to have been relatively barren or hopelessly antediluvian in the attention it gave to child care.

The inevitable question about the span of years implied in my use of the word "the child" must be answered by relying again on the conceptions of the nineteenth century. The word was used loosely to cover the years from infancy to what we now call early adolescence. The many intermediate stages of growth and the sub-cultures subsequently defined by students of the child and advertising campaigns were only beginning to be articulated about 1900. They have consequently very little claim on the scholar working earlier than in that part of the century. Even when differentiation by age appears, the character desired for the child at any age was so constant that there is little substance to set off one stage of growth from another.

I should like to acknowledge my indebtedness to Dr. Gunnar Dybwad, former director of the Child Study Association of America, for giving me unrestricted access to the archives of the Society and to Warren Susman of Rutgers University and Barbara Welter of Hunter College for their criticisms.

B. W.

CONTENTS

ILLUSTRATIONS

I
THE CHILD REDEEMABLE
(1830-1860)

1

The Stakes of the Game

WHEN George Santayana characterized America as a remarkably idealistic civilization, he meant to emphasize two tendencies of national character: a prodigious fantasy about bending society and nature to man's power, and an equally impressive wish to live by the highest moral principles. Critics of America are usually quick to observe its willful and ambitious qualities, but have been less sensitive to the strength of its recurrent idealism. For a supposedly practical and anti-reflective people, Americans have been extraordinarily concerned with their moral and religious justifications to themselves and the world. The ideals spawned by Puritanism and the Declaration of Independence have pledged us to awesome tasks of human redemption and require us never to take the world as we find it. But in America even men who are relatively unaware of these formal ideals become consciously hostile to inherited tradition and cloying circumstance. The instability of American life induced by the tempting chances as well as noble ideals of the day, has been terribly taxing to our energy and patience, our wills as well as our consciences.

Life in America has thus taken a dreadful toll for its high rewards. We have been constantly preoccupied with the conflict between our desires and our ideals, between our intense coarser ambitions and our utopian aspirations. We have ceaselessly worried about national failings, are forever "taking stock," defining the "national purpose," and setting "goals for Americans." What other nation insists that the lowliest life in the most distant community anywhere in the world is never too small to be ignored by conscience, to be tested by some ideal standard of fitness or justice, and, if found deficient, put right? This cry for redeeming every life—most deeply, perhaps, for abolishing death itself—has become so strong that our sense of national failure almost matches our pride of achievement. We have suffered in almost every generation in our history from both the boasts of confidence men and the cries of critics about the tears of one child or the wretched state of all mankind. Battered at by "experts" and bewailed by moralists, the American child caught in this debate has become an incarnation of the will and conscience of every generation of parents. The history of the changing notions of the child and of the debates about child-rearing is, therefore, an important chapter in our ceaseless national inquiry about what is wrong with America and what America needs in order to be put right.

The great public nurture debate began in America well over a century ago, when a call went out to citizens to save their children from the sins and errors undermining the republic. As the reform campaigns of the 1830's went, the informal movement for children's rights was a minor enthusiasm, even more variegated and occasional than many of the more familiar crusades of the time. For more than a century, European and American reformers—descending principally from Rousseau or Locke—had been demanding new respect and special care for children. By 1830 a sizeable body of speculative literature about the problems of child care had slowly accumulated but, thereafter, the older and isolated intellectual concerns about the proper raising of children merged into a flood of popular criticism. Powerful evangelical religious energies of a millenialist or perfectionist strain, as well as phrenological or utilitarian ideals, were used to justify various schemes of saving the child and to satisfy the growing demand for reliable advice about his nurture. By 1835 an American writer on "childhood education" already complained about "the current of popular treatises on this subject that almost daily issues from the press."[1] Such popular "currents" are seldom, if ever, primarily inspired by disinterested intellectual curiosity. Writers of the era were not reluctant to confess that their concern about American children was generally related to feelings of anxiety and *malaise* about the nation during the 1830's. As Marvin Meyers' analysis of the conservative and nostalgic features of the era in *The Jacksonian Persuasion* suggests, Americans were stirred to take a deeper interest in reforms of every

[1] John Hall, *On The Education of Children,* 2nd ed. (Hartford, 1836), p. 41.

sort because they sensed such strong challenges to their assumptions about the ideals of the republic. Fifty years after the Revolution, national life was viewed as betraying the heritage of an Olympian age. Nascent industrialism, the pretensions of oligarchy, aristocracy, or democracy, and the taxing instabilities of a highly competitive, expanding society made men fear for the distant ideals of 1776. A once-simple, virtuous American character seemed dirtied or tempted by a host of vices and every evidence of vice represented a failure to live up to the mission in republican morals and manners established by God and the Founding Fathers of 1776. A superabundance of sermons, tracts, pamphlets, and speeches circulating from a fast-growing press called citizens to all sorts of holy work, which was given emphasis by yet another cycle of American "new-light" evangelicals. Men could thus be as concerned about the badly fed child as others were with the enchained slave, and equally convinced that this blow or that, once struck for "the right," would usher in the millenium which America had long awaited.

Whatever their goals, in trying to understand the sources of national anxiety and in planning a way back to the paths of the moral life, Americans were, on the whole, ill-served intellectually by the popular moralists of the age of Jackson. What have, by now, become familiar limitations on democratic enlightenment were already discernible in the young republic. Certainly, Tocqueville's remarks at the time about a democratic culture's preference for easy and encouraging ideas rather than difficult and demanding ones had much justice and pertinence when applied to the students of the child.

The popular moralists of Jackson's age whom we shall be discussing wrote for a general public whose intelligence, education, and sophistication were probably not much greater than theirs. Influenced as many of these writers were by a simple, intense, Christian piety, their advice about the child tended to be abstract and hortatory. Choices seemed simple: the child was God's or Satan's, a glory to the republic or its shame and corruption. Argument was predominantly apocalyptic and eschatological and even if, occasionally, it was more temperate, no sizeable body of facts about the physical and emotional development of children existed to help control any argument.

Although he might start by posing issues in the most stark or grandiose terms the pamphleteer or tract writer of Jackson's time was often what we now call a middlebrow moralist. He was only superficially skillful in interpreting ideas for the general public. More familiarly, he was likely to rush into print with an assuring meliorism against those deep conflicts and contradictions of American life which bred an anxiety he and his audience were unable to bear. Sensitive to the repeated antagonisms in American life between self and society, man and nature, past and present, father and son, man and God, a few critics of the time were skeptical about American optimism and ironic about reformers and panaceas. They eschewed the easy optimism of the programmatic radical as well as the conservative's confidence in the wisdom of history and tradition. But men like Hawthorne and Melville and, at times, Thoreau were less read or less heeded than the dozens of more popular middlebrow moralists whose names will be cited in this book. If Americans combined a fierce will for success and an impetuous Christian conscience that right prevail, their nurture writers did not face the possibility that such conflicting traits were likely to lead to personal or national disaster. Instead, they outlined idealistic reconciliations of will and conscience. In the debates about the child before the Civil War, Americans began to argue that harmony between child and society, success and Godliness were possible without sacrificing either the child's individuality or the adult's fixed principles. A realistic assessment of the deeper perplexities of child-rearing in Jacksonian America is, therefore, extremely difficult to establish directly from Jacksonian nurture and nursery literature. Fortunately, we have one brilliant exposition of the basic issues with which we shall be concerned in another source, Hawthorne's masterpiece *The Scarlet Letter* (1850).

Although this novel is not, of course, primarily about children, the fate of the one child in the story does illustrate some of the classic problems of child and parents in American culture. *The Scarlet Letter* is set in Massachusetts Bay in the seventeenth century, but from his opening chapter on the old Salem Customs' House of 1840, Hawthorne makes it clear that the novel is a judgment on Jacksonian America and an assessment of continuous tendencies of American character. As D. H. Lawrence and other critics have emphasized, Hawthorne presents Hester Prynne, the heroine, as no curiosity from Puritan times but as embodying a recurrent American radical conception of the self. Her will in her fullest fantasy rejects all moral and social limits. It was a will even more characteristic perhaps of Americans in Hawthorne's own time than in the Puritan commonwealth that still lived under the restraints of Christian idealism and Calvinist law. Like Ahab in Melville's *Moby Dick,* however, Hester in her madness is essentially what Richard Chase has called a false Prometheus. Her story is a warning to those who, like Hester's Puritan persecutors, invoke the absolute claims of society and of moral law. But it is also, we must remember, a rejoinder to those who, like Hester, spinning the American fantasy of perfect freedom, dream of an individualism transcending the limits of law and custom, albeit usually in the name of the highest ideals of humanity.

Some critics have seen in Hester traces of Anne Hutchinson or of Margaret Fuller, that extraordinary "emancipated woman" of the circle of Transcendentalists, and still others of Hawthorne's relatives. Whoever her actual correspondent is, Hester is characterized for us primarily by the "A" she is condemned to wear. By the laws of God and man she is an adulteress. Beyond that, she is also "America," the new world casting off the rules of the old, or the Antinomian, pure to her own spirit while rebelling against the letter of the Calvinist law. Like other Antinomians, however, her reading of her spirit may bring her to speak the right words, reason and human redemption, but her adultery and her later fantasy of self-justification suggest moral and social chaos, wrath and will without justice.

Hester is no mean person but a spirited and gifted woman, frustrated by an unhappy marriage to a worthy man, Roger Chillingworth. She cannot love Chillingworth, however, and she takes as a lover Arthur Dimmesdale, the pious, brilliant, but weak, Puritan minister. Aware of the demands his calling places on him and unwilling to force him to confess his complicity in their crime, Hester has borne and raised his child, Pearl, in stubborn silence. Condemned by the Puritan elders for refusing to let the law punish her partner in sin, Hester must wear the scarlet "A" as a sign to all of her adultery. Although Hawthorne detests the cruelty and hypocrisy of the Puritans, we must remember that he does accept their judgment of the adultery and is not, as some liberal critics have implied, completely "on her side" against society and law.

At first Hester accepts her punishment, convinced like a good Calvinist that her conduct proves she is damned. In her earthly life she will be an outcast and a warning to others. But by isolating her from society the Puritans set loose Hester's extraordinary will and speculative temperament. As time passes Hester, alone and introverted, begins to reject the idea that her adultery was a sin and thinks of it instead as a legitimate revolt against society and its repressive customs and religion. The weary, pitiful woman becomes the proud,

Satanic rebel. She richly embroiders the letter "A" on her dress and it glows ever more brilliantly. Hester dreams of turning her humiliation into liberation and of leading all the world's oppressed to a new freedom that will supersede age-old laws and beliefs that have crushed or limited humanity. Ominously, however, the more the letter glows the more Hester loses her femininity. She puts up her lustrous hair under a cap, for example, rejects womanliness and reconciliation with her fate and instead serves a destructive, abstract, and masculine rationality.

Her child, Pearl, already carries the burdens of illegitimacy and the price of not knowing a father: she has no place in society and is as much an outcast as is her mother. She is potentially wild female energy because no man in the household gives law and sexual balance or contrast and thus keeps her from misjudging or ruining her life. Pearl is described with words suggesting that a dangerous exotic freedom is active in her. She gets on poorly with other children and seems to have more in common with the forest animals than with human beings. She thus reminds us of the excesses of her mother's passion but, as Hester's rebellion grows, she becomes an embodiment of her mother's dream of denying the judgment of society by escape to a "new life." Pearl is the future, the American fantasy of will fulfilled through the child.

The bolder Hester grows, the stranger Pearl acts. Her mother thinks that Pearl will be the new human nature, unfrustrated and perfect. But the child's fate is not completely sealed. Her energy need not be corrupted if her parents will decide to open to her the balance between will and conscience that neither of the competing absolutisms, Puritan society and Hester's dream, will bring. Pearl seems to be only the ideal future to the rebellious Hester; yet, inescapably, she is the past; she is her parent's guilt and their frustration; she is their failure, not so much in loving, as in refusing to accept the moral and social consequences of their love.

Pearl's fate hangs in the balance when Hester, at the height of her fantasy, plots her escape. Meeting Dimmesdale in the forest, Hester lets her luxurious hair fall loose and she tears and throws away the scarlet letter from her dress. Suddenly, her womanliness, so long repressed, seems to return with overwhelming force, but Hawthorne suggests that Hester's resurgent sexuality should not mislead us, much as we may sympathize with it, for the successful escape of the lovers would cut Pearl off from all hope of achieving a tolerable humanity. Happiness is possible for her only if her father accepts her publicly, if Hester and Dimmesdale honestly face their responsibilities for their love and open to Pearl the life in society that as a conscienceless, fatherless child or as a creature of her mother's absolute will she cannot possess.

In the forest scene, the transfigured Hester calls to Pearl to come to her and her father, to lawless freedom. The child refuses and points instead to the scarlet letter lying on the ground, like the present and future pointing to the past. Her gesture implies that her tie to her mother and father must be, however painful, first through their guilty love, not through the freedom that seems promised by Hester's loosened hair. In escaping, Hester would not redeem Pearl but would have to sacrifice the child's recognition of her and all control over the child. The price of the full freedom of the child is really that it no longer recognizes or knows even its parents, and rejects their law and love. Hester can make Pearl the free self she dreams of only if she is willing to lose all the mother's claims and rewards. Hester's rebellion for absolute freedom thus brings more rebellion, not the dreamed-of triumph of a morally perfect individual capable of love. Hester agrees, however, to put up her hair and to pin on the scarlet letter; Pearl runs quickly to her. Seemingly, she knows and will accept Hester as a humanly imperfect creature as long as she and Dimmesdale agree to become openly her parents within the limits set by society.

When their plans for escape are frustrated and the dying Dimmesdale publicly acknowledges Pearl and Hester, recompense and reconciliation become possible. The weight of the sin becomes eventually only a vague memory of the past. As the years pass, both Hester and Pearl eventually find peace and happiness.

Hester, Dimmesdale, and Pearl at first seem caught in a hopeless situation. The inflexible laws of a society over-intense about conscience, or over-certain about what conscience permits the law to do, conflict with the equally absolute claims of Hester's will. Pearl is in danger of becoming, like the possessed Hester and Chillingworth, a monster whose will serves an abstract vision of life called justice—but meaning vengeance. Such independent wills can exist only by alienating, destroying, or unsexing everyone standing in their way. Without parents, Pearl is potentially without pity, without sympathy, without love—deficiencies that actually kill the maddened rationalist, Chillingworth.

Yet an overly censorious society, in justifying Hester's passionless marriage and frustrating her powerful nature, has led Hester to adultery with a man whom she misjudges as lover and mate, for Dimmesdale is not her equal sexually or morally. Paradoxically, the absolute moral law of Puritan society also leads to its antithesis, the untamed Pearl. It makes possible the duplicity and hypocrisy of Dimmesdale and places high-spirited individuals like the young Hester at the mercy of all that is repressive and vindictive in the community.

In its concern with Pearl and her parents, *The Scarlet Letter* exposes two of the strongest conflicting tendencies of American life: the claims of the free individual, deeply impatient with all limits on life, and the contrary demands of an inherited, inflexible code of Christian character and republican social faith. In Hawthorne's time, the growing American aspiration for perfecting child nurture can be viewed as the obsession of a highly ambitious people, repeatedly tempted by the dream that human will can triumph over every mundane limit yet equally hopeful of making the child the incarnation of a moral law and Christian orthodoxy that are, in fact, inimical to any such fantasy.

The nurture reformers who wished this extraordinary double destiny for the child thus started out with an impossible task. They wanted to guarantee that every child could be as just in resisting the world as he was powerful in commanding it, or, put another way, that a child could be raised without sacrificing Christian faith and morality, wordly success, and the happiness implied in the American ideals of 1776.

Given such awesome *hubris* that the conquest of nature, the transformation of man's history, and the creation of a pure Christian-republican paradise lay within America's grasp, the very way in which moralists defined the alternatives for the child doubled anxiety about his possibilities and deepened frustration with his failures. However monumental the job of creating an American both fully powerful in will and perfectly pure in spirit, the nurture writers of the time called American parents to just such work with their children.

2

The Will and the Word

ONE of the first obstacles that the pious had to overcome in devising a new nurture was the long-standing Calvinist belief that the infant child was already intrinsically limited by a heritage of sin and that sin expressed itself most vividly in excess or pride of will. A playful, energetic, pleasure-loving child would surely be on the road to perdition. Unless some way around the still-strong doctrine of infant depravity could be found all meliorist aspirations might be fruitless.

If there was any constant in the religious outlook of evangelical American Protestants in the early nineteenth century, it was their awareness of the conflict between man's will to escape his innate sinfulness and his desire to enjoy the lures of the world. For two centuries, American Calvinists had battled to reconcile human will and God's Word, to save the world from Satan and to make it fit for saints, albeit increasingly worldly ones. Although expressed differently by proliferating Protestant sects and constantly reformulated by theologians and ministers, by 1800 Calvinist views of the child and of a human destiny under God's stern judgment had demonstrated remarkable staying power.

This heritage included Jonathan Edwards' famous words that unrepentant children were "young vipers and infinitely more hateful than vipers."[1] Another view was they were "not too little to die . . . not too

[1] Jonathan Edwards, *Works,* 4 vols. (New York, 1881), Vol. 3, p. 340.

little to go to hell."[2] Isaac Watts' well-known songs had told how the busy little bee improved each shining hour but also sounded many sad notes such as:

That I am led to see
I can do nothing well
And whither shall a sinner flee
To save himself from Hell.[3]

Despite the prestige and weight we now give the more congenial "modern" ideas of the American Enlightenment, in the very hour of the triumph of American independence in the 1780's there had begun a remarkable resurgence of Calvinist views and religious conservatism that Dixon Ryan Fox called "The Protestant Counter-Reformation."[4] So pervasive was the influence of this evangelical neo-orthodoxy that the small and slow accumulation of Enlightenment notions of the child as inherently pure and deserving happiness came under attack. For the next half-century, orthodox ministers would also invoke the convenient spectre of Jacobinism to strengthen their demands for strict discipline and early religious training of the child.[5] The future of the nation as well as the child's soul were said to be in danger. The "atheism, licentiousness, and intemperance," of the time, the growing lax discipline in the home, and overemphasis of intellect were all seen as causes of the French Revolution and the maladies of the American republic. As late as the 1840's, Americans were warned that they could avoid the triumphs of atheism and radicalism only by "seizing upon the infant mind and training it up under moral and religious influence."[6]

Despite this attack, orthodoxy in the early nineteenth century had to give way on the Calvinist view of the child even in its Arminian version that a soul could choose to be saved. If unrepentant children were damned, then a campaign to teach them and their parents the discipline necessary to transform or save their souls and American society was essential. The new Christian nurture worked out in the three generations after 1800 necessarily had to pay increasing atttention to en-

[2] James Janeway, *A Token for Children,* quoted in Sanford Fleming, *Children and Puritanism* (New Haven, 1933), p. 66.

[3] Isaac Watts, *Divine and Moral Songs for the Use of Children* (first published in 1715; reprinted: London, 1848), p. 29.

[4] Dixon Ryan Fox, "The Protestant Counter-Reformation," *New York History XVI* (January, 1935).

[5] Merle Curti, *Social Ideas of American Educators* (New York, 1935), pp. 55-60, a discussion of the menace of the French revolution.

[6] Mr. Welch, "Our Country," *Parent's Magazine,* 2 (October, 1841), p. 25.

vironment and the claims of the world, as well as the demands of God. The result was to brighten the view of the world and to temper the Word of God as they affected ideas of the nature and destiny of the child.

The need for a new basis for Christian nurture seemed confirmed after 1830 by the ceaseless complaints of both American and foreign observers about spoiled, corrupted, and unruly children. Although remarking that "the independence and fearlessness of children were a perpetual charm to my eyes,"[7] even Harriet Martineau, the English radical writer, and no Calvinist, found in both America and England a threat of improper routine to the child's character. Satirically she asked:

> How can a boy, not predisposed that way, hope to grow up consumptive, if some pains are not taken with him in his childhood? . . . we must use artifice to circumvent the stomach. In one hour we must come upon it unexpectedly with a dose of fruit and sugar; then, if the regular dinner have been taken, astonish the digestion, while at work upon it, with the appearance of an extra lump of cake and presently some gooseberries . . . Let us subdue mere nature at her first start, and make her civilized in her beginnings. Let us wipe the rosetint out of the child's cheek, in good hope that the man will not be able to recover it. White, yellow and purple—let us make them to be his future tricolor.[8]

The disorder of the American home was also attacked by Fredrika Bremer who claimed that the American mother showed her love for her children "principally by spoiling them."[9] Mary Duncan's fears brought the question of unruly children back to the theme of excess liberty when she remarked ". . . to see sensible people smile with secret admiration at the spirited exhibition of rebellious will on the part of their offspring excites in an English mind, a sense of lurking danger."[10]

---

[7] Harriet Martineau, *Society in America,* 2 Vols. (New York, 1837), Volume II, p. 271.

[8] Harriet Martineau, "How to Make Home Unhealthy," *Harper's Monthly* I (October, 1850), p. 602.

[9] Fredrika Bremer, *The Homes of the New World,* 2 Vols. (New York, 1853), Volume II, p. 455.

[10] Cited in Arthur W. Calhoun, *A Social History of the American Family,* 3 Vols. (Cleveland, 1913), Volume I, p. 55. There is an excellent full survey of foreign opinion in G. R. Clay, "Children of the Young Republic," *American Heritage XI* (April, 1960), pp. 46-53.

American critics ratified these opinions and launched their own wide attack in the 1830's on the corruptions in the home. One great enemy was "Fashion," for it had spoiled the child and "distorted" his nature. Everywhere the proper republican simplicity and Christian order had been violated. The child was wrongly nursed,[11] wretchedly fed, overdressed, too closely supervised while playing, and overtaxed intellectually. At its worst "Fashion" had made the child into an artificial, spoiled, or excessively grave household pet or live doll.[12] In the best homes, therefore, one found the very vices besetting the nation, a growing love of luxury, indulgence of the senses, affected manners, and unbecoming worldliness. *Godey's Lady's Book* satirized the use of oversophisticated standards and social frills in the education of a young girl:

"I HAVE BROUGHT MY DAUGHTER TO YOU TO BE TAUGHT EVERYTHING."

Dear Madam, I've called for the purpose
  Of placing my daughter at school;
She's only thirteen, I assure you,
  And remarkably easy to rule.
I'd have her learn painting and music,
  Gymnastics and dancing, pray do,
Philosophy, grammar and logic,
  You'll teach her to read, of course, too.

I wish her to learn every study
  Mathematics are down on my plan,
But of figures she scarce has an inkling
  Pray instruct her in those, if you can.
I'd have her taught Spanish and Latin,
  Including the language of France;
Never mind her very bad English,
  Teach her that when you find a good chance.

[11] On daily routine see Monica Kiefer, *American Children Through Their Books* (Philadelphia, 1948); Anne L. Kuhn, *The Mother's Role in Childhood Education* (New Haven, 1947); Elizabeth Wilson, *The Hygienic Care and Management of the Child in the American Family Prior to 1860,* unpublished MS thesis (Duke University, Durham, N. C., 1940); and Robert Sunley, "Early Nineteenth Century American Literature on Child Rearing" in Margaret Mead and Martha Wolfenstein, *Childhood in Contemporary Culture* (Chicago, 1955).

[12] Typical of numerous attacks was the most interesting book by Mrs. A. J. Graves, *Woman in America* (New York, 1843), pp. 94-95; also "A Supplement to a Plea for Children," *Ladies' Magazine* 8 (Nov., 1835), pp. 597-604; Matthew Carey, "Fashion," *Ibid.,* 7 (April, 1834), pp. 148-52; W. A. Alcott, *The Young Mother* (Boston, 1836), pp. 236-37.

What the Well-Dressed Child Would Wear (1840's)

On the harp she must be proficient
  And play the guitar pretty soon,
And sing the last opera music
  Even though she can't turn a right tune.
You must see that her manners are finished,
  That she moves with a Hebe-like grace;
For, though she is lame and one-sided,
  That's nothing to do with the case.

Now to you I resign this young jewel,
  And my words I would have you obey;
In six months return her, dear Madam,
  Shining bright as an unclouded day.
She's no aptness, I grant you for learning
  And her memory oft seems to halt;
But remember, if she's not accomplished
  It will certainly be your fault.[13]

A "modern catechism adapted to the times" that appeared in a workingman's newspaper also suggests that the spoiled or corrupted child was not exclusively a problem in America's comfortable or fashionable homes:

> Who is the oldest man? The lad of fourteen who struts and swaggers and smokes his cigar and drinks rum, treads on the toes of his grandfather, swears at his mother and sister and vows that he will run away and leave "the old man" if he will not let him have more cash.[14]

A generation later, when the number of neglected children had increased, especially because of immigration, the Children's Aid Society was created in New York City. The cause of immorality among poor children was traced to an improper environment; but the slum child was to be saved less for his own sake than because he was a potential threat to society. As Charles Loring Brace of the Society warned, "This dangerous class has not yet begun to show itself as it will in eight or ten years, when these boys and girls are matured. . . . They will have the same rights as ourselves. . . . They will poison society."[15]

Confronted initially by, on the one hand, a Calvinist demand for

---

[13] *Godey's Lady's Book* XLVI (May, 1853), p. 457.

[14] *The Man,* March 21, 1834, p. 104.

[15] Charles L. Brace, *First Annual Report of the Children's Aid Society* (New York, 1854), pp. 12-13. The contrast between the emphasis on saving the child in the "nice" family for his own sake and those in the slums for the sake of society became even more apparent after 1890; see below pp. 131-35.

supreme efforts by parents to convert their children and, on the other, increasing reports of conditions in the best homes and "streets" that corrupted character or enlarged the effects of innate depravity, the course of the nurture "expert" was clear. He had to suggest a way to develop the child's will that would do justice to American ideals of individualism while, at the same time, saving that freed and expanded will from indulging in the corruptions plaguing American society.

It would be tempting to think that the new ideals of the child that emerged by about 1860 were the result of a clear-cut battle of liberal idealists against religious obscurantists and authoritarians, the heirs of Calvin fleeing the field and the banners of reason and enlightenment, suddenly freshened, flying ever higher. But this would distort the facts. Instead, finding themselves called upon to prepare the American child for a destiny of liberty, worldly success, and, at the same time, obedience to God, Americans created gradually within the context of respectable Protestant traditions a new status for the child. Popular Christian moralists steadily drifted toward a primary concern with the flexible character of the child, always within the context of religion, however less precise its creed and less demanding its duties.[16] Parents began to be urged "not to press too closely upon children such non-essential points as form the distinguishing particularities of the various sects of Christians."[17] Jacob Abbott's widely read book of Christian instruction, *The Young Christian,* professed to explain Christian duty "as based on those great fundamental principles of faith, in which all evangelical Christians concur."[18]

Respectable theologians by 1830 were already questioning directly the strict Calvinist notion of infant depravity and the accompanying stress on conversion as the sole aim of religious education.[19] Lyman Beecher for example, had contended that Calvin's belief in election or predestination did not imply that any particular child was certainly damned. Although infants were liable for punishment, this did not *necessarily* mean that they would be sent to Hell. Furthermore, no

[16] E. S. Bates, *An American Faith* (New York, 1940), Chaps. 22, 28 on general changes in American religion in this period.

[17] Louisa Hoare, *Hints for the Improvement of Early Education and Nursery Discipline* (Salem, 1826), p. 151.

[18] Jacob Abbott, *The Young Christian* (New York, 1851), p. x.

[19] "Dissertation on the Sinfulness of Infants" (a letter), *The Christian Disciple and Theological Review* 2 (Aug., 1814), pp. 245-50; "Familiar Considerations Addressed to Parents on the Duty of Requiring Their Children to Study the Holy Scriptures," *Ibid.,* 5 (May, June, 1817), pp. 140-44, 168-70.

exact knowledge of who was saved or damned could be gained since this was known only to God.[20]

Ideas like Beecher's began to spread against an opposition slow to give way but without any practical alternative doctrine to meet the claim that the materialism and radicalism of the age had brought about a crisis in child-rearing that was endangering the child's soul and the ideals of the nation.

It is perhaps risky to speculate about the hostility to children that the belief in infant damnation and strict training seems to express. In part, of course, the belief that the unrepentant child's soul was lost had genuine claims as an idea, even on loving parents, but it is likely that the responsibilities and expense of many unwanted children created or intensified hostile feelings towards offspring. Whatever inspired them, the orthodox were reluctant to dampen the fires of Hell awaiting the child who had not started the arduous training needed for saving the soul or testing whether God had chosen a soul to be saved.

The methods of conversion originally had been devised for adults but they were particularly effective with immature and easily impressed children.[21] Orthodox training emphasized the sense of sin, fervent and constant prayer, deeply stirred feelings, strict parental care, authority and restraint. Infants were "by nature sinners, and show us that . . . the wicked are estranged from the womb, they go astray as soon as they be born, speaking lies."[22] The presses of the American Tract Society helped advance the cause of orthodoxy and poured out countless editions of long tales for children about the lives of fallen boys and girls whose only hope lay in throwing themselves onto an omnipotent God's stern mercy.[23] "Memorials" of a Christian life like the *Memoir*

[20] Lyman Beecher, "Future Punishment of Infants not a Doctrine of Calvinism." *Spirit of the Pilgrims* I (Jan., 1828) pp. 42-52. This debate was carried forward until the early twentieth century. Behind arguments like Beecher's and much of the general Protestant views of the child in this period lay the pervasive influence of the Scottish or "Common Sense" philosophers. The still-underappreciated weight of this group of eighteenth-century thinkers with American writers on morals, religion and education can begin to be assessed from H. W. Schneider, *A History of American Philosophy* (New York, 1946). Among men's "faculties," the Scottish writers listed a God-given moral faculty or conscience which men perceived by common sense awareness of their failings.

[21] The actions of children at a revival are noted in "Dr. Porter's Letters," *Spirit of the Pilgrims* 5 (May, 1829) p. 261.

[22] Rev. Allan Hyde, *Essay on the State of Infants* (New York, 1830).

[23] One estimate of the number of pieces of literature printed by the A.T.S. reaches more than 68 million tracts. See E. D. Branch, *The Sentimental Years* (New York, 1934), p. 323.

of Henry Obookiah[24] and the early volumes of *The Youth's Companion* stressed the wicked temptations of life, the heavenly rewards for the pious, and the punishments for the unconverted. These books and magazines made use of a theme that Harriet Beecher Stowe was later to make famous in the character of little Eva, one that Dickens and many others also used, the child who was too pious and good to be kept alive by mere human love and understanding. The kingdom of children like Nathan Dickerman[25] was not of this world. Given what seems to have been the very high rate of infant mortality, such books were built on sad facts too familiar in many families.

It has been said that "the deep conviction of sin, the intense emotional reaction which invariably accompanied 'satisfactory' conversion, the lack of any real assurance of acceptance with God, were all entirely out of harmony with child nature"[26] and that the danger of "atrophy of the religious sense" under a puritanical system of nurture makes it "hardly possible to exaggerate the harm that may be done by premature emphasis on the darker side of religious experience."[27] As true as we may now believe these claims to be, the consciousness and weight of sin must in part have been relieved by conversion itself; furthermore the certainty of principle and sense of purposefulness in a Calvinist milieu could have also established compensations for the child beyond any harmful effects of his training for conversion.

Even if the orthodox parent denied the appealing idea that no one could know with certainty what child was damned, all children, nevertheless, had to be tested for capacity for conversion and watched for signs that they were saved. Paradoxically, perhaps unintentionally, the need to test the child for the ability to transcend the world implied the actual importance of decisions about and concern with the very world the pious denigrated.

A more vexing paradox for parents was the limit to which piety and other-worldliness could be permitted to go. Little Nathan or little Eva might be so lacking in a will for life that parents could anticipate none of the usual flattering achievements of more worldly American children. This failure might not trouble those who strictly

[24] American Tract Society, *Memoir of Henry Obookiah* (New York, circa 1835).

[25] G. D. Abbott, "Memoir of Nathan Dickerman" in J. S. C. Abbott, *The Child at Home* (New York, 1833). These two Abbotts were the conservative brothers of the more famous and more liberal Jacob Abbott.

[26] Fleming, *Children and Puritanism*, p. 188.

[27] W. B. Selbie, *The Psychology of Religion* (Oxford, 1936), p. 182.

preferred piety to success. But with even pious parents probably deeply involved in a daily competitive and materialistic life, a second entirely different model and code of behavior was inevitably set for the child, one that urged him not to brake his will but to use it to the utmost on the world. The inner conflict in young Americans between the will for righteousness and will for success must have been extraordinary and without recognizing its strong sources in American home life, we probably cannot fully understand the complex play of moralism and materialism in American culture well into this century.

Pious parents who were troubled at reconciling the will and the Word in their offspring had available an impressive, if diverse, array of "experts." Among the more conservative writers on the child was the President of Amherst College, Dr. Heman Humphrey. His book, *Domestic Education* (1840) was a catalog of errors for the day and a guide for perplexed mothers and fathers. In his narrower moments, fretting over a growing laxness of parental discipline, he called for absolute rule by the father, accountable to "no earthly power." Fathers should try to control the child diligently by the age of four months and were to continue until the child was twenty-one. Any child who remained at home after reaching that age was still to be treated as a minor.[28] Yet, although he believed parents could not add anything to the nature God had given the child at birth, in *testing* the child's capacity for conversion even Humphrey rejected excessively demanding methods. He advised a gradual increase of demands on the child and not merely to make him pious.[29] Possibly a "moral instinct," properly nurtured, could provide a sense of right and wrong at two years.[30] Mothers should thus become interested in ethical as well as religious development for they could make the infant "rise and shine and sing" or "sink and wail."[31] But the most probable effects of the "enlightened" training demanded by Dr. Humphrey are suggested by one child's response to his mother's reassurance that Heaven was like an eternal Sabbath, "Oh dear, what have I done that I should go where there is an eternal Sabbath."[32]

Humphrey's advice was given in broad abstract statements, and tended to be largely sermons. The simplest matters of daily routine were inseparable from cosmic concerns about the child's nature and

[28] Heman Humphrey, *Domestic Education* (Amherst, 1840), pp. 25, 37, 41.
[29] *Ibid.*, p. 183.
[30] *Ibid.*, p. 78.
[31] *Ibid.*, p. 71.
[32] *The Christian Examiner* 2 (July, 1825), p. 291.

destiny in Humphrey as well as the other chief "school" of writers on the child who gradually gained ground after 1830. These moralists were often connected with the humanitarian and perfectionist movements of the time and although overwhelmingly professing Christians, were less suspicious of the will, more confident about the world, and less literal about the Word than Humphrey.

Such nationally read writers as Mrs. Lydia Sigourney or Jacob Abbott usually had a Congregational or Presbyterian background. They refused to go as far toward religious heterodoxy as William Ellery Channing or Bronson Alcott but, nevertheless, they gradually abandoned much of the orthodoxy of their fathers. Jacob Abbott, for example, father of Lyman Abbott, was a young instructor at Amherst College when Dr. Humphrey was President. He left that center of orthodoxy, perhaps under the influence of his wife who was a close friend of Mary Peabody Mann. He then moved continuously toward more "modern" beliefs. By 1840, the year of Humphrey's *Domestic Education,* Abbott and others were writing optimistically in the spirit of that early appeal made in the *Christian Disciple,* that the future of children was less a question of their intrinsic nature but "necessarily dependent on their parents and others around them."[33] Mrs. Sigourney and others depicted heaven not as a demanding "eternal Sabbath" but the home of God the kind father and friend, the source of mercy, love, and goodness. Natural and worldly joys were also slowly coming to have a legitimate place in the life of the pious child. By 1832 evangelical literature was using new themes typified by such rhymes as:

I love to join the joyful play
To sport beside the shady pool
To watch my kite soar far away
But more I love the Sunday School.

For there I meet my teacher's smile
And read and learn the Holy Book
And, oh my heart doth feel the while
That God is pleased on us to look.[34]

Mrs. Sigourney's classic, *Letters to Mothers,*[35] stated that the central problem of nurture was "how the harp might be so tuned as

[33] "On the Influence of Education as a Source of Error," *Christian Disciple* (Sept., 1814), p. 264.

[34] American Sunday School Union, *Hymn Book* (Philadelphia, 1832), p. 14.

[35] Lydia H. Sigourney, *Letters to Mothers* (Hartford, 1838).

not to injure its tender and intricate harmony." She wrote about the "waxen state of children's minds," of the body as "a miniature temple," and of love, proper environment, and pure example as the final determinants of the child's glorious destiny. Every trace made on "the soul of the babe . . . will stand forth at the judgement." The mother with her "mission so sacred" should learn to "feel with Rousseau" that "the greatest respect is due to children" for the "ark of the nation" as well as the child's soul rested in her hands.[36] Without love, simplicity, and delicacy, without the mother recognizing that the child was simply incapable of conforming to adult standards, the child's potentialities as "an erring being" could triumph and ruin him.[37]

Complete rejection of the belief in depravity or innate tendencies to wickedness did not appear generally in popular literature until just before the Civil War. There were, however, harbingers of a future fuller liberalism in the work of early Pestalozzians like Joseph Neef and William Maclure,[38] the Temple school and the writings of Bronson Alcott,[39] the translation of Mme. de Saussure's *Progressive Education,*[40] Almira Phelps' *Observations,*[41] and the advanced ideas expressed in Woodbridge's *American Annals of Education and Instruction,*[42] but these were isolated and occasional items, not a steady literature.

Horace Bushnell's *Views of Christian Nurture* (1847) is often taken as a high-water mark of these ideas. But Bushnell had solid roots in the orthodox tradition. This important student of the newer pedagogy of his day did not abandon the notion of depravity. He be-

[36] Mrs. Sigourney, "Duty of Mothers," *Southern Literary Messenger IV* (Dec., 1838), p. 786, recommended by the editors to Southern female schools as a repository "of all that is pure in sentiment and sublime in morals."

[37] Sigourney, *Letters to Mothers,* p. 36.

[38] W. S. Monroe, *The History of the Pestalozzian Movement in the United States* (Syracuse, 1907). Unlike his predecessor Rousseau, Pestalozzi was essentially anti-egalitarian. See Curti, *Social Ideas of American Educators,* p. 99. This, and the usual claims that Rousseau caused the French Revolution, may have made him more acceptable than Rousseau himself.

[39] Bronson Alcott, *Observations on the Principles and Methods of Infant Instruction* (Boston, 1830); also his several articles in the *American Annals of Education and Instruction.* Elizabeth Peabody, who was to found the first American kindergarten in 1867, has left her favorable reflections on Alcott's school in *Record of a School* (Boston, 1836).

[40] Mme. de Saussure, *Progressive Education* (Boston, 1835); translated by the famous American teachers and educational reformers, Emma Willard and Almira Phelps.

[41] *Observations Upon an Infant During its First Year* by a Mother in Saussure, *op. cit.,* pp. 323-48.

[42] This magazine first appeared in January, 1826, as the *American Journal of Education.* In 1831 the name was changed to the *American Annals of Education and Instruction.*

lieved that a proper nurture could counteract mere "tendencies" to depravity if nurture began while wickedness was weakest—that is, in infancy. "Weeding out" sin was the new metaphor. Religious and moral instruction was to be slow and patient and the traditional orthodox notions of flailing at evil and rapid readying for conversion were deprecated. In general, authoritarian and repressive techniques were to yield to a more wholesome guided growth of the child's moral life. Kindness, love, and tender care by a mother who exemplified all the virtues would adequately prepare the child for salvation and a life of moral responsibility.[43]

By the 1850's, the decade after the publication of Bushnell's study, public objections to ideas that the child's potentialities were limited by innate sinfulness became more open and frequent. By 1850 the Swedenborgians were trumpeting that "at birth the child is . . . but an incipient receptacle of that thought and affection, the proper protection, nourishment, and exercise of which are capable of forming it into an angel; and this, indeed, is the ultimate design of its being."[44] Other writers, calling for recognition of the "rights of the children," expressed fears "that we are sacrilegiously interfering with the ways of Providence in . . . arbitrarily mapping out the travels of an immortal soul" which is "a law unto itself" deserving appropriate freedom in the nursery.[45] And another protest against improper treatment of the child warned that "a baby is a complex and wonderful work of art" and "whoever produces a pale and diseased child should at once be put to death without talk; the evidence is complete."[46]

By 1850, there existed a less hostile and less repressive attitude towards the child's will; yet what image of character and faith, what "truth" was this new freedom to serve? The Calvinist had warned that, even in the noblest claims for freedom, there lurked the vices of worldly pride and materialistic egotism. Would the "diseases" that had plagued the republic as it built its power and wealth thus be strengthened rather than diminished by a new freedom for the child? Or could some way be found to prepare the now redeemable child to serve more noble causes?

---

[43] Horace Bushnell, *Views of Christian Nurture* (Hartford, 1847). See Fleming *Children and Puritanism,* pp. 195-207 on Bushnell's importance.

[44] "Errors of Education," *The New Jerusalem* 23 (August, 1850), p. 296.

[45] Paul Siogvolk, "The Rights of Children," *Knickerbocker* 39 (June, 1852), pp. 489-90.

[46] "About Babies," *Putnam's Monthly* 6 (August, 1855), p. 143.

3

The Sweeter Service of God and Morality

ONLY powerful wishes and evasive abstractions could have nurtured the illusion that the Jacksonian writers on the child were successfully reconciling a new freedom with traditional morality. They themselves thought they had provided a way to do justice both to the individuality of the child and their inherited religious and moral ideals. The basis for a new, seemingly more benign nurture had been prepared by modifying the notion of infant depravity. Yet, though the methods of child-rearing were to be more loving and tender, the character desired for the child was not significantly different from long-established conceptions of the ideal American, Christian citizen.

What is most striking in the years of debate before and after Bushnell is that however much writers differed on methods of nurture, they all urged that every available means be used in the struggle to save the child and the country for "the truth." However radical in their theology and their view of man, even the Swedenborgians agreed that "all true freedom is acquired only through a knowledge of and obedience to truth."[1]

Both traditionalist and enlightened nurture reformers envisioned the child as a potential servant of some universal moral imperative, usually an absolute moral law, ordained by God, in whose light he was to make the vital decisions determining both his religious destiny and his worldly happiness. All writers agreed that the child was to

[1] "Religious Education of Children," *The New Jerusalem* 9 (April, 1836), p. 267.

be trained consciously and carefully to develop well-defined ideals and the will to live by them. The child himself was advised to

> Commence life with the fixed determination ever to give your voice and your influence in behalf of that which is right. Be ever ready to make sacrifices of your own rights and your own convenience to promote the welfare of the community. Let the principle be planted in the depths of your heart that you are not to live for yourself alone, but for influence in the world, for usefulness. Be ever ready to deny yourself in all needful ways, that you may make others happy, and that when you die, you may feel that you have not lived in vain.[2]

The key figures in this indoctrination were, obviously, the parents. But were parents themselves ready for their new, awesome responsibilities? Freud's classic observations a half-century later about relations between parents and children have strengthened the belief that the supremacy of the father in giving the child clear laws and strong ideals was a fact of momentous importance in the lives of nineteenth-century children. Malinowski's convenient "Freudian" sketch of the child's early years in such patriarchal families can serve here as a scale against which the new American methods of nurture might be tested.

> . . . in our society, irrespective of nationality or social class, the father still enjoys the patriarchal status. He is the head of the family and the relevant link in the lineage, and he is also the economic provider. As an absolute ruler of the family, he is liable to become a tyrant, in which case frictions of all sorts arise between him and his wife and children. The details of these depend greatly on the social milieu. In the wealthy classes of Western civilization, the child is well separated from his father by all sorts of nursery arrangements. Although constantly with the nurse, the child is usually attended to and controlled by the mother, who, in such cases, almost invariably takes the dominant place in the child's affections. The father, on the other hand, is seldom brought within the child's horizon, and then only as an onlooker and stranger, before whom the children have to behave themselves, show off and perform. He is the source of authority, the origin of punishment, and therefore becomes a bogey. Usually the result is a mixture; he is the perfect being for whose benefit everything has to be done;

[2] Rev. John S. C. Abbott, *The School Boy* (Boston, 1839), p. 175.

> and, at the same time, he is the 'ogre' whom the child has to fear and for whose comfort as the child soon realizes, the household is arranged. The loving and sympathetic father will easily assume the former role of a demi-god. The pompous, wooden, or tactless one will soon earn the suspicion and even hate of the nursery. In relation to the father, the mother becomes an intermediary who is sometimes ready to denounce the child to the higher authority, but who at the same time can intercede against punishment.[3]

In America a century ago, most fathers were away during the long day, and the mother inevitably had great influence in inculcating the child's religious and moral ideals. The father undoubtedly had formal and ultimate authority, but how often could it have been used?

In city homes, for six days a week, fathers went to work earlier and returned later than we do, so the child was closer to his mother or, in wealthier homes, to a "domestic" or nurse. There were no telephones to secure the father's advice about the child and the threat to "call father at the office" could not be made. Children in more comfortable homes went to sleep earlier and often ate by themselves. All this kept the father in the background in the early life of the child. Sunday was father's only day at home. It may well be, however, that this full day at home and his few hours at home during the week, made the tangible power and prestige of the near-stranger on those occasions more impressive to the child than a more familiar, easy-going supervision at home during the entire week.

In American farm families, we should expect to find greater closeness of children and both parents than in city homes. With farmhouses being presumably cruder and simpler dwellings than city homes, the nearness to the mother and father and to older children and animals increased the opportunity to observe or overhear the most intimate scenes. Often children in farm houses and in poorer homes everywhere slept with each other and in many cases, especially during infancy, even with the parents for warmth and convenience of suckling. Even on a farm, however, the youngest children did not work too near the father and, like some urban children, they may have seen him only at meals. But he could easily be recalled from the fields or the child might be sent out to him. Whatever the ultimate or formal supremacy of the father, in most homes during the child's earliest years the mother was

[3] Bronislaw Malinowski, *Sex and Repression in Savage Society* (New York, 1959), p. 36.

Waiting for Father

probably far more important than the father as an immediate source of ideals and as a disciplinarian.

The reappraisal of American family life that took place after 1830 brought two conclusions about authority in all types of homes: both fathers and mothers were failing the republic but fathers were neglecting their duties, while mothers were merely inexpert at theirs. The principal emphasis of the nurture writers was for *mothers* to reform themselves in order to accept new and portentous responsibilities. In fact, if we accept and generalize the judgment of one student of New England society in this period, the American mother was now to take the lead in most matters connected with the child.[4]

In the new tide of "domestic reform," the American mother was placed under the sternest pressure. She was to give up wealth, frivolity, and "fashion," to conquer weaknesses and ailments, sloth and insensitivity, and acquire a discipline and knowledge preparing her for a great calling. The reason was simple enough: the mother was the obvious source of everything that would save or damn the child; the historical and spiritual destiny of America lay in her hands. Her own states of mind, body, and soul were of utmost importance. The "new mother's" place was in the home as the most powerful figure in affecting American society. What were "women's rights" compared with such influence?[5]

By 1840 maternal associations in rural New England were becoming active to help rededication to the holy, healthy hearth.[6] The *Parent's Magazine* and *Mother's Assistant* printed frequent glowing reports from the members of seemingly orthodox mother's associations who were convincing their children of their sinfulness and bringing them, through prayer and meditation, to "public profession of their faith in Christ."[7] Stories were printed about a poor convict, fated for prison since youth because his mother had not had the help of a maternal association.[8]

---

[4] Kuhn, *op. cit.*

[5] *Ibid.*, pp. 28-35.

[6] See the descriptive article, "Maternal Associations," *Parent's Magazine* 1 (May, 1841), pp. 205-07. A. C. Curtis, "Extracts from the Report of the New Hampshire Maternal Association, *Parent's Magazine* 1 (Dec., 1840), pp. 81-85.

[7] Wayland Maternal Association, "To the Editors of the Parent's Magazine," *Parent's Magazine* 1 (Feb., 1841), pp. 129-30.

[8] "An Interview with Convicts in the New Hampshire State Prison," *Parent's Magazine* 1 (June, 1841), pp. 234-38.

The general complaint was that mothers were ill-informed and badly disciplined, insufficiently attentive to the right ideas, and often too affected by the same moral ills that threatened the child. The usual explanation for "paternal neglect"[9] was less that father was corrupt but that he was ". . . eager in the pursuit of business, toils early and late, and finds no time to fulfill his duties to his children."[10] While at home fathers were also said to be too impatient. They rushed through meals and scarcely ever spoke to the family. Guides like Theodore Dwight's *The Father's Book,* which catalogued these failings in detail, urged fathers to reassume their responsibilities.[11]

Foreign observers sensed deep differences between American and European fathers and mothers. Fredrika Bremer claimed that woman was "the center and lawgiver in the home of the New World."[12] Tocqueville, attributing women's status to the uncertainty of life in American society and the special training in independence and vigor thus demanded for daughters, stated that nowhere had he seen women "occupying a loftier position."[13] These observations strengthen the impression that whether the goal of the new nurture was religious conversion, the good citizen, the moral man, or the honest entrepreneur, the new mother as "lawgiver" was to lead the way with the father necessarily only her auxiliary. But new rules needed new methods.

In brief, mothers were increasingly to abandon formal precept, preaching, and formalistic methods and to rely on the direct experience of the child as the most effective source of education. We are by now so accustomed to linking such empirical methods, classically alleged to derive from Locke or Rousseau, with progressive or permissive moral ideals that it may be difficult to recall that, historically, the notion that men's ideas and character are derived solely from their experience has not logically committed parents or teachers to any particular ethical or religious outlook.[14] In America, as shown most

---

[9] Rev. J. S. C. Abbott, "Paternal Neglect," *Parent's Magazine* 2 (March, 1842), pp. 147-49; see also President Wayland, "Paternal Duty," *Mother's Assistant* 12 (May, 1848), p. 110; Rev. A. B. Muzzey, *The Fireside* (Boston, 1856), pp. 217-18.

[10] "The Father," *Parent's Magazine* 2 (April, 1842), p. 174.

[11] Theodore Dwight, *The Father's Book* (Springfield, 1834).

[12] Fredrika Bremer, *America of the Fifties* (New York, 1924), p. 72.

[13] Alexis de Tocqueville, *Democracy in America.* 2 Vols. (New York, 1945), Volume II, pp. 192-214.

[14] The startling diversity in the use of Locke's ideas is sketched in Merle Curti's "The Great Mr. Locke, America's Philosopher, 1783-1861" in *Probing Our Past* (New York, 1955). See also p. 18, fn. 20 *supra.*

notably by Jonathan Edwards (1703-1758), it was possible also to use Lockeian theories of knowledge for instilling a religiously orthodox view of life.[15]

In 1831 Dr. Thomas Gallaudet published his book on the religious training of children. Its purpose was to teach mothers how to instill traditional religious ideals with new empirical techniques.[16] Gallaudet is most famous in American history as a teacher of the deaf but he was also one of the leading, yet religiously orthodox, empiricists about childhood education in his day.

Gallaudet preached early Bible reading and the strict Sabbath and used florid prose to emphasize their importance for the child. The mother was to inculcate such ideals, however, by exploiting the child's sense-impressions of daily life and by leading him gradually from facts he had observed or knew to accept happily God's word and service. Rather than overwhelm the child's mind or overtax "tender emotions" with rote learning of ideas beyond his comprehension, the mother was to watch for the child's every expression of curiosity that could be turned to good account, and she was not to exceed the child's demonstrated ability at any stage of development. The dark notes possible in such empiricism are best shown by the notion that the child could better appreciate the glory of the immortality of the soul by having him touch a dead child's cheek and hands—"I touched his cheek and it was cold as ice. I took hold of his little hand but it was stiff."[17]

In every aspect of strategies like Gallaudet's, the mother's own piety and prayers were of foremost importance, since example rather than precept had greatest effect on the child. Her godliness alone, Theodore Dwight emphasized, would convince the child that she "not only spoke of God's goodness, but daily meditated on Him . . ."[18]

Gallaudet and men like him[19] asked the mother to take the lead in family religious observances, especially to begin religious training very early.[20] *Parent's Magazine* suggested that attending family worship at the age of nine months would give the infant a valuable incipient sense of the importance of religious life.[21] Another writer rhapsodically

---

[15] Perry Miller, *Jonathan Edwards* (New York, 1949).

[16] Rev. T. H. Gallaudet, *The Child's Book on the Soul* (Hartford, 1831).

[17] *Ibid.*, p. 49.

[18] Theodore Dwight, *The Father's Book*, p. 50.

[19] *Ibid.*

[20] "The Time to Begin," *Parent's Magazine* 1 (March, 1841), pp. 162-63.

[21] Almira Phelps, "A Mother's Journal," *Ladies' Magazine* 8 (Aug., 1835), pp. 441-449.

described a year-old child's behavior during grace at meals.[22] Constant themes were early church-going,[23] the beauty of death, religious instruction appealing to a child's growing imagination and active senses,[24] and solemn Sabbaths with a full program of observances.[25] If conversion was the goal, the mother was to maintain what would have amounted to a constant camp-meeting atmosphere in the home, ceaselessly working on the child with prayer and plea towards adoption "into the family of Christ."[26]

Commenting, however, on such overzealous early religious and moral instruction, Mrs. Sigourney asked, "Why commence a warfare against nature almost as soon as she develops herself?"[27] On the contrary, no demand should be made on a child that he was incapable of fulfilling and whatever demands the child himself made, either in fractiousness or ebullience, were to be understood as an outburst of natural energy that should be gently corrected or, if possible, tolerated rather than being ruthlessly suppressed. The mother was to help the child fulfill natural needs and to encourage his capacity for a moral life. If the child developed badly it was a reflection on the parents who had "ruined the seed," rather than proof of the child's essential depravity.

What was wanted was still obedience—to parents, to elders, to conscience, to God, to "just government,"[28] to the Golden Rule—without breaking the will, "a mighty power given by God, too sacred to be tampered with, too noble to be broken, a power to be directed, not destroyed."[29] In T. S. Arthur's words, "The real object of education is to give children resources that will endure as long as life endures, habits that will ameliorate, not destroy; occupations that will render sickness tolerable, solitude pleasant, age venerable, life more dignified and useful, and death less terrible."[30]

---

[22] "Family Scenes No. 2," *Parent's Magazine* 2 (Dec., 1841), p. 81.

[23] Muzzey, *The Fireside,* p. 179.

[24] R. C. Waterston, *Thoughts on Moral and Spiritual Culture* (Boston, 1842); "Leading Children to God," *Mother's Assistant* (Dec., 1846), pp. 141-42.

[25] Humphrey, *Domestic Education,* Chap. XI.

[26] "The Conversion of my Little Daughter," *Mother's Assistant* 4 (April, 1844), pp. 74-81.

[27] Sigourney, *op. cit.,* p. 42.

[28] *Ibid.,* p. 15. "The degree of her diligence in preparing her children to be good subjects of a just government, will be the true measure of her patriotism."

[29] "Miss Martineau on Education," *op. cit.,* p. 609.

[30] T. S. Arthur, *The Mother's Rule* (Philadelphia, 1856), p. 298.

According to Mrs. Sigourney, the wise mother had deliberately to inculcate desirable virtues because the child, left to itself, would err.[31] She was to be constantly at the center of the child's life and take the most minute interest in all his activities, trying especially to save the infant from "all those conflicts of feeling which must continue, as long as it remains doubtful who is to be its guide."[32] Ultimately, the child was to be prepared for "submission to the Eternal Father," described however, as a God of love who sanctified the mother's teaching of the softer moral virtues through explanation, example, and above all the creation of good habits. The "utterly helpless" child could thus learn "strength of character," "self-government," industriousness, and especially benevolence. "As reason develops . . . parental authority naturally relaxes its vigilance."[33]

Environment, persuasion, example, precept, carefully formed habits were thus stressed by both the orthodox and the more benign nurture enthusiasts. Using gentle methods adjusted to the child's capacities, the mother was never to lose sight of her "mission," her clear moral purposes, and the need for firmness and dignity.[34] Minute prescriptions inculcated for the child's salvation were gradually abandoned in favor of general principles of religious and moral life. Writers complained that closely drawn regulations could "destroy all that freedom and naturalness which, after all, constitute the greatest charm both in mind and manners and without which there is little scope for the varieties of individual character."[35] Spontaneity, joy, affection thus slowly moved to a higher status than singleminded piety and literal following of "the law." But those joyous qualities we would admire in the child today were not yet sanctioned fully for their own sake. We cannot escape the impression that the new realism in nurture was largely first envisioned as a more effective means of fulfilling the child's destiny of obedience to the laws of God and the rules of moral righteousness.

Harsh and minute prescriptions gave way to general, more benign principles of behavior because Americans could not anticipate that a closely drawn code of behavior appropriate to a traditionalist society,

---

[31] Sigourney, *op. cit.*, p. 36.

[32] *Ibid.*, p. 35.

[33] *Ibid.*, p. 36.

[34] Mrs. J. Bakewell, *The Mother's Practical Guide in the Early Training of Her Children*, pp. 130-131.

[35] "Young Ladies' Friend," *New York Review* 1 (Oct., 1837), p. 398.

would serve the child well in a fast-changing world. The call for more affectionate and tender care also suggested a way of winning the life-long love of offspring who in America had no need to remain indefinitely at home under the rule of a patriarch whose favor determined their chance in life. Both the generality and mildness of the new rules of nurture thus reflected the instability and unpredictability of American life, a culture in which everything in life was a problem and a gamble, a world in which men so radically opposed history and nature that the possible rewards of life put increasing stress on experiment, on resisting tradition and narrowly defined rules. Minute authoritarian codes were not so much right or wrong as they were useless. The detailed prescriptions of a traditionalist society were outmoded. With the fluidity of society and the sanctions for the freed will in America, as Tocqueville observed, ". . . the family in the Roman and aristocratic signification of the word, does not exist."[36]

Margaret Mead has suggested that this dissociation of present and future from the past required parents to "play the world by ear" and tended to make them "allies of infancy" rather than surrogates of a prestigious past.[37] With greater choice open to the child, with more possible roles to consider, more ways of life to choose from, many situations and difficulties were likely to arise far from home which could not be anticipated or provided for in advance. If, understandably, the first tendency of parents was to make the child in their own image and to tie him as closely as possible to ways of life and ideals with which they were familiar, adults might also remember how much in their own childhood the day's need and yesterday's commandment had conflicted. Every parent himself had probably departed far from the practices and ideals of his own home. At best could parents do more than give the child general principles and hope that these would provide him with the guidance he needed for an unknown future? And if mere man-made rules were weak, a supplementary sense of sin might force on offspring some recognition that in facing the temptations of life, God as well as his parents stood in judgment on him. However much the world might applaud or reward him for leaving the straight road of character and faith marked out by his parents, there was always divine recompense at the end to reckon with.

[36] Tocqueville, *op. cit.,* Vol. II, p. 192.
[37] Margaret Mead, *The School in American Culture* (Cambridge, 1951).

4

Food for Body and Spirit

WITH the child conceived as "a plot of ground in which weeds will spring up the more abundantly, the less good seed we sow in it,"[1] the need for specific advice to the gardeners became great. Increased knowledge, or what passed for knowledge, and a greater sense of the power and responsibility of the mother also intensified the desire for information and advice that the predecessors of Drs. Spock and Gesell helped to fulfill. In 1826, Dr. William Dewees of Philadelphia published the first edition of the most famous of the early American textbooks in pediatrics.[2] Its appearance was another indication of the extent to which the child's needs were being distinguished from those of adults. The range of advisers included doctors like Dewees and, later, Chavasse,[3] Andrew Combe and the phrenologist Fowler,[4] and the influential Mrs. Sarah Hale, editor of the *Ladies' Magazine* and later of *Godey's Lady's Book,* who took special interest in providing mothers with detailed rules on daily problems.[5]

---

[1] Mrs. J. Bakewell, *The Mother's Practical Guide,* p. 15.

[2] Monica Kiefer's study cites several earlier "catechisms of health" in the late eighteenth century in her chapter "Young Victims of Kitchen Physick."

[3] P. H. Chavasse, *Advice to Mothers on the Management of their Offspring during the periods of infancy, childhood, and youth* (New York, 1844).

[4] Andrew Combe, *A Treatise on the Physiological and Moral Management of Infancy,* 2nd ed. (Edinburgh, 1841), and also his articles: "To Mothers and Nurses," *Parent's Magazine* 1 (July, 1841), p. 245-46, "Frequency of Nursing," *Mother's Assistant* 3 (Jan., 1843), pp. 11-13. Also Orson S. Fowler, *Love and Parentage Applied to the Improvement of Offspring,* 40th ed. (New York, 1844).

[5] See "A Supplement to a Plea for Children," *Ladies' Magazine* 8 (November, 1835), pp. 597-604; "Childrens' Dresses" *Ibid.,* 6 (Oct., 1833), p. 463; "The Good Dinner," *Ibid.,* 6 (Jan., 1833), pp. 38-40.

The most striking characteristic of this varied group was their emphasis on the connection between daily tactics and moral strategy. Even physicians like Dewees and Dr. W. A. Alcott of Boston, cousin of Bronson Alcott and a voluminous writer on child and home, gave practical advice with constant doses of moral lessons.[6]

These writers suggested that their regimens really spelled out the "laws of nurture,"[7] and that these were important parts of the "laws of health."[8] This common phrase marked that intense American concern for health and health fads[9] before the Civil War, a concern which contrasted vividly with shocking living conditions, epidemics, fevers, and high infant and adult mortality rates.[10] One writer at the time warned that good health must be cultivated or "the American race fails."[11]

As that warning implied, the well-being of the body was seldom justified for its own sake. Doctors like Dewees and Alcott stressed the importance of the relation between physical health and soundness of moral character.[12] The phrenologists went so far in the same direction as to verge on materialistic explanations of character traits, but they vigorously denied this intention. The accepted motif was that proper care of the body was a way of strengthening the higher claims of the spirit.[13] By thus refusing to press their ideas about the physical nature of the brain to their logical conclusions, the phrenologists managed to

[6] William A. Alcott, *The Young Mother* (Boston, 1836), p. 207 and Appendix F; *The Young Wife* (Boston, 1837), p. 314. An outline of the knowledge necessary for mothers included "Paley's Theology" and numerous volumes on zoology, physiology, and natural history. On the moral emphasis of the phrenologists see George Combe, *The Constitution of Man* (Boston, 1838).

[7] The work of the phrenologists was obviously influential here, too. See O. S. Fowler, *Education and Self Improvement* (New York, 1844), p. 48.

[8] Catherine Beecher, *Suggestions Respecting Improvements in Education* (Hartford, 1829); William Alcott, *The Laws of Health* (Boston, 1857).

[9] A. F. Tyler, *Freedom's Ferment* (Minneapolis, 1944), pp. 440-42.

[10] R. H. Shryock "The Yellow Fever Epidemics" in D. Aaron, *America in Crisis* (New York, 1952), pp. 51-72.

[11] "The Murder of the Innocents," *Atlantic Monthly* 4 (Sept., 1859), p. 345.

[12] Fowler's very popular work, *Education and Self-Improvement* (NB p. 48), went into the relation between physical and spiritual nurture in ecstatic detail. The answers of the phrenologists to the charge that they were atheistic materialists as well as their general influence on popular notions of health and moral improvement, can be found in John D. Davies, *Phrenology, Fad and Science* (New Haven, 1955). In his list of works that parents had to read to cope with the problems of the child, Dr. Alcott suggested that Combe could be read without "the phrenological part," (Alcott, *The Young Wife,* p. 314); also Sarah J. Hale, "What Good will Phrenology do the Ladies?" *Ladies' Magazine* 5 (Oct., 1832), p. 474.

[13] On these matters Humphrey was also most enlightened. See *Domestic Education,* p. 61.

maintain the supremacy of man's "higher faculties" and "immortal destiny."

However evasive the basic premises, physical care and nurture of mind and soul now seemed inseparable. Proper care of the infant required that no relevant daily problem be left unexamined. Every change in the child's physical development was to be noticed and used to best advantage. As the home guidebooks, cookbooks, and lectures of the time began to take special notice of the child's peculiar physiology and psychology,[14] their writers became intensely interested in his clothing, feeding, play, and nursery conditions, and his physical relations with the family, his friends and even domestic help. However moralistic this intense interest in physical effects on character and the soul, it obviously stimulated the search for fact about the child's distinctive natural needs and errors of the day were ceaselessly catalogued.

Harriet Martineau represented a Spartan approach to daily faults. In line with her belief that physical improvement, like moral growth, depended on keeping environment and discipline simple and pure, she gave her American audience extensive advice on child care. Her article reprinted in America entitled "Herod in the Nineteenth Century,"[15] in effect summarized the themes of her famous book, *Household Education.*[16] She was aroused by the report of forty-thousand child deaths in England in a single year. Nearly half of these children were under five. As a first remedy for the situation she called for more nursing by mothers, and attacked the tendency away from breast feeding that women justified in the name of delicacy and fashion. After the child was weaned, milk was still to form an important part of the child's simple diet.[17] She urged that all sweets and rich, spicy adult foods be dropped from the child's fare.[18]

The wrong regimen would also be sure to include suckling whenever the child demanded it, active rocking producing giddiness, sudden weaning, crowded, unclean nurseries with poor ventilation, bare

[14] "Dr. Grigg's Lecture," *Ladies' Magazine* 4 (Nov., 1831), pp. 514-18. For the important "ideological" cookbooks, see especially Lydia M. Child, *American Frugal Housewife* (Boston, 1836) and Eliza Leslie, *Miss Leslie's Complete Cookery,* 38th ed. (Philadelphia, 1851).

[15] Harriet Martineau, "Herod in the Nineteenth Century," *Once A Week* 1 (Sept., 3, 1859), pp. 195-98.

[16] Martineau, *Household Education* (Philadelphia, 1849).

[17] Martineau, "Herod in the Nineteenth Century," *op. cit.,* p. 196.

[18] Cf. Fanny Fern, *Fresh Leaves* (New York, 1857), pp. 108-09. Humphrey, *op. cit.,* pp. 190-99.

legs in cold weather, strict decorum in the streets, and "a little gentle amble with a hoop" for severest exercise.[19]

Harriet Martineau's satires were in fact a catalog of generally proscribed practices of the day, for Dr. Combe, Dr. Alcott, George Ackerley, and Catherine Beecher[20] stressed the same themes. They were equally convinced that nursing followed nature's pattern,[21] and was thus essential. Milk from the breast might even supply the child with the mother's own moral virtues.[22] Mother's milk and simple diets after weaning were to be supplemented by stopping the constant use of medicines, laxatives, and drugs often cited as a growing menace to children.[23] One writer wailed that "Godfrey's Cordial has slain its thousands."[24] The forbidden list also included cake and fruits, pastry or "confectionary," coffee, tea, liquors, gravy, spices, preserves, even meat at times. The simplest foods and drinks were best: milk, clean cold water, wheat bread and vegetables.[25] Such "natural foods" were contrasted with "distorting" diets that the ignorant or fashionable mother gave to the child.[26]

---

[19] Harriet Martineau, "How to Make Home Unhealthy," *Harper's Monthly* 1 (Oct., 1850), p. 602, Cf. Sigourney, *Letters to Mothers,* p. 78; Alcott, *The Young Mother,* pp. 33-36.

[20] W. Alcott, *The Young Housekeeper,* 4th ed., (Boston, 1839), Chap. XIII; Catherine Beecher, *Letters to the People on Health and Happiness* (New York, 1855), a syllabus of the errors of the day; George Ackerley, *On the Management of Children* (New York, 1836).

[21] Andrew Combe, M. D., "Frequency of Nursing," *Mother's Assistant* 3 (Jan., 1843), pp. 11-13; "Hints to Young Mothers," *Ladies' Magazine* 7 (Feb., 1834), p. 52. On this and the related problems of effects of nursing on women and bottle feeding ("bringing up by hand") see what seems to have been a summary view in Alfred Donne, *Mothers and Infants, Nurses and Nursing* (Boston, 1859).

[22] Almira Phelps, "Remarks on the Education of Girls," *Godey's Lady's Book* 18 (June, 1839), p. 253. A detailed analysis of these and other nursery matters has been made by Elizabeth Wilson in her unpublished M. S. thesis, *The Hygienic Care And Management of the Child in the American Family Prior to 1860* (Duke University, Durham, N. C., 1940). Since both this study and Miss Kuhn's, previously cited, go into fuller detail on the matters I have restricted myself here to highlights.

[23] Catherine Beecher, *A Treatise on Domestic Economy,* rev. ed., (Boston, 1842), pp. 215-16; "Caution to Parents," *Parent's Magazine* 1 (May, 1841), pp. 203-05.

[24] T. Searle, *Companion to Seasons of Maternal Solicitude* (New York, 1834), p. 212.

[25] "Family Scenes No. 1," *Parent's Magazine* 2 (Sept., 1841), pp. 12-13. Alcott, *The Young Housekeeper,* Chap. XIII. Alcott was a crusader for vegetarianism and his views reflect this bias.

[26] Alcott, *The Young Wife,* pp. 173-74.

Faulty diets had stimulated all those worst moral tendencies of children that should be brought under control.[27] In short, cooking "as a means, indirectly, of forming human character" had "a bearing on the prospects of the individual, for eternity as well as time" and should "become a matter of consequence in the work of education."[28]

If the diet of the child was to be simplified for moral purposes, the freedom of his body was to be increased for similar reasons. Swaddling and overdressing in "caps, hats, bonnets, cravats, pelisses, frills, muffles, gloves, ribands, and other paraphernalia"[29] were all forbidden. More freedom was necessary if parents wanted strong bodies and moral growth.[30] Dr. Humphrey cited George Washington and Benjamin Franklin as symbols of what virtues the "right to creep" might produce in a child.[31] Martineau warned about excessive "pinning." The moral justification for simpler clothing was that fancy dress encouraged vanity, irresoluteness, and faith in expensive deceiving ornaments rather than in simplicity and directness of character. Fancy dress was, in short, false colors.[32]

Unrestricted exercise for the child out of doors was a corollary belief. Physical ebullience was declared a natural tendency in the child rather than a sign of wickedness.[33] Not only was physical exercise not dangerous, but it would help "harden"[34] the body against the effects of animality and prevent moral flabbiness and laziness. A growing excessive moral justification for play implicit in these new ideas was satirized by Moncure Conway. He complained that overdidactic writers too often conceived of play in the spirit of the man who said, "Now boys, I've brought you out here to enjoy yourselves,

[27] "Overfeeding of Children," *Ladies' Annual Register* (Boston, 1839), p. 69; Alcott, *The Young Mother,* p. 122.

[28] "Should Females be Employed in Cookery," *Ladies' Magazine* 7 (Nov., 1834), pp. 483-84.

[29] Dick, "The Clothing of Children," *The Family Magazine* 4 (1837), pp. 461-462. Alcott, *The Young Mother,* p. 49: "Management of Infants," *Parent's Magazine* 2 (Sept., 1841), pp. 3-4; Kiefer, *op. cit.,* pp. 183-85, a contrast of old and new clothing.

[30] "Physical Education of Women," *Ladies' Magazine* 4 (Jan., 1831), pp. 30-36; "Dresses for Infants," *Godey's Lady's Book* 40 (Feb., 1850), p. 142.

[31] Humphrey, *Domestic Education,* p. 63.

[32] "Boarding Schools," *Ladies' Magazine* 4 (April, 1831), p. 146; "From a Mother's Diary," *Ibid.,* 4 (June, 1831), p. 129.

[33] Alcott, *The Young Mother,* p. 238.

[34] The idea of "hardening" had been proposed by Locke. Simplicity and vigor rather than indulgence in daily routines would create "character" and thus resistance to temptation. "Hardening" was an attractive ideal for those convinced that a Spartan environment was the best influence on a child's character. See Humphrey, *Domestic Education,* Chap. VIII for a favorable view and Alcott, *The Young Mother,* p. 293 for a criticism.

BREAKFAST FOR A YOUNG LADY.—"Waiter, you may bring me a Steak, and a Lamb Chop, and a bit of broiled Chicken, and, and, that's all, Waiter, except an Omelet and the Rolls and Muffins; and the Coffee, Waiter, let it be very hot and strong."

—and if you don't enjoy yourselves pretty soon, you'll catch it, that's all."[35]

All these new notions about food, clothing and play meant that the mother could let no detail of general household management escape her eyes.[36] If maids had to be used, she should scrutinize them carefully.[37] The proper reason for servants was to free mothers to take complete care of the child.[38] Writers warned constantly against the dangers of nurses. Even at their best they were inadequate substitutes for the mother herself. The characters and "habits" of nurses might expose the child to corrupting influences.[39]

In these discussions and related matters, our present-day frankness and directness about natural infant sexuality would have shocked readers a century ago. Considerations of "delicacy," "morality" and the absence of knowledge about their psychological importance made references to toilet training and sexual development less frequent and more censorious than we are accustomed to. Only one reference to sex education, for example, appeared in T. L. Nichol's appropriately entitled work, *Esoteric Anthropology*.[40]

Since moral virtues were associated with cleanliness, order, and regularity of all habits, it is not surprising that doctors like Dewees stressed the earliest possible rigorous toilet training; control by the age of one month was Dewees' goal![41] Even bladder and bowel control represented moral victories, and regular or controlled "habits" as making life easier for mother and child were usually viewed as subsidiary ideals at best.

What we call infantile masturbation was classified in a familiar way: it was the first sign of moral and physical degeneration. According to Miss Beecher, the cause was probably the "low and depraved character" of many nurses or a "licentious domestic."[42] Similarly, corruption could come from "wicked companions." Once discovered, the perversity had to be stopped as quickly as possible. The best pro-

[35] Moncure D. Conway, "Children and their Literature," *Southern Literary Messenger* XVIII (Nov., 1852), p. 684.

[36] Alcott, *The Young Wife,* passim.

[37] Catherine Beecher, *The Evils Suffered by American Women and Children* (New York, 1846), pp. 13-14.

[38] Sigourney, *Letters to Mothers,* pp. 84-87.

[39] Combe, *Treatise on Infancy,* pp. 221-32. Louise Hough, *The Science of Man* (Boston, 1849), p. 160, expressed common fears and warnings, basically, if veiledly, sexual.

[40] Dr. T. L. Nichols, *Esoteric Anthropology* (New York, 1853), p. 404.

[41] Dewees, *op. cit.,* p. 237; Donne, *op. cit.,* pp. 169-70.

[42] Beecher, *loc. cit.*

tection against nurses was to hire none. Wicked children were to be kept away and the child himself warned of madness and hell fire if he continued to touch his genitals. However, less drastic preventive measures and more matter-of-fact attitudes towards the problem had also begun to appear in the literature. Dewees suggested, for example, that the child should not be left in bed long. Games and other interests would also circumvent "precocious development of the sexual instinct."[43] Another writer was wise enough to warn that excessive open concern about the problem might intensify rather than lessen the child's curiosity.[44]

Thus even with the most intimate matters of child care that one could discuss with parents there began to appear, occasionally, a less moralistic and more matter-of-fact tone. Overwhelmingly however, in sexual and other matters, the concern was to find a more rational regimen for the body which would both make clear and strengthen the supremacy of the spirit.

[43] Dewees, *op. cit.*, p. 251.
[44] Searle, *Companion*, p. 269.

5

Spare the Rod and Save the Child

HOWEVER much parents sensed the perils and uncertainties of American life, they were assured by their nurture experts that they need have no fear about their offspring if children passed the first test of loyalty to principle, namely, obedience to parents, the authors of their ideals.

Few practical problems in the home were probably more taxing to morally zealous parents than disobedience and bad conduct. What better suggested the parents' failures to "school the will" properly and the child's likely ruinous future than defiance of their authority? The old-fashioned stress on "breaking the will" in more conservative and orthodox writers may have been an extreme position, but there was universal belief that a disobedient child reflected in the worst possible way on his parents. A primary objective, whatever the method of nurture, was thus to assure an obedient child.[1]

Writers like Dr. Humphrey, understandably, thought that the root of disobedience lay in depravity and "evil tendencies." It followed that undue leniency or "bribes"[2] to fractious children might strengthen rather than correct any depraved tendencies that resistance to orders had already exposed. Excessive leniency would also plant doubts about the parents' authority and wisdom;[3] it enlarged rather than lessened

---

[1] "The New England Home," *Monthly Religious Magazine* 26 (Dec., 1861), pp. 341-57.

[2] Moncure Conway called the giving of bribes "foul Benthamism" ("Children and their Literature," *Southern Literary Messenger XVIII* [Nov., 1852], p. 683).

[3] Humphrey, *Domestic Education,* pp. 23-25.

the child's unreasonableness,[4] and threatened both family order and the safety of society.[5]

On the other hand, others argued that occasional ebullience or fractiousness did not imply final ruin. Throughout the 1830's and 1840's writers took notice of the growing number of suggestions that whipping not be used as a means of punishment until all other gentler means of training had failed. T. S. Arthur advised parents, "Young children often do wrong merely from the immaturity of their reason or from a mistaken principle."[6] Harriet Martineau called for "shouting hours"[7] and George Ackerley argued against fears of noisy children at play:

> The noisy mirth of childhood ought never to be met with a frown for it ought always to be recollected, that it is not only natural to them, but actually necessary for the full and healthy development of every organ of the body . . . every effort to restrain them in their youthful gambols is as unnatural as it would be to confine the deer in the midst of the forest.[8]

Romping children were thus either acting "naturally"[9] or were even symbols of "Christian Liberty" (in Bushnell's phrase).[10] The child's natural energy was thus at least receiving greater credit than previously.

But how draw the line between "natural" and "unnatural," tendencies or "Christian liberty" and the devil's pleasure? And what was the proper procedure when the child crossed the line? Opinions ranged from the view that harsh punishment would seldom, if ever, be needed if good examples were set for children[11] by their peers, to the

---

[4] Mrs. J. Bakewell, *The Mother's Practical Guide,* p. 48.

[5] S. G. Goodrich, *The Young American* (New York, 1842), pp. 8-9.

[6] T. S. Arthur, *op. cit.,* p. 298.

[7] Harriet Martineau, "Herod in the Nineteenth Century," *Once A Week* 1 (Sept. 3, 1859) pp. 195-98. Miss Martineau was given the unflattering sobriquet "female Godwin" by the famous editor Sarah J. Hale, *Woman's Record* (New York, 1853), p. 740.

[8] George Ackerley, *On the Management of Children* (New York, 1836), p. 61.

[9] Alcott, *The Young Mother,* p. 238.

[10] Bushnell, *op. cit.,* pp. 339-40.

[11] William Alcott, *A Word to Teachers* (Boston, 1833), p. 27.

notion that the rod should be held in reserve and used only for extreme offenses.[12]

A notable phase of the debate about corporal punishment was started by Horace Mann's proposal that the use of rod be severely limited in the common schools of Massachusetts. Mann was attacked for excessive softness and radicalism, among other charges, in exchanges between him and some Boston school masters.[13] In the South, Braxton Craven, the educational reformer, had announced his opposition to "punishments that mortify" (dunce blocks, leather spectacles, etc.), excessive use of the rod "with but little discretion," and insufficient use of small "privations" of privileges and of "the great instrument of school order and obedience . . . moral influence." By "carefully cultivating the nobler principles of the heart, and by avoiding occasions of offense," severer punishments could be averted "except in rare cases."[14] In administering punishment in the schools, teachers were thus expected to act like enlightened parents,[15] and a Young Ladies' Seminary informed parents, ". . . the discipline will be strict, yet mild and parental, being founded on appeals to the moral sense . . ."[16]

In 1847, the same year as Bushnell's *Christian Nurture,* Lyman Cobb published his influential book, *The Evil Tendencies of Corporal Punishment*. It was, like Bushnell's work, a summary view since many writers had already taken a stand on using the rod. Most critics cited by Cobb refused to give up corporal punishment entirely, especially if they were religiously orthodox.[17] Those who reluctantly con-

[12] Jacob Abbott, "Punishments," *Mother's Assistant* 1 (Feb., 1841), pp. 74-77; Lyman Cobb, *The Evil Tendencies of Corporal Punishment* (New York, 1847), Appendix; Humphrey, *Domestic Education,* p. 56; a general review is in Branch, *The Sentimental Years,* pp. 295-99.

[13] Association of Masters of the Boston Public Schools, *Remarks on the Seventh Annual Report of the Honorable Horace Mann* (Boston, 1844).

[14] Edgar W. Knight, ed., *A Documentary History of Education in the South before 1860,* 5 Vols. (Chapel Hill, 1953), Vol. 5, pp. 241-42.

[15] There was, understandably, a growing contemporary literature on relations between school and home in this era when free elementary education was quickly expanding. Two articles sketch the general issues: Jacob Abbott, "Duties of Parents re the Schools where their Children are Instructed," *American Institute of Instruction* (1834), pp. 81-98; and David Mack, "The Claims of our Age and Country upon Teachers" *American Institute of Instruction* (1839), pp. 137-54.

[16] M. C. Garber, "Sketch of Madison Schools" (ms), Indiana State Library. This and other items on the Midwest were made available to me by Professor David Donald.

[17] An example is the well-known orthodox minister Hubbard Winslow, "On the Dangerous Tendency to Innovations and Extremes in Education." *American Institute of Instruction* 5 (1835), esp. p. 183. Also Matthew Hale Smith, *The Bible, The Rod and Religion in Common Schools* (Boston, 1847).

Prelude to Punishment

ceded that sometimes the rod would have to be used suggested that it be combined with a "you cannot know how much this hurts me" speech. A whipping without a lesson would be unjust because it would leave the rational basis for punishment unclear to the immature child and its empirical cause might not be impressed on his conscience. Cobb himself was revolted by free, thoughtless, and frequent whipping. Such punishment revealed a tyrannical father or mother, not a devilish child. Parents had to abandon mere caprice to consider rationally whether whipping, one of many methods of punishment, would help create self-disciplined, responsible human beings.[18]

Two scenes from the literature of the era illustrate enlightened ways in which punishment could be administered. One is an account of Mrs. Robinson, a fictional English model-mother used as a guide for magazine readers. Although Mrs. Robinson used the best methods in raising her children, a moment arrived when a disobedient son had gone too far. She thought whipping was vindictive, but she was at her wits end. After explaining why he needed a caning, Mrs. Robinson

[18] Cobb, *op. cit.*, pp. 32-33.

made an appointment for the event with her little boy for the next day and sent the sister for a whip. When the sister showed it to him, she cried and kissed her brother. The mother then hung the rod where the boy could see it and meditate upon it. Next day she again explained why the whipping was necessary and read an appropriate story from the Bible. After explaining the story she asked, "Would you rather have God punish your mother or have her punish you?" The poor child's choice was a foregone conclusion but before this torture finally ended both knelt and prayed.[19] We can only speculate about whose guilt in this account was greater, the child's or the mother's. That corporal punishment now had to be examined and justified so elaborately and joined with this extreme appeal to the child suggests how much anxiety and guilt about methods of nurture were already being thrust onto parents.

The other scene, from Catherine Sedgwick's best seller of 1835, *Home,*[20] illustrated how parents might completely spare the rod and yet save the child.

The events in the second chapter, "A Glimpse at Family Government," take place a few years after the marriage of Mr. and Mrs. Barclay, exemplary young Americans who had spent their first evening after their wedding in Bible reading and prayer in their new home. One day, several years later, when their children were playing peacefully indoors, a son, Wallace, suddenly becomes enraged at his sister's kitten for having torn his new kite. In temper, Wallace catches the kitten and throws it into a pot of water boiling on the hearth.

His action shocks and horrifies the family. But Wallace is not beaten or starved or physically mistreated in any way. The child has to recognize his wrong and repent by his own efforts. For the next two weeks, except when at school, Wallace has to stay in his room to learn to govern his passions. No one shows anger or takes revenge on him. He is punished, interestingly enough, with the same enlightened techniques penologists who had followed Beccaria and Bentham had suggested for adult criminals: isolation, maintenance of physical decencies, reflection on the crime, change of heart, return to society. Wallace has been shut away to think about his deed for, the author comments, "How much worse than a consumption is a moral disease." Social ostracism, the sorrow of those who love him, his offense to peace and

[19] Mrs. M. O. Stearns, "The Restored Family," *Mother's Assistant* 4 (May, 1844), pp. 97-119.

[20] Catherine Sedgwick, *Home* (New York, 1835).

love in the family—actual experiences, not abstract exhortations—are the burdens on his conscience.

At last, Wallace asks to speak to his father. He wants to be forgiven and to be taken back into the family. Mr. Barclay asks if he has gained strength to resist the sin of temper. Wallace replies that he knew his father would want proof of his regeneration, "so I had to wait till something happened to try me." Twice at school a friend had tried to provoke him to fight. The second temptation made him raise his fist to hit his friend:

"Oh, Wallace!"

"But I did not, father, I did not, I had to bite my lips though so that the blood ran."

"God bless you, my son."

Seeing his opportunity to use moral maxims now that they could be related to what the child actually felt and thought, Mr. Barclay explained how important such trials were. Virtue and good were only possible with free will; it was better to be virtuous through temptation than to be incapable of sin. Wallace then says that he most worries about future failure because he knows the weakness of his character and the lures of the world. Giving way to either his vices or the world's ways would never permit him to become a moral man.

At this point, Mr. Barclay invokes precept and example to strengthen the tendency to virtue that his enlightened discipline had set in motion. The father prefaces his lesson with the reassurance that "We must always remember, my son, that virtue and vice produced by circumstances is not to be counted to the individual. It is the noble struggle and resistance against them that makes virtue." As a moral being one can expect temptation but Wallace has help available to strengthen his conscience.

His loving family, the people closest to him, believe in him and know that he can control his temper; they depend on him not to fail. Next, as an American who lives in those northern states of the Union in which there is a society of equals, he will be reminded that it is his responsibility not to encroach on other people's rights. The benefits of this free society and the protection of its laws were at the disposal of only the virtuous man. The finest men in American history have also set Wallace an example. They have shown him that self-control can certainly be won: George Washington's best victory was over his greatest personal fault, his temper.

Like Wallace, Washington had a fine home, and good parents, whom he hated to make unhappy. But, more important, Washington was pious and received much strength from his religion. The example of Washington then suggests even a higher model for Wallace. Which of the apostles is his best guide? With a final rush that completes the hierarchy of heroes who glorify the free happy service of the moral law, Wallace finishes this catechism. His final inspired answer is, "St. John, because he controlled himself as any man who loves Christ and his father in Heaven."

Mr. Barclay gladly forgives Wallace, now an obedient child, supposedly without a broken will. The child embraces the law through his own efforts, using his own knowledge and ideas which his father has merely skillfully set in motion. Wallace and his father go downstairs and enter the dining room together for the first time in weeks. The child, the family, the nation, even the heavens are again happy and harmonious.

Whether parents followed Mrs. Robinson or Mr. Barclay, punishment had to fit the crime and no one rule could cover all circumstances. Whatever the punishment, it was to be used with proper understanding of the child as a being capable of moral improvement or regeneration. Love and gentleness were regarded as the greatest positive inducements for the growth of good character[21] just as mother love would also be the source of those wise restraints on "excesses" caused by innate tendencies to depravity or by unfortunate environmental influences.[22] Kisses, hugs, and frequent embraces were recommended[23] and the mother's kisses were given magical power over the child's destiny. Such love and affection when combined with "appeals to conscience and reason," persuasion, precept, good examples, firm and consistent treatment, and especially reminders of the pain that wickedness caused others, were to be used to guarantee that conscience would control the child and the man.

How effective a brake on disorderly children the image of the loving upright parent could be has been suggested in Freud's reflections on the first work of the super-ego. The superego whose full job is "self-observation, conscience and ideals" is, in its earliest stages,

> the vehicle of the ego ideal, by which the ego measures itself, towards which it strives, and whose demands for ever-

[21] "Introductory Address," *Parent's Magazine* 1 (Sept., 1840), pp. 7-8.
[22] Humphrey, *Domestic Education,* pp. 42-48.
[23] Lydia M. Child, *The Mother's Book,* 2nd ed., (Boston, 1831), Chap. II, Dwight, *The Father's Book,* pp. 31-33.

> increasing perfection it is always striving to fulfill. No doubt this ego-ideal is a precipitation of the old idea of the parents, an expression of the admiration which the child felt for the perfection which it at that time ascribed to them.[24]

We can infer from this how realistic the new ideals of punishment were. The strong sense of guilt we associate with what David Riesman calls "inner-directed" morality need not have been linked to the cold and cheerless upbringing that we too often associate with the "Victorian" nineteenth-century family. If authority in the home was basically loving, the child who openly expressed hostility probably suffered inwardly for it. His feelings of guilt might grow intense if parents refused to punish him harshly or quickly for bad conduct, so that the pain and fear of little Wallace in further offending his loving parents may have been far more effective in disciplining him than harshness which would have permitted the child to hate more openly and rebel again. Quick strong punishment, when justified, probably allows the child to feel that he has paid his debts, while gentler methods in excess would keep the child's sense of guilt alive and active. By not being permitted to express his aggressiveness openly against the world, the child is left with increased guilt. Where the new nurture was practiced, its enthusiasts seem shrewdly, if unwittingly, to have gambled that on the whole the inner penalty to the child for abusing the love and trust of parents was a more effective control on his conduct than the memory or fear of a beating by a vengeful father or mother.

[24] Sigmund Freud, *New Introductory Lectures on Psychoanalysis* (New York, 1933), pp. 92-93.

6

Fit for Children to Hear

CHRISTIAN orthodoxy about punishment and other matters created a problem for those tending to regard the will of children in a more kindly and tolerant way, to sanction or enlarge the ordinary joys of childhood, and to regard happiness as a legitimate aim of education. Increasingly, the new nurture suggested that the natural and the divine, heaven and history were less opposed to each other than in traditional Pauline and Calvinist theology. Yet, if challenged on the issue, many Americans on the eve of Darwinism would probably still have defended the propositions that a personal God was the sole source of moral truth and that Christian morality was intended to help man rescue himself from an imperfect nature and the inherent corruptions of human history.

How far could one go, therefore, in approving the natural interests of the child without either giving freedom to the forces of evil or modifying seriously the classic Christian antagonism between the flesh and the spirit? The problem was implicit in appealing to "nature" for justification of the child's enthusiasm and energy, the lessening of physical punishment and the new daily health regimen emphasizing a robust and healthy body for its own sake. All nurture reformers had simply denied that there need be any conflict between concern for the soul and care of the body.

Besides implied challenges to Christian asceticism made by growing emphasis on natural strivings and care of the body, a formidable intellectual apparatus was available by 1850 to open critics of Christian orthodoxy. Since the time of Kant and Hume, a century earlier, there had developed the strongest and most many-sided intellectual case against traditional religion that Christianity had ever faced. By 1850 the Higher Criticism had joined philosophy in challenging the supernatural foundations of biblical knowledge, the claim that the Word originated, as it were, beyond the world.

No writer on child care could have hoped to gain a respectable and large audience if he seemed to challenge directly the supremacy of the Word. Those who tried to school the nation in moral matters or in the "laws of health" had to be careful not to offend Christian sensibility about the worth of the body or the perils of the "natural." Considering the steadily increasing secularism and materialism of American life, the acute public sensitivity at the time about rising dangers to the claims of the soul and spirit was perhaps an overreadiness to denounce in others worldly ideals it itself had already guiltfully adopted.

In many ways, therefore, the possibility that man was only a natural creature had been widely sensed and had aroused fear and anxiety even before 1859, the year of the *Origin of Species*. The danger of a thoroughgoing naturalism to man's special status in God's creation insinuated itself recurrently into the writings on the proper care of children. Concern centered on the question, "What was to give distinction to human nature, or distinguish the 'human essence' from the rest of nature if the character, health, and development of children seemed increasingly entirely dependent on natural or environmental influences?"

If writers on child care for the adult audience were periodically hard-pressed to avoid the charge that they were sensualists or materialists the writer of children's literature was in an even more difficult position. The vexatious problem of the nature of human identity came into revealing focus in a debate about moral tales for children in which the "order of nature" was reversed and animals or fairies were involved in human situations and spoke and acted like human beings.[1] In dignifying the animal or the magical these tales seemed to degrade the human. By the 1830's the attack had achieved much success—and much criticism for, as one writer put it in "A Lament for the Fairies,"

[1]Fantasy tales like Perrault's famous stories had appeared in America near the end of the 18th century. The attacks at this time, 1830-1860, were reminiscent of the earlier opposition of Maria Edgeworth and Mrs. Trimmer. On this earlier hostility to fairy tales see Blanche E. Weekes, *Literature and the Child* (New York, 1935), p. 56.

There never has been any fun
Since fairies went away.[2]

Attacks on such stories were part of a largely evangelical assault on "fiction" that began after 1760 and continued well past the middle of the nineteenth century. Powerful fiction, it was said, might lead the individual to take a "morbid interest" in wickedness or immorality. Even worse, he might question or doubt his unique human responsibility and identity by indulging in fantasies of himself as another person. Or he might deny his separateness from animal nature by identifying with an animal character. In *Father and Son,* that classic biography of a mid-nineteenth-century evangelical English boyhood, Edmund Gosse tells how his parents, who were members of the fundamentalist Plymouth Brethren, abhorred "fiction." They thought that exposure to fancy or make-believe would corrupt the child by leading him away from single-minded devotion to a God who had created only one world and one truth with fixed categories of being and identity. In another famous work, Fanny Price, the serious, pious heroine of Jane Austen's *Mansfield Park,* refuses to participate in a play being staged by the pleasure-loving members of her family and their guests. Fears of not being at all times her own true self obsess her. The real world's temptations were great enough as it was and the pleasure that fantasy gave was pleasure taken irresponsibly, almost as animals might take it, without consideration of what was morally fit for a man or woman.

Even the spreading reform notion that religious purity and moral duty could be learned by the child gradually and pleasantly through an appeal to his imagination, interests, or emotions did not automatically imply permission to read Aesop, La Fontaine or their imitators. The more literal-minded of the nurture writers with a gentler disposition to children conceived of religion or morality as truth given once and for all time. They could not fully sanction spontaneity and imagination because they led from single-minded clarity about morals and religion. Religious or moral education was to "school the will" in the light of unchallengeable ideas. By placing facts before the child, by backing them with strong and patient authority, without permitting any departure from them, the child's intellect, one of his "faculties," would become tied to truth—and truth, once firmly planted in the individual, would forever control the will. On the issue of the truths of human nature even a utilitarian radical like

[2] Cited in Kiefer, *op. cit.,* p. 19.

Harriet Martineau could speak for others of her generation when she wrote, "As spiritual people we look down with much contempt upon the man who would in anything compare us with the lower animals. His mind is mean and must be quite beneath our indignation."[3]

The benign opponent of corporal punishment, Lyman Cobb, argued in one of his textbooks that "dialogue between wolves and sheep, cats and mice . . . is as destructive of truth and morality as it is contrary to the principles of nature and philosophy."[4] Mrs. Cobb in another work assured her readers that "In this as well as in the other series nothing has been permitted to find a place which is false, unnatural, or unphilosophical or any details of conversation among animals which never did and never can take place."[5] Another writer asserted that since "the pure mind of a child loves truth"[6] fiction could only lead it astray or strengthen "evil tendencies." According to *The Christian Examiner,* what fiction children did read should be severely limited because it excited "their minds and expectations to impossible things."[7]

These attacks do not seem to have stopped the steady revival and growth after 1830 of a children's literature in which the scope for imagination and fantasy was greater than that for an obvious moral to the story. Books like *Andersen's Fairy Tales, Swiss Family Robinson, The Green Mountain Boys,* and the works of Captain Marryat began their popularity.[8] *Alice in Wonderland* was also to appear shortly and challenge the notion of a world in which "impossible things" did not happen, although at the end of her adventure Alice did find Wonderland absurd and untrue and left it in vexation at its perversity.

Those who defended the new, imaginative literature for the child contrasted it favorably with "Peter Parleyism." Under the name of Peter Parley, S. G. Goodrich had written many popular didactic and moralistic books for children. Peter Parleyism was attacked for making an insufficient appeal to the imagination. Children would outgrow fiction, and fairy tales were harmless. Given only dry fact and no

[3] Harriet Martineau, "How to Make Home Unhealthy," *Harpers Monthly* 1 (October, 1850), p. 618.

[4] Lyman Cobb, *Juvenile Reader #2* (Philadelphia, 1832), Preface.

[5] Mrs. C. S. Cobb, *Cobb's Toys,* (Sandy Hill, New York, 1836), Preface.

[6] Association for the Improvement of Juvenile Books, *First Reading Lessons for Children* (Philadelphia, 1830) p. v.

[7] "Books for Children," *The Christian Examiner* 5 (Sept., 1828), pp. 402-20.

[8] F. S. Mott, *Golden Multitudes* (New York, 1947), a study of best sellers.

sympathy with "the invisible," children would end by feeling nothing and believing in nothing but sense-objects. Fairy tales did not distort life or corrupt men; the world did. The purpose of literature should be "to make us sensible of our position on earth and our kindred with heaven, and to excite in us, the earnest purpose and humble hope so to think, to feel and to live, as not to belie our high calling."[9]

This antagonism to literalness and hard fact in education is reminiscent of the belief of writers who, echoing Rousseau and other Romantics, emphasized the sentiments as the source of morality and the basis for religion.[10] Whether their defense of fantasy came directly from American Transcendentalism, a theologically liberal Christian pietism, or from Rousseau or the German idealists and English poets of the previous generation, the intention should not be misunderstood. Like the rationalistic or evangelical critics of fairy tales, their goals were still "character" and "faith." If appeals to the sentiments and imagination of the child, like a softer discipline and more rational diet, would strengthen the chances of redemption, then by all means let the child read fairy tales about "impossible things." In sum, one could even defer to the child's imagination (and, by implication, to energies of nature) by placing it in the realm of the spirit.

The pre-eminent concern that children learn clear moral lessons, on whatever psychological basis, is apparent in every type of children's story before the Civil War. Although a more imaginative literature for children was making considerable headway by 1860, only in the generation after Appomattox did writers for the child create books and stories that adults still care to remember and children still seem to read.[11] In fact, the old-fashioned didactic and moralistic qualities of even the more imaginative popular tales of the generation after 1830 now make those stories seem largely literary curiosities.

Comparing literature *for* the child with books *about* children at the time reveals a difference in tone. While parents were urged to become more realistic about the child's needs and to abandon preaching and over-didactic moral and religious instruction, the children were not themselves allowed to enjoy any significant freedom from moralism and homily in their books. This lag, which was to disappear after the Civil War, may seem purely fortuitous but since several of the more

[9] "Books for Children," *Living Age* 1 (June 15, 1844), p. 301.

[10] See, for example, the complaint of William Russell against the mechanical and literal in education in "The Infant School System of Education," *American Institute of Instruction* (1830), pp. 97-121.

[11] See Part II for details.

notable enlightened writers on nurture also wrote for children yet in a more "conservative" style, we can question the depth of the proclaimed happy confidence that expert knowledge and greater freedom would work wonders in saving the child.

Most books on conduct written for boys and girls at about 1850 had the same essential theme—the fulfillment of the individual by identifying with unquestioned truths of morality and religion. This happy goal could be reached only if the child began by giving complete obedience and love to his parents in thought as well as in deed.

Peter Parley advised, "It is of infinite importance that you should watch over the internal state of your mind, and not suffer dislike, alienation or indifference to extinguish your regards. . . . A child's pleasure should be to please his parents."[12] Reverence, rather than mere respect, was owed to parents for the love and care the child received from them. In the presence of his parents the child should act as though they were king and queen. Parley dismissed as one of "the fallacies of the young," the belief that "fathers have flinty hearts."[13] Obedience implied that "You must give up your own will and sacrifice your own predilections, and perform the things that are difficult as well as those that are easy."[14] Filial piety was illustrated by the "sublime and striking" reply of the child who was urged by guests to eat something his father had forbidden him to touch. After all, since the parents were away from home, they wouldn't know. "Very true," the child said, my parents are not here, "but God and my conscience are."[15]

Although in the nurture books of Jacob Abbott, S. G. Goodrich, T. S. Arthur and others, it was the mothers who were at the center of home life, in books for children written by the same authors, the father was clearly in control of the family. This difference is not surprising for it had not been decreed that the mother formally replace the father. She had, for the sake of practicality, stepped into roles in the nurture literature that the American father could not play well. One of the mother's primary duties was still to teach the child that he owed supreme respect, love, and obedience to his father. And even if mothers were actually taking on or sharing his powers, there was no incentive to attack the formal rights of the patriarch. Certainly many writers even hoped, as we observed, that the father would merely resume his

[12] Peter Parley, *The Parent's Present* (Boston, 1835), pp. 43-44.
[13] *Ibid.*, p. 50.
[14] *Ibid.*, p. 49.
[15] *Ibid.*, p. 50.

duties and it was a secondary consideration that it be as an enlightened Mr. Barclay or as a stern surrogate of God.

The possibility that the enlarged practical role of mothers as "lawgivers" and the merely formal supremacy of the father would lead to conflicts in the child's life was unthinkable, for it was simply assumed that with child, mother, and father all dedicated to "the right," the family would always be harmonious. The child would follow the example and teaching of his mother and she, in turn, would encourage deference to the perfect father. Few nurture writers, seemingly, could yet proclaim that the American mother was to be superior to or a reformer of her husband as well as her child, although campaigners for women's rights were already emphatic about who actually ruled the roost.

The perfect child from the perfect home was to use constant introspection and tests to measure how well he lived up to the first principles learned from either mother or father. The well-educated child will "know how to choose the right," and having made his choices, "all his faculties operate to realize his will. . . . He is nerved for the fight, he can breast himself manfully against every assault, he will triumph victoriously over all opposition, for he feels himself strengthened to every good word and work, both in the inner and outer man." Such a person "in after life will stand the test of every trial."[16]

Dr. Alexander described the young Christian

> . . . he is so much in the habit of noticing his moral exercises; he so frequently communes with his own heart, that he comes at length to be an acquaintance with himself, and can pronounce, with humble confidence, on his present state and future destiny. Such a character is venerable and immovable. Changes may occur; prosperity or adversity may come; but he walks in too high a region to be unduly elated by the former, or sinfully depressed by the latter. What a calm delightful enviable summit. It is like the mountain covered with verdure upon whose top rest the mild beams of glory; whilst in the figurative language of Goldsmith, "the midway storm thunders and rages below."[17]

The typical hero of children's literature stood for "character," being absolutely dedicated to principles of truthfulness, purity, and

[16] "Education in New England," *North American Review* 47 (Oct., 1838), pp. 282-83; 285-86.

[17] Dr. A. Alexander, *Advice to a Young Christian* (New York, 1843), pp. 80-81.

devotion. He was a person who lived up to his ideals and constantly proved his self-reliance and dedication by going through trials and ordeals by which he mastered himself and acquired the virtues that the child could find listed in almost any manual of conduct: conscience, justice, honesty, faithfulness, truth, obedience, industry, patience, etc.[18]

The voice of orthodoxy, Reverend John Abbott, was realistic enough to warn boys how much his notion of the moral life required of them:

> When you come out into the busy world you will find many occasions for the exercise, not only of great decisions of character, but also many trials in doing that which may be very painful to you. You will often find that which is wrong, to be popular, and but few, and they perhaps reviled and persecuted, advocating that which is right. . . .The mass of men are corrupt and take the easy way or they are too meek. Make yourself felt for the right. Resolve that your voice shall be ever heard, and your influence felt in behalf of justice and mercy, whether the cause be popular, or unpopular.[19]

Young men were also warned by the less stringent T. S. Arthur to overcome temptation by consciously developing and perfecting their "characters as immortal beings."[20] The child's progress from "reformation to regeneration"[21] inevitably exposes him to "temptations to evil" which "are far more powerful than allurements to good."[22]

Mrs. Sigourney emphasized the degree of consciousness with which a boy dedicated to principle must live. "Let every boy dread the first advance of vice, for the descent is swift, like the swollen and headlong torrent, sweeping every landmark away."[23]

The character recommended for girls was based on traditional womanly ideals. The virtues of propriety, marriage, home-making and motherhood were chiefly praised in the girls' conduct books,[24] and Mrs. Lydia Child summed up the feminine virtues neatly as purity of heart and correctness of principle. The girl attained them by prayer

[18] Jacob Abbott, *The Rollo Code* (Boston, 1841); cf. the later code of the Boy Scouts ". . . trustworthy, loyal, friendly," etc., etc.
[19] John S. C. Abbott, *The School Boy* (Boston, 1839), p. 177.
[20] T. S. Arthur, *Advice to Young Men* (Boston, 1853), p. 75.
[21] *Ibid.*, p. 78.
[22] *Ibid.*, p. 93.
[23] Lydia H. Sigourney, *The Boy's Book* (New York, 1845), p. 95.
[24] Lydia H. Sigourney and others, *The Young Ladies' Offering* (Boston, 1848); Lydia M. Child, *The Girl's Own Book* (New York, 1833).

and remembrance of God, practice of the Golden Rule, frank and open dealing with all, acting at once on good resolutions, politeness and amiability at home, love of brothers and sisters, knowledge proper to a woman, and neatness of person.[25]

Jacob Abbott's extremely popular books for boys and girls used most of the themes that dominated even the more imaginative children's literature before 1860. Life was a trial and the world a place of temptation in which one must make right prevail; youth was a time of preparation for manhood or womanhood when one's highest goal was to keep fresh a sense of duty, especially, respect for one's parents; life promised every material and spiritual success if the child could improve himself by watching for failings, by shunning the corrupting influences of bad companions, and by remembering the certain punishment that would follow immoral or improper conduct.

In his preface to a series of monthly story books, Abbott outlined his constant concern:

> . . . the end and aim of all will be to impart useful knowledge, to develop the thinking and reasoning powers, to teach a correct and discriminating use of language, to present models of good conduct for imitation and bad examples to be shunned, to explain and enforce the highest principles of moral duty, and, above all, to awaken and cherish the spirit of humble and unobtrusive but heartfelt piety.[26]

If there was any single symbolic hero of the age it was little Rollo—only nine years old, yet the perfect realization of Abbott's ideals. Rollo was the spiritual heir of the Christian hero of *Pilgrim's Progress*. If his world was less terrible than Bunyan's and his earthly rewards more important, his character was just as disciplined and flawless, as Abbott demonstrated in the first series of books about the adventures of a young person to achieve mass popularity in America.

In *Rollo on the Atlantic*,[27] which started the *Rollo in Europe* series, Rollo and his younger sister, Jane, have been called to Europe to join their traveling parents. Jane, passive, dependent, nervous, is frightened to travel the Atlantic, but Rollo is fully confident and reassures his sister. He is almost happy about the challenge when their uncle is unable to find suitable adults with whom they can travel from New York, for "It is right . . . that a boy at that age should begin to

[25] Child, *op. cit.*, p. 283 ff.
[26] Jacob Abbott, *Harpers Monthly Story Book* (New York, 1854), Preface.
[27] Jacob Abbott, *Rollo on the Atlantic* (New York, 1858).

feel something like a man, and to desire that opportunities should arise for exercising the powers which he finds thus developing themselves and growing stronger every day within him."[28] The first test of self-reliance soon begins: their luggage is lost at the pier. After escorting them aboard the boat, Uncle George rushes off to find the trunk. The children are alone and frightened and Jane begins to cry. Rollo steels himself:

> He perceived that the time had now come for him to show by his acts that he was really able to do what he had been so eager to undertake. He determined, therefore, instead of yielding to the feelings of fear and despondency which his situation was so well calculated to inspire, he would nerve himself with resolution and meet the emergencies of the occasion like a man.[29]

He diverts Jane's attention and the trunk arrives, but not Uncle George. By now it is too late for him to make proper arrangements for the children. The ship sails but no one aboard has been asked to take care of them. They are on their own and Rollo decides that he will follow Uncle George's rule: watch to see what adults do if what you have been taught seems inadequate.

Soon everyone goes to lunch, the children follow and all goes well because Rollo and Jane follow Uncle George's advice. After lunch, in one of the salons, they meet a beautiful woman who casually asks them questions about their troubles, but takes no real interest in the stranded children. She waltzes off and loses what beauty she at first had in their eyes. A more plain-looking woman, however, does take them under her wing. The reader learns that such real goodness is often hidden, that appearances are to be distrusted. By the time the Rollo books appeared, the excessive moralizing associated with the older, but still popular English stories of Maria Edgeworth, Mrs. Barbauld, and Mrs. Trimmer,[30] had declined. The child was now permitted sometimes to draw the moral for himself, but it was clearly suggested. This freedom merely carried out the current dictum that "the right" would be more effectively grasped if the child discovered it himself rather than learned it abstractly from adults.

---

[28] *Ibid.*, p. 31.

[29] *Ibid.*, p. 40.

[30] See below, p. 63ff for an example of Maria Edgeworth's work. See also Kiefer, *op. cit.*, for a survey of evangelical and Rousseauian moral and religious tales.

Rollo takes a stroll and is tempted to ask about the ship's bells and to climb the rigging. He controls his curiosity and soon finds out during a conversation with the ship's surgeon that such questions and conduct are frowned upon. He has learned, again from experience rather than precept, the wisdom of self-control and that he was "not to violate the proprieties of life by obtruding himself into places where he ought not to go."[31]

One of the perennial bad boys of these stories soon appears. Hilbert is a victim of "fashion"; he is spoiled, thoroughly disobedient, and rude. He refuses, for example, to go to his sick mother when she calls for him. Rollo tries to reassure her that Hilbert will come to her although he has no basis for saying this. The author points out that the reader will have to discover for himself the rightness or wrongness of this half-truth. He says nothing of the fact that Rollo has involved Hilbert in a lie and has perhaps exposed him to punishment which he did not really deserve. But the certainty that the moral order of the world would be wrecked if one lie were told has at least been questioned for the reader. The propriety of telling a lie under certain conditions has become a topic for debate, probably because the duty to be decent and polite to Hilbert's mother has conflicted with Rollo's duty always to tell the truth.

After this first meeting with the bad boy, Rollo's conduct is constantly compared with Hilbert's. A storm breaks but Rollo does not go out on deck. He uses his own good sense, follows the official warnings, and sees the storm very well from inside while Hilbert rushes out and is drenched by a wave.

The children soon meet the worst temptation. A lottery is to be held on board. Hilbert takes one of the chances. Horrified, Abbott has no reticence this time in calling his action a sin. Rollo, of course, abstains and advises Hilbert to do the same, but then a Mr. Chauncey buys a chance and offers to give it to Rollo. Naturally, Rollo graciously refuses this less direct temptation and is praised. The lottery has been fixed ("this is always the way") but somehow the fixers are foiled and the prize goes to a poor Irishwoman to whom Mr. Chauncey had given his ticket after Rollo had refused it. Hilbert is furious at his own stupidity in not taking the ticket when Chauncey offered it to him but vows to try again. It is the essence of wicked people not only to sin but never to learn goodness even when sin fails to pay.

[31] *Rollo on the Atlantic,* p. 104.

Finally, the ship arrives at Liverpool. Due to another series of circumstances, all the adult friends Rollo has made on the boat fail to reunite the children with their parents. Left on his own again, Rollo takes Jane in a cab to the best hotel and is delighted to find that he has guessed correctly; his parents are there. He is overjoyed in the reunion and feels justified in his belief in himself and his ideals.

It goes without much comment that this story is far beyond what we now think children would find interesting. The situations are mechanical and contrived, the characters are two-dimensional. Whenever the author required a moral decision, invariably the good boy chooses the right thing and the bad boy gets the proper recompense. The choice between good and bad is usually clear and unambiguous. There is little real obstacle to the child's will to truth and his triumph over temptation and difficulty. The child who most identifies with truth, who is most deferential to the morality and wisdom that comes from adults wins at every crisis. The good is never defeated; it always wins because it is good. The great and constant lesson of the Rollo series is that merit lies in moral fitness and righteousness. Be good and all will be granted; be bad and you lose both the world and heaven.

Considering the extent to which materialism and immorality were constantly attacked as the chief vices of the Jacksonian republic we might expect greater realism about business life and the lures of wealth than one in fact finds in children's literature. Instead the children's works are dominated by the so-called Federalist-Whig rhetoric: all working people and employers, being Americans, have their mutual interests at heart; the rich man is wealthy because he has "character" which also makes him the exemplar and best friend of the laborer. Moralism and abstraction again obscure the possibility that honesty and success are incompatible with each other. Sinful businessmen or unjust practices are exceptional and both, in God's time, will yield to righteous men or to God's punishments. Even the Horatio Alger stories of the next generation were more sceptical about the business world than the children's stories of the 1850s.

A good example of the latter comes from the vast collection of Sunday School stories published by the interdenominational American Sunday School Union. In *Bosses and their Boys or the Duties of Masters and Apprentices,* two young men are apprenticed to Mr. Stone, "a fair sample of manufacturers, and merchants and capitalists generally. He was willing to do well by those who were disposed to do well by him."[32] Rich men are at once characterized by superior moral qualities rather than merely by money. In this story, the good boy works hard and diligently, resists temptations, maintains good principles, shuns evil associates, saves his money, and is advanced in rank and wages. He is "one who would make his employer's interest his own," and is among those who are the "favorites and favored."[33] He learns that "success that is not built on merit is not worth having."[34] The young hero's conduct toward his parents is exemplary. He repays them for sacrifices they made for him by sending home his first extra dollar, by repairing their home, by loving them and his church. Eventually, the boss helps him and his friend to start their own business. One of these boys marries the boss' daughter and inherits the old firm, from all of which comes the final moral, "I have been greatly blessed; and I trust I have been mindful always that every good gift cometh from the hand of God."[35]

This tale, like many others, put a premium on the so-called Puritan virtues of diligence and thrift. William Makepeace Thayer, who was as popular an author as Jacob Abbott, promised that the child would find in *The Bobbin Boy* "an unusual example of energy, industry, perseverance, application and enthusiasm in prosecuting a life purpose."[36] For the much-read Aimwell series the author adopted the general motto "Precepts may lead but examples draw," and stated that, in particular, his story *Clinton* was "designed mainly to illustrate by example the importance of early habits of obedience and industry."[37]

In the newer, more imaginative literature of the 1850's, one of the great favorites, *John Halifax, Gentleman,*[38] was still essentially the same story of a poor boy who, although orphaned early in life, bravely dedicates himself to purposes higher than fortune and social rank and, by not seeking wealth as a good in itself, triumphs over early poverty and misfortune.

Mrs. Barbauld and Maria Edgeworth, famous English writers of an older *genre,* had been constantly republished for several generations in America. Many of their moral tales were especially concerned with

[32] American Sunday School Union, *Bosses and their Boys* (Philadelphia, 1853), p. 139.

[33] *Ibid.,* p. 138.

[34] *Ibid.,* p. 139.

[35] *Ibid.,* p. 143.

[36] William M. Thayer, *The Bobbin Boy* (Boston, 1860), Preface.

[37] Walter Aimwell, *Clinton* (Boston, 1858), Preface.

[38] Dinah M. M. Craik, *John Halifax, Gentleman* (London, 1857). See also the American editions of Harriet Martineau's tales illustrating "the truths of Political Economy."

practical virtues. In one of Mrs. Barbauld's happier *Lessons for Children,* a little boy on his way to school thinks of playing all day, but none of the animals he invites will join him: "What, is nobody idle! Then little boys must not be idle either."[39] Maria Edgeworth's *Waste Not Want Not* was still reprinted in several collections of stories in the 1840's and 1850's. It stresses how the virtues of thrift and diligence distinguish a good child from a bad child. The convention of personifying virtues and vices had an ancient literary lineage and even in children's literature long preceded her work. On the eve of the Civil War Jacob Abbott was obviously still using it with characters like Rollo and Hilbert. Maria Edgeworth however, had been heavily influenced by Rousseau and tried to appeal to the child's imagination and sense of fact. Her talent as well as her desire to be more realistic place her moral tales among the best, but they will probably still seem arch and over-didactic to modern readers. Although her plot and characters were not flat, the moralism was always apparent.

In *Waste Not Want Not,*[40] a wealthy, kindly man, Mr. Gresham, retires and decides to adopt a relative as his heir. He sends for two nephews Hal and Benjamin. Hal is spoiled and extravagant because of his fashionable upbringing; Benjamin is thrifty because he comes from a simple home. Although wealth in the Federalist-Whig rhetoric might often be sentimentally deprecated as making for burdens and unhappiness, it was also admired when it made benevolence possible and in Mr. Gresham's case, money had come to him as a reward for his virtue. On arriving at his uncle's home, Benjamin admires the sampler in the hall, "Waste Not, Want Not," but Hal declares, "I think it looks too stingy to servants; and no gentleman's servants, cooks especially, would like to have such a mean motto always staring them in the face."[41]

The test of the boys' characters thus begins. Some packages for Mr. Gresham have to be unpacked. Benjamin carefully unties the string and saves it but Hal, at once, cuts the knots. An appropriate moral is drawn about haste and thrift. A few days later both boys receive tops as gifts, but without strings. Ben, of course, has some string, but Hal must use his hat band. He breaks his top and then the top Ben kindly lends him. Next, Lady Diana Sweepstake's sons arrive. (The family name alone guarantees that they are perfect friends

[39] Anna L. Barbauld, *Lessons for Children* (New York, circa 1856), p. 72. These tales had first been published in 1760.

[40] Maria Edgeworth, *The Fireside Story Book* (New York, 1853).

[41] *Ibid.*, p. 5.

for Hal.) He goes off to play with them, but Ben stays behind with Mr. Gresham's daughter who has sprained her ankle by tripping over the piece of string Hal had thrown on the floor while opening the package.

News of an archery contest reaches the Gresham's. Hal, envying the young Sweepstakes, thinks that he and Ben must have fancy costumes for it. The boys approach their uncle who gives them a choice of the special costumes or new coats for everyday wear. Hal chooses the costume and Ben the coat. At the contest all kinds of disasters overtake Hal, his friends and their fine suits. Plain Ben steps up to the target. Defeat threatens him, too, for the string of his bow snaps, but he digs into his pocket, finds his trusty piece of string, fits it to his bow, shoots his arrow and wins the contest and, supposedly, his uncle's fortune and the reader's admiration.

If readers of these famous samples from a voluminous literature would thus be constantly assured that virtue brought more than its own rewards, so would they find it equally certain that wickedness would bring ruin. In fact, scarcely any stories of the age would not fit the description of the famous eighteenth-century storyteller Arnaud Berquin that in his tales, "virtue is constantly represented as the fountain of happiness, and vice as the source of every evil." [42] In one of Mrs. Barbauld's tales a cock betrays his brother to a fox who eats both; in another, two boys put a rope across a path to trip people. Their first victim sprains his ankle and turns out to have been rushing to fetch the surgeon to bleed the boys' father who had suddenly taken very ill. "I do not know whether their father died or not; I believe he got well again." [43]

Peter Parley told children about a boy named Ralph, who lied about a mirror he has broken. From this (as the reader might suspect) he went on to stealing trifles, then larger items. He was finally caught, was sent to prison and died. The story ends, "If they [little children] have ever been wicked, let them confess it frankly, and do so no more, and they will be forgiven." [44]

In *The Christ Child*, [45] Heinrich, raised in the slums, with a drunkard father and an epileptic mother, has to care for his little sister,

[42] Arnaud Berquin, *The Looking Glass for the Mind* (New York, 1849), Preface.

[43] Mrs. Barbauld, *op. cit.*, pp. 126-29, 168.

[44] Peter Parley, *Juvenile Tales* (Philadelphia, 1833), p. 58.

[45] Lydia M. Child, *Flowers for Children* (New York, 1846).

Gertrude. Heinrich is contrasted with Wolfgang, a boy made a bully by a corrupt environment. One Christmas Wolfgang steals some apples and nuts. He is so perverse that he reproaches himself for not remembering the poverty of the brother and sister and stealing something for them also. He makes amends by pilfering some oranges for them but the person whom he has robbed tries to arrest all three children. Heinrich and Gertrude are horrified to learn that their oranges are stolen property. Although near starvation, they still follow the moral law, "Good children will never eat what they know is stolen."[46] A stranger intercedes with the police for all three and arranges to send them and the sick parents to a home outside the corrupting city. There the law of love and reform by moral suasion are the rules and Wolfgang seems to respond to this humane environment.

After a time, a job is arranged for him in town. He returns to the place of temptation for the test of his new principles and slides back into evil, selling shoddy merchandise. Heinrich and Gertrude come to town to sell baskets and entrust Wolfgang with several which he promises to sell. This act of faith finally turns the tide against the forces of Satan. Wolfgang is fully redeemed by his own will; he could not resist the example of perfect goodness and confidence that Heinrich and Gertrude had set for him. "She told him that through temptation and struggle, bad men become good and good men become angels."[47]

A child who, unlike Wolfgang, remained unrepentant might escape the consequences of bad conduct at first, but eventually he and others suffered for it. In this relentless universe there were no exceptions. In *Aunt Fanny's Story Book* two little brothers wet their hair with cologne and then cut it. They put on adult clothes and drag them on the floor, spill water on the rug, and polish the brass with a wet glove and tooth powder. One then takes a razor and tries to shave the younger brother and severely cuts him. Both finally get justified beatings.[48]

The child who was skeptical about due recompense for evil or about the world's respect for true worth was reassured in stories like Mrs. Stowe's *Art and Nature.*[49] Fanny, one of three daughters, the child of hidden virtues, is contrasted with her sisters who are their

[46] *Ibid.*, p. 22.
[47] *Ibid.*, p. 48.
[48] *Aunt Fanny's Story Book* (New York, 1852), "The Mischievous Boys."
[49] Harriet Beecher Stowe, "Art and Nature," *Godey's Lady's Book* 18 (Dec., 1839), pp. 241-44.

vain mother's favorites. They are spoiled, and fashionable and, as the corrupt world would judge, ideally eligible girls. In this Cinderella-like tale, the charming cousin, George Somers, finally chooses Fanny as his wife, ". . . do what you would with her, she would always come out herself after all."[50] Her real worth, although less obvious, is more valuable than her sisters' flash, and in the end, wins its just reward.

Even when better written or more exciting in plot, the vast majority of children's stories before 1860 thus strengthened the lessons in absolute morality and the inflexible ideals parents were urged to teach. This general tendency to moralism was evident even in a *Parent's Assistant* that purported to be a book of facts for children:

> Question: When does old age commence?
> Answer: At different periods according as we live temperately or intemperately. Drunkards and gross eaters become old at fifty, while persons of virtuous and temperate habits do not become old at sixty.[51]

In some older tales, the moral was stated; in other, more "modern" books it might be merely suggested. The moral comes eternally either with a somber warning about evil or with affection and hope about the triumph of the good. As Peter Parley told his vast audience, "So, my little readers, may you be ever true to your friend, and if any of you are at any time unfortunate or in danger, may you have some sure and kind friend to protect and save you.[52]

---

[50] *Ibid.*, p. 242.
[51] *The Parent's Assistant* (New Haven, 1849), p. 29.
[52] Parley, *Juvenile Tales,* p. 24.

7

What Teacher Thought

THE major education journals, textbooks, and school reports after 1830 tell a story chiefly of struggles between partisans of religious or secular common education,[1] and between defenders of strict or enlightened pedagogical methods. These battles were, understandably, related to the larger conflicts of the age about the child's nature in the light of Christian orthodoxy and newer ideas.[2]

The spread of common school education after 1830 started a full-scale American debate about educational theory that has continued with enormous vigor down to today. It had been traditional in America and elsewhere to treat the problems of education as a branch of moral philosophy or epistemology. But with the growth of the teaching profession and school administration the new important education journals, such as *The Common School Assistant, The American Institute of Instruction,* and Henry Barnard's *American Journal of Education,* came to be dominated by men and women for whom education was a vocation. How they became spokesmen for

[1] The typical complaint about the divorce of "positive religion" from the Common Schools is in Rev. W. F. Kremer, "Catechetical Instruction" *Mercersburg Review* 6 (April, 1854), pp. 205-223. For a contrasting view of educational purposes and a specific protest against those who "weep" over the absence of sectarian religious teaching in the public schools see Executive Committee of the Western Literary Institute and College of Professional Teachers, "Education in the West," *The Christian Examiner* 23 (Nov., 1837), pp. 194-207.

[2] Of the few principal educational journals after 1830, the annual proceedings, *American Institute of Instruction* has the clearest clash of views. The other journals were founded largely to propagate enlightened ideas and were, consequently, dominated by faith in new techniques and "Education."

the extension of common school education in the United States is a complex story. Lawrence Cremin has emphasized ideology: the force of American ideals drawn from the Declaration of Independence and the frontier; Sidney Jackson, more effectively, has written of political and social conflict among diverse groups which agreed on the necessity for extending common education, but differed on what should be taught, for what purpose, and at what cost. Too often our notion about this aspect of American history has been too simply one of "Reformers" and "Reactionaries." In fact, like the debate about the nurture of the child, the struggle for free schools was largely about the forms of public education rather than about whether public schools should be established at all. Too much seemed at stake in American society for anyone to ignore the powers of education. But this is not our story here. What is more relevant to the history of child nurture is that with the concurrent growth of the Common School, the spread of Sunday schools (originally secular institutions) and the founding of Infant Schools,[3] society was establishing for the first time powerful agencies to share parents' work with young children and to provide for openly confessed deficiencies in training at home. With more people and more points of view thus involved in raising the child, the conflict of ideas about the aims of nurture grew more intense.

Given some superiority in experience and mind and their stake in their new ideas, enlightened theorists of child nurture rapidly dominated the growing teacher's literature so that it was often more "advanced" than the average home or parents' magazine. William A. Alcott seemed to set themes of liberation and change when he told teachers, as he had told parents, to "study the nature and seek the happiness of the little ones committed to their care."[4] But, like other reformers and parents professing new ideas, Alcott was only seeking new, more effective ways to instill older virtues and traditional subjects: manners, morals, and knowledge. Similarly, if seemingly conservative leaders bewailed the absence of "positive religion" in the common schools,[5] it was not because they feared only for the child's soul. In the words of Theodore Dwight Jr.:

[3] The nationwide interdenominational American Sunday School Union was founded in 1824. See Curti, *op. cit.*, p. 203. On infant schools see "Infant Schools," *Ladies' Magazine* 3 (Nov., 1830), pp. 224-26; 5 (April, 1832), pp. 179-82.

[4] Alcott, *A Word to Teachers*, p. xvi.

[5] Kremer, *op. cit.*

> to separate these . . . [religious, moral, intellectual instruction] is to tear sound education limb from limb. They cannot be divided with impunity. We must present sound and consistent principles to the young, or they will never form sound and consistent characters . . . Who can pretend that the mind is not exposed to perversion, when trained by a deist, an immoral man, or a teacher who passes for either.[6]

In other words, the "conservative" wanted the same broad instruction as others did, but enforced by full religious teachings. In general, sectarian religious teaching was gradually declared to be incompatible with publicly supported education.[7] Jacob Abbott as early as 1831, thought moral and religious education were distinct from each other. Love of God was useful and desirable, but religion was "not the only foundation" of morality.[8]

What then was? If the school was going to share or supplement the work of the home, teachers—like the newly dedicated mothers with perfect homes—had to be noble, their school room environment pleasant, their examples and precepts good, and their text books moral and truthful. With such goals shared, the most ardent believer in strict religious training and the apostles of gentle suasion could agree with Horace Mann's words:

> Educate, only educate enough, and we shall regenerate the criminal and eradicate vice; through the schools we shall teach mankind to moderate their passions and develop their virtues; let us but conquer the world of knowledge that is lying at our doors, and then, and then only shall we be able in the words of the Laureate to 'ring out the false and ring in the new.'[9]

What is being claimed here is that, whatever his particular view of religion in school, no one really dissented from the ideal of an education "based on the characters of men . . . , conducted in accordance with the established principles of nature, revelation and provi-

[6] Theodore Dwight, Jr., "A Review of Cousin's Report on Education in Prussia," *Literary and Theological Review* 2 (June, 1835), p. 329.

[7] Butts and Cremin, *A History of Education in American Culture,* pp. 215-17, 257-59, 272-73.

[8] Jacob Abbott, "Moral Education," *American Institute of Instruction* (1831), pp. 63-64; F. A. Packard, *Thoughts on Popular Education* (Philadelphia, 1836), a leading statement of the opposing view.

[9] Quoted in George E. Hardy, *Literature for Children* (New York, 1892), p. 5.

dence."[10] The idea of the divine mission of teachers to lead "the progress of Christian civilization"[11] and the notion that "whoever has the charge of a young mind should be a moral educator"[12] became the natural corollaries of the new ideas about mothers and their mission.

Teachers, however, were to instruct in the traditional intellectual disciplines as well as in moral matters and almost from the outset of the common school revolution the demand arose for enlarged curricula.[13] Such newer goals for schools as preparation for an active life in the service of society, development and cultivation of morals, and formation of character[14] should not have set school against home, for both shared these ideals. Differences arose about a paradox that was to plague American education continuously. If the schools were to share with the home the new powers of redemption, was it not logical that they had to make strong intellectual and moral demands on the child? Yet parents continued to balk at the school house discipline actually needed to reach the goals set for American education.

What demands any school program ought to make on a child were indicated in a review of Horace Mann's 4th Annual Report. The reviewer agreed with Mann about the dangers of insanity if intellectual training began while the child's emotions were immature.[15] Others commented that too much "analysis" would destroy the "essence" of the child because it tried ". . . to develop the flower before the stalk is grown."[16] Children were to be prepared to acquire knowledge as they needed it, and not to be loaded like "beasts of burthen."[17] These are only samples of numerous complaints against what was thought to be the excessive weight of school work.[18] Para-

[10] Rev. Elysha White, "Introductory Discourse," *American Institute of Instruction* (1837), p. 13.

[11] David Mack, "Claims of Our Age and Country upon Teachers," *American Institute of Instruction* (1839), p. 54.

[12] Warren Burton, "Best Mode of Fixing the Attention of the Young," *American Institute of Instruction* (1834), p. 51.

[13] Braxton Craven of North Carolina advised: Spelling, reading, writing and orthography, arithmetic, geography, composition and grammar, American history, bookkeeping, mensuration, algebra, natural philosophy, English poetry, geometry, chemistry and physiology. These were to be introduced over a nine-year period. Edgar W. Knight, ed., *A Documentary History of Education in the South before 1860,* 5 vols. (Chapel Hill, 1953), Vol. 5, p. 242. Butts and Cremin, *op. cit.,* p. 213.

[14] Henry S. McKean, "The Ends of School Discipline," *American Institute of Instruction* (1835), pp. 131-52.

[15] "Murder of the Innocents," *Atlantic Monthly* 4 (Sept. 1859), pp. 345-56.

[16] H. N. Hudson, "Education," *Democratic Review* 16 (May, 1845), p. 480.

[17] T. B. Fox, "The Meaning and Objects of Education," *American Institute of Instruction* (1835), p. 194.

[18] Kuhn, *op. cit.,* pp. 99-103.

doxically, therefore, at the same time writers were urging the increased responsibilities of the school for redeeming American society, one aspect of reform thought, tenderness about the child, was conflicting with another reform tendency, to provide the highest possible intellectual improvement. The ensuing conflict between what the schools were asked to do in theory and the actual demands the community at large permitted them to make upon the child was and has remained a particularly vexatious problem.

The complaints against the "overloaded child" at school resembled those against the "distorted" child in the home with his fussy dress, poor food, and unnatural manners. The bright child was described at times almost as if he had a disease: "If a child exhibits any symptoms of precocity, it should be immediately taken from books and permitted . . . such amusements as will give rest to the mind and health and vigor to the body."[19] Other observers also claimed that "mental power" meant more than mere knowledge.[20] But all failed to distinguish premature or dessicating intellectualism from the demands necessary to intellectual thoroughness or scholarly seriousness. Instead, in the name of health, happiness, or "real-life," a species of anti-intellectualism soon insinuated itself into discussions and planning of schools. Existing American tendencies to invoke narrow "real-life" or utilitarian standards of intellectual and moral judgment were thus reinforced, and, as Tocqueville had observed, to the derogation of ideals of scholarliness and disinterested philosophic thought. The growing anti-theoretical, anti-intellectual, anti-critical strain was certainly reassuring to getting-and-spending parents who understandably feared the new powers coming to teachers with common-school expansion. But the degree of the workday teachers' and ministers' hostility to encouraging intellectual and critical independence in students should also not be underestimated.[21] Between 1830 and 1860 the attacks on intellectual demands in the schoolroom launched by spokesmen for home, church, and school were wide-ranging. Precociousness was unnatural, and "forced feeding" of ideas even worse for the child than grown-up diets or too-early religious or moral training. At stake were his general health and future growth, including

[19] S. B. Woodward, "Treatment of Scholars," *North Carolina Journal of Education* 1 (July, 1858). Cited in Knight, *op. cit.*, 5, p. 258.

[20] Butts and Cremin, *op. cit.*, p. 268.

[21] Richard Hofstadter, *Anti-Intellectualism in American Life* (New York, 1963), pp. 55-117.

the strength of his physical frame and mental balance, and his capacity for feeling and for a moral life.[22]

These assaults, it must be reiterated, often came in the name of would-be generosity and enlightenment about the child's nature. We even find in these early reformers future themes such as "Life considered as a school, becomes a model for our schools."[23] The anti-intellectualism mixes, therefore, with well-founded criticism of rote recitation[24] or uninviting schoolrooms.[25]

Under all such proto-progressivism and would-be safeguards for the child's well-being we came back eventually in the teachers' literature to "the law" to be written on "the infantile heart."[26] That insistent, transcendent theme of both nurture and education reform should have united schools and home in a great common national effort at moral regeneration. Mutual antagonisms and fears, however, were strong, and ideals, however sacrosanct were abstract and distant in comparison. In contrast with the home, schools brought different classes of children together; "other children" could foster "evil examples" and corrupting associations. Since the schoolmarm was beginning to replace the schoolmaster in the 1830's[27] it was only natural, also, to wonder about her competence, especially whether she, let alone a schoolmaster, could give an individual child a mother's love and attentiveness. Part of the justification for the change to women teachers seems in fact to have been that they would obviously be better able than men to act with "loving tenderness".[28] Even with this new ideal of a teacher, schools were still unlike the home in other respects. They were allegedly overcrowded and poorly or badly staffed, so that much more might be done intellectually for the child

[22] Goodrich, *Fireside Education,* p. 81, "The Young Lady's Friend" (a review), *The Christian Examiner* 22 (March, 1836), p. 93; "The Murder of the Innocents," *Atlantic Monthly* 4 (Sept., 1859), pp. 345-56; "Causes of Insanity," *Ladies' Magazine* 7 (Jan., 1834), p. 79; Humphrey, *Domestic Education,* pp. 74-75.

[23] W. H. Furness, "Introductory Lecture," *American Institute of Instruction* (1835), p. 5.

[24] T. H. Palmer, "Evils of the Present System of Primary Instruction," *American Institute of Instruction* (1837), pp. 209-39.

[25] W. Russell, "The Infant School System of Education," *American Institute of Instruction* (1830), pp. 98-99.

[26] "Infant Schools," *American Annals of Education* 3 (July 1833), pp. 296-304.

[27] Butts and Cremin, *op. cit.,* pp. 283-84.

[28] Horace Mann, *Lectures on Education* (Boston, 1848), p. 74.

in an enlightened home.[29] Mothers might even start school subjects at their hearths.[30]

No sooner, however, were these intrinsic tensions between school and home mentioned than leading reformers of the day denied that conflict was inevitable or unyielding to a little thought and good will. One writer hailed the infant school as an aid to and substitute for parental care.[31] Samuel Goodrich tried to calm fears with semantics: the school was, after all, a kind of seminary; the parent a type of teacher; and the school itself, "the great auxiliary of the fireside."[32] Abbott asked parents first to select teachers carefully and then to cooperate, to understand, and to be kind to them; but for reassurance, he left no doubt about the pre-eminence of the home.[33]

With an improved school thus declared to be simply the perfect home enlarged, no conflict seemed logically possible. Teachers, for example, were to watch the child constantly, like parents, for signs of failure of character and correct them at once. With a parentlike appreciation and study of the child's nature, though the great goal was difficult, teachers could help teach virtue without breaking the will and could aid the home in bringing the child to the discipline appropriate to the service of American and Christian ideals.

As far as curriculum was concerned, it was common belief that there was a relatively fixed body of knowledge and certain basic "skills" to be mastered eventually by all students. This belief and the rough standardization endemic to an early system of wide public education created a curriculum that was the same for all children at given ages. Intellectual mastery came through conquering the material in textbooks under the teacher's guidance and drill.

By 1850, there were already six principal kinds of schoolbooks: readers, spellers, arithmetics, grammars, histories, and geographies.

[29] *The Mother's Assistant* ran a spate of articles criticizing the excessive influence and growing use of common schools for younger children. See the following: William A. Alcott, "There is no School like the Family School," 3 (Jan., 1843); Mrs. M. O. Stevens, "The Restored Family," 4 (May, 1844); Charles Holden, "The Family School," 3 (Nov., 1843).

[30] Sigourney, *Letters to Mothers,* pp. 104-05.

[31] "Infant Schools," *Ladies' Magazine* 5 (April, 1832), p. 182. One important purpose of the Infant School was to "rescue" the children of the poor and the immigrants from becoming threats to society.

[32] Goodrich, *Fireside Education,* p. 64.

[33] Jacob Abbott, "Duties of Parents Re The Schools Where Their Children Are Instructed," *American Institute of Instruction* (1834), pp. 81-98. The ideal teacher is sketched in: David Mack, "The Claims of our Age and Country Upon Teachers," *American Institute of Instruction* (1839), pp. 137-54; Samuel R. Hall, *Lectures in School-Keeping* (Boston, 1829); David Page, *Theory and Practice of Teaching,* 15th ed. (New York, 1853).

By 1829, Noah Webster's famous spellers (1st ed., 1783) had dropped explicit moral catechisms and religious lessons,[34] but standardized texts down to 1900 continued at least to suggest the same moral ideals found in parents' manuals and children's story books combined with each grade's quota of factual information.

Mark Sullivan's description of these early textbooks, however sentimental, has much truth in it. The young "were led from beautiful maxims for children to the best thoughts of a long line of sages and poets."[35] As early as 1830, however, a painless road to such wisdom was being sketched. The preface to *First Reading Lessons for Children* explained,

> Believing that the infant mind is very early susceptible of impressions which may be lasting, the compilers feel engaged to offer to the public this little volume, . . . in which we desire to combine purity of sentiment with beauty of style, as to render them attractive to the youthful mind, and at the same time tend to invite to the attainment of those branches of knowledge, whereby the intellectual faculties are called into action, and which prove a source of rational and social enjoyment.[36]

Such ideas were also combined with conceptions of the child as a "pure, unsullied sheet . . . ready to receive any impression that may be made upon it."[37]

Some of the most revealing of the "impressions" that might come from the schoolroom have been examined by Ruth Miller Elson in a study of American textbooks before 1865.[38] The conception of history common to most textbook authors was that of C. A. Goodrich: History

[34] See Kiefer, *op. cit.,* for a discussion of earlier textbooks; American Book Co., *A Brief Outline of the Evolution of the American Textbook* (New York, 1935); R. R. Reeder, "The Historical Development of School Readers and of Method in Teaching Reading," *Columbia University Contributions to Philosophy, Psychology and Education,* Vol. 8 (May, 1900).

[35] Quoted in Mark Sullivan, *Our Times,* 5 vols. (New York, 1927), Vol. II, p. 12; a brief discussion of early textbooks follows.

[36] *Op. cit.,* pp. iii-iv.

[37] Renssalaer Bentley, *Pictorial Primer* (New York, 1842), p. 5.

[38] Ruth V. Miller, *Nationalism in Elementary School Books Used in the United States from 1776-1865,* doctoral dissertation, Columbia University, 1952. This study confirms the evidence presented here of the essential conservatism of the goals sought through new methods of nurture. The textbooks studied stressed: the rejection of Europe, the exaltation of the Anglo-Saxon and scorning of the immigrant, the moral failure implicit in poverty, the acceptance of one's own station and duties as God's will, the ignoring or attacking of reform movements, the rightness of class distinctions (even after Jackson), and the heroism of Hamilton and Clay. See her Conclusion, pp. 394-401. This dissertation has recently been published. Ruth M. Elson, *Guardians of Tradition* (Lincoln, Neb., 1964).

> . . . sets before us striking instances of virtue, enterprise, courage, generosity, patriotism, and by a natural principle of emulation, incites us to copy such noble examples. History also presents us with pictures of the vicious, ultimately overtaken by misery and shame, and thus solemnly warns us against vice.[39]

American history provided a special moral lesson, revealing the march of a unique people toward fulfilling the idea of liberty under God's constant guidance and aid. Essentially this nationalistic theme, drawn allegedly from the works of George Bancroft,[40] represented a secularized and broadened Puritanism: the idea of the divine election and calling of all Americans.

The generation from the Declaration of Independence to the Constitution was conceived as one in which freedom was completed and handed on to future Americans to preserve and enjoy. The great work was done, for liberty had already been achieved. The Revolution required Americans constantly to test the moral state of the nation and the individual against the standards set by the men of 1776:

> If you seek to know why your countrymen have outstripped all the nations of the earth . . . the reason is easily found. The founders of this nation were honest, true men. They were sincere in all they said, upright in all their acts. They feared God and obeyed the laws. They wrought constantly and vigorously at the work they had to do and strove to live at peace with their neighbours. . . . Above all they insisted, from the very first, on being free themselves, and securing freedom for you, their children. If you follow the example they set, and love truth, honor, religion, and freedom as deeply and, if need be, defend them as stoutly as they did, the time is not far distant when this country will far excel other countries in power, wealth, numbers, intelligence and every good thing, as other countries excelled it before Columbus sailed away from Spain to discover the New World.[41]

America was thus finished and perfect, without extremes of wealth or poverty, an asylum for the oppressed, the bastion of private

[39] C. A. Goodrich, *A History of the United States of America* (Hartford, 1833), p. xii.

[40] A. Goldberg, "School Histories of the Middle Period" in E. Goldman, ed., *Historiography and Urbanization* (Baltimore, 1941), p. 175.

[41] John Bonner, *A Child's History of the United States,* 2 vols. (New York, 1855), Vol. II, p. 319-20.

property and opportunity—in other words, like the perfect child, it was a model creature of the law.

The child who loved his country would copy the virtues of the heroes who made and preserved it. "The holy influence which Washington's name and character will exert upon the world is doubtless incalculable; while human society lasts they will never cease to shed their blessings on mankind."[42] Franklin, the next ranking hero, and the Puritans were models of temperance, thrift, industry, and patriotism. As self-made men they resisted the temptations of luxury, money, speculation, and inflation. Their ingenuity and enterprise pointed the way to a material achievement of which Americans were justly proud. At all times in the past the nation had also received God's help and rewards. In the future it remained to extend Christianity, the institutions of American civilization, and the principles of liberty of the perfect Constitution.[43] Only loyalty to the pure truths and principles that inspired the Fathers assured future material progress and the success of the republican enterprise.

These conceptions of the nation and of its history thus strengthened and supplemented the ideas of individual destiny that parents and teachers were urged to instill in the child. America was the moral individual written large. Nation and child, because of unswerving loyalty to ideals, could confidently face constant trial and temptation in a hostile and corrupt world of inferior nations or evil companions, unfriendly to the great moral experiment as well as to the virtuous man.

---

[42] S. G. Goodrich, *The First Book of History* (Boston, 1831), p. 119.

[43] Cf. A. Weinberg, *Manifest Destiny* (Baltimore, 1935). The gap that separates the public views of the America of a century ago from our own can be fully appreciated by going through these textbooks. Texts other than history books were equally nationalistic.

8

Life *vs.* Law

THE briefest way of stating the dilemma of the American parents and teachers so concerned about both redeeming and protecting the character of the child is that they were trying to maintain traditional and unyielding principles in an uncertain, unstable world. Their inherited Christian, republican code of character and faith became an amalgam of incompatible elements. It was absolute while life was relative. A strong otherworldliness, for example, did not mix well with an intense desire to get as much from the world as possible. How, on the other hand, guarantee the victory of "the truth" without giving the child at least some of the worldly wisdom that the pure and pious affected to despise and which, once learned, might tempt and corrupt him?

Throughout the pre-Civil War literature on the child there is at least the sense of the conflict between the pristine ideals of the Christian republic and its present temptations, its new hopes for its progeny and the weight of the world poised against the redeemed child. Yet perilous as the principled life often seemed, pessimism or skepticism about human nature in general yielded to optimism about nurturing individual possibilities. The sense that American life offered constant temptations to break all rules, an accurate appraisal of what probably awaited the child, was never really brought into balance with the belief that only absolute moral rules were worth having. And yet did not these high spiritual goals go far to account for the feelings of the peril to principle that so troubled the Jacksonian moralists? Where every turn in life is calculated by some master scheme for redemption, life, logically, seems posed in uncompromising terms. Then only absolute self-discipline will suffice against the risks of lurking corruption and damnation. On the one hand, the self is tempted to cast off all limits; on the other, it binds itself to impossible law. The effect is to aggravate the individual's feelings of guilt while stimulating his power-hungry fantasies. Any material or worldly achievement must inevitably carry with it a feeling of betrayal for having paid too high a price, in lives wasted and ideals forsaken, to reach one's goal. In model children of the time, however—in Wallace, Rollo, and Benjamin—the relentless will and the demanding perfect law were made to seem to coincide, thus adding to the moral illusions of the age. The idea that one could live relatively decently amid the conflicting ideals and desires of American life, without constantly reaching for absolutes, whether of religious or mundane success, was one seemingly beyond the wish or understanding, ultimately beyond the moral style of both the popular moralist and his audience.

Still, however unrealistic the picture of their choices and chances in life, acceptable model children by the 1850's had all the virtues that their heirs today allegedly lack. They had, to use the modern jargon, "values" and ideals and these gave their lives "purpose" and "meaning." Their characters were like rocks. They had the ability to resist temptation, the easy way, the lures of the world. They did not go 'round about but straight through. Preeminently, they were people with at least a genuine aspiration to principle. Many had moral dignity and some were even capable of tragedy.

But inseparable from these qualities that may now seem, nostalgically, so admirable, there was, we must not forget, a persistent moral fanaticism, a crippling hunger for absolutism, for the hundred per cent return on a hundred per cent investment in life. Later in the century this old American character faced a world which forced it to confront its illusions and ask if the old guides to spiritual and worldly success were really working, whatever nurture or story books promised.

II
THE CHILD REDEEMER
(1860-1900)

9

A Bridge of Sighs, 1860-1880

AMERICANS in both North and South responded to changes brought by the Civil War by looking back on the years preceding Sumter as a golden age, a time of virtue and innocence, after which the nation had continuously moved away from the South's idyllic "Greek Democracy" and the North's peaceful "agrarian republic."

The nation seemed to forget the sense of *malaise* of the generation after 1830, the attacks on money madness and unscrupulous politicians, the fears of atheism and "upstart radicals," and the sense of loss of old ideals. Instead, the former golden age, the Revolutionary generation, was lengthened and the two generations after 1815 came under the enlarged halo of innocence. This transformation after 1865 was helped by the full arrival of a new generation of political leaders at the helm of the nation. The great men of the years after 1815, the Clays, Websters, Calhouns, and Jacksons, who began to leave the national scene about 1850, had almost fully yielded to their successors by the war's end. With so large a number of dead heroes and battle shrines and the shocked feeling that the war had cut the republic off from their wisdom, the material for new or recast myths was abundant. Writers as different as Twain, Whitman, and Henry Adams became convinced that something precious had left American life—and Henry James' contrasting hope that the Civil War, terrible as it was, would bring Americans to a less innocent and more temperate sense of life's possibilities was unique.

But in their more vigorous and open dedication to the possibilities of money, Americans of the gilded age were almost as naive as their predecessors who had such faith in moral and religious nostrums. They seldom sought money as an end in itself but to have it serve their larger appetites for freedom, power, and love.

After the nation's exhausting bout of idealism before and during the war, and stimulated by the war-induced prosperity in the North, money after 1865 seemed a more realistic measure of success than the distant rewards of heaven. In the gilded age, money became the most powerful and obvious weapon with which Americans tried, pathetically at times, to overcome the stubborn harshness of the world. Of course, there came a euphemism for money—"economic opportunity"—and after Appomattox and under this guise, the vulgarities of money became more powerful and more open and created grave problems of adjusting the old Christian republican code to the demands of a complex industrial society. The anxiety about American life, the continuing sense of *malaise,* expressed by major writers was equally obvious in popular literature, including books for parents and children.

Three popular children's books of the generation 1860-1880 compared with pre-war works show a dramatic change in mood about the world and in conceptions of personal character: Martha Finley's *Elsie Dinsmore* (1867), Louisa May Alcott's *Little Women* (1869), and Horatio Alger, Jr.'s *Bound to Rise* (1873).

Bound to Rise[1] was one of the most popular of the Alger series. Its immediate striking characteristics are its secularism and the association of what had long been largely spiritual traits such as resoluteness and forthrightness with worldly ends and rewards. In *Bound to Rise* there occur only two or three minor references to God, religious duties, or church. As though he was conscious of breaking new ground, Alger claimed that his books "treat of real live boys who were always up and about—just like the boys found everywhere today."[2] "Pious," "holy," "pure," "diligent at prayers and Bible study" and similar phrases that filled the child's books only a generation earlier gave way to "red-blooded" and "manly" as the principal words of praise. The "Vigorous Life" was as important in Alger's gospel of wealth as it

[1] On Alger and Dime novels see Merle Curti, "Dime Novels and the American Tradition" in *Probing Our Past,* pp. 172-88; H. R. Mayes, *Alger: A Biography Without a Hero* (New York, 1928); E. L. Pearson, *Dime Novels* (Boston, 1929); A. Johannsen, *The House of Beadle and Adams* (Norman, Oklahoma, 1950).

[2] Horatio Alger Jr., *Bound to Rise* (New York, 1873), Foreword.

was to be to the anti-materialistic Theodore Roosevelt a generation later.

The Alger story was certainly more realistic than most juvenile books before the Civil War, for the hero's character and world were more complex and less idealized than in Jacob Abbott's Rollo books. But even if Alger admitted that the world, in many cases, permanently defeated the virtuous, the triumphs of the hero were probably all the more tempting to readers, given the more realistic setting.

In *Bound to Rise,* the father of Harry Walton, the hero, is no model for his son for he is a failure. He "was one of those men who can do a great many things creditably, but do not have the knack of conquering fortune." Harry, on the other hand, is already superior to his father in having abundant energy and ambition. He is a student in the nearby country school. Like the sketch of the hero's character, the image of the school is greatly changed from the pre-Sumter era. The teacher emphasizes performance rather than intrinsic virtues. There is no moralizing and there is comparatively light punishment for cheating and lying.[3] Harry himself wants to succeed at school not because of the inherent virtues of excellence, but because "his ambition had been stirred by the offer of a prize, and he was resolved to deserve it." On graduation day he wins the award.

Following graduation, Harry has to choose a career. In analyzing his decision Alger contrasts life on the farm and in the city. Before the Civil War the city was clearly associated with vice and temptation but now Alger, joining the national tendency to question the prestige of the farm, shows life on the land more realistically. Some country people are depicted as mean and corrupt and rural life as harsh and frustrating. Harry's father, however honest and a man of character, is pressed to the wall and is forced to go heavily into debt to the miserly local Squire. The city is still dangerous—"Country people are not robbers. Burglars stay in the cities"—but it represents more opportunity than the farm can offer and Harry concludes, "I must leave home if I want to rise in the world." Alger added a direct warning, lest all country boys should think that there were far greater opportunities in the city than in fact existed: there was only room for a few and one should not be hasty in imitating Harry.

Harry's discussion about leaving home shows less formality between children and parents than one can find in books before the

[3] See Edward Eggleston, *The Hoosier School-Boy* (New York, 1883) for a more famous but similar portrait.

Civil War. There is no reverence or awe for parents or any obvious cowing of children. There is as much give and take, jocularity and joshing at home as in the schoolroom. However more "permissive" this atmosphere, when parents finally speak, they still speak with full authority but Harry's mother and father seem to share authority. Both warn Harry that he is likely to fail if he leaves home but, nevertheless, they give him their permission. Despite an offer from the mean rich Squire for Harry's services, his father prefers to recognize his son's talents for "something better." Harry gets his chance in life because his parents decide to let him go out into the world. But this seeming willingness of the parents to bow to the child's talent is ambivalent. Harry is permitted to leave home to make his own destiny, but also to earn enough money to pay Squire Green's exorbitant charges on the new cow Harry's father had to buy.

These first themes in Alger are clues to the general change that takes place between 1860 and 1880 in American children's literature, a change similar to the earlier transition in adult books from the picaresque to the *Bildungsroman.*

As men abandon traditionalist society for a life of accelerated change and innovation, in the accompanying picaresque literature heroes' characters remain relatively unchanged, although their adventures awaken in them and in the reader a sense of the largeness and diversity of the world and invite speculations about the adequacy of the wisdom of fathers. In the history of American children's books, the child's picaresque as found in Alger books, rapidly gave way to a juvenile *Bildungsroman:* a young hero starts life naively and open to experience and acquires his character gradually through changing, deliberated responses to an uncertain world for which neither his early family life nor social traditions prepare him. In nineteenth century literature repeatedly the "young man from the provinces" leaves the traditionalist village or family home of centuries to test his will and character in "the world." What marked such encounters in modern times, as Hegel had emphasized, was man's developing self-awareness, his idea of his separateness and individual worth, not merely before God, but before all men and regardless of his status and tradition at birth. Defiance of society and tradition became justified in the name of some ideal of character or dictate of reason superior to claims of class, religion, or race. In the mundane motto, careers were to be open to talents.

In the Rollo books, Rollo has been impeccably schooled in inflexible moral precepts by perfect parents and his adventures are merely ways of showing that however diverse and tough the world may actually be there is no need to abandon or change first principles. They are completely compatible with experience and are certain to bring success. In the Alger books the world broadens and beckons. Fame and fortune have new prestige, but they are reached largely by fidelity to traditional ideals. Much of the child's character, however, is free of any heavy weight of moralism and open to some influences of the world. As Harry starts his journey from the provinces to the city, the life of Franklin, the self-made man, a life justified by the claims of will and reason, was "the chart by which he meant to steer in the unknown career which stretched before him." He would be guided by ". . . the wise precepts with which he (Franklin) had shaped and molded his life." Harry's character, in the picaresque style, will remain fixed even though his world is constantly changing and challenging.

Harry's adventures also introduce a second new theme in children's books. The generation 1830-1860 had established ideas of the child as a redeemable creature. Now the child because of superior energy, purity, or magic will become a redeemer of adult failures. From this point on (circa 1870) the sentimental notion that somehow it is better to be a child than an adult, that the best standards of life are those of naive and innocent children becomes an increasingly powerful theme in American culture. Before the War there was no question that a boy should strive as much as possible to grow up and become a man, and a girl a woman. The principles of maturity, to be learned through gentler nurture, were ideals worthy of children. The child had been increasingly viewed as an innocent but the aim of nurture was to bring that innocence to maturity and to leave childhood behind. The adult had confidence in his standards and raised the redeemable child to live by the same ideals. But if Harry makes good he will fulfill his own destiny *and* save his family. Indeed, unless he succeeds, the adults in the family will be lost. The notion that the child can save the adults or redeem their failures is, moreover, built around a boy like Harry who is not a paragon like Rollo but has obvious, if minor, faults that do not lower his moral prestige or impede his success, "Even our hero shared the common weakness"—of carving initials on his school desk.

Harry's adventures bring him into touch with exotic people and new ideas and he is far more flexible and less moralistic than Rollo in meeting new experiences. An old insane man tells him a fantastic story that Harry merely finds amusing rather than a repulsive lie or "misleading fiction." The hero is constantly tempted and taunted and, finally, robbed by a young man named Luke, who hates "old sayings." When Luke asks Harry to play billiards, he refuses because he is saving his money for his parents; he says nothing about having moral scruples against gambling. Harry may have the guidance and comfort of his principles but he is more troubled than earlier heroes by the opinion of others. "He knew he was right, but it was disagreeable to be called a miser." Offered a cigar, he refuses it simply, without any sermonizing, because, "I don't think it would do me any good." When he decides to continue his journey after his first job is cancelled, Alger comments,

> This was good philosophy. Waiting passively for something to turn up is bad policy and likely to lead to disappointment; but waiting actively, ready to seize any change that may appear is quite different. The world is full of chances, and from such chances so seized has been based many a prosperous career.

Although one must be virtuous to be successful, to virtue one must now add "the breaks."

Harry's next job is with a traveling magician who openly admits that his business is to deceive people. Harry seems untroubled by this and laughs at an old lady who becomes upset by the magician's ventriloquism. He has no qualms about working with a man who is a trickster, perhaps because the magician is essentially an honest and decent man.

When bringing a doctor for the magician who has taken sick, Harry gives a lift to a stranger who repays his kindness by robbing him of his savings of forty dollars and his new coat. The robber, however, leaves Harry his old warm jacket from which he forgets to remove a wallet with ninety-seven dollars. By pure luck, Harry ultimately profits for being kind to the thief; his principles do not dictate trying to return fifty-seven dollars change. When he returns to the magician the landlady is surprised, having predicted his desertion with the horse and wagon. "So he had come back after all and falsified her prediction. Such is human nature, that for an instant she was disappointed." Virtue now can not only be unappreciated, it can be positively envied, and a few pages later comes another break in the old moral certainties, "Worldly prosperity doesn't always go by merit. Plenty of mean men prosper."

Harry returns home with his savings for a visit, just in time to save the family from the Squire whose fault is living by a principle, the rule that "A contrack's a contrack. It's the only way to do business." Alger concludes the story, ". . . I am quite aware that I have hardly fulfilled the promise of the title. He (Harry) has neither lived long nor learned much as yet, nor has he risen very high in the world. In fact he is still at the bottom of the ladder. I propose, therefore, to devote another volume to his later fortunes . . . which will be entitled *Risen from the Ranks* or *Harry Walton's Success*."

If the world gives way slowly before fallible but worthy Harry Walton, and is less quick to judge him and others harshly, it seems to be in positive conspiracy against the ideally moral Elsie Dinsmore. Elsie is one of the first of the poor little rich girls. She is perfectly good, though not especially bright, and is obsessed by love for God and Jesus, and by thoughts of her duty. Unlike little Eva, although too good for this world, she still has to live in it. This child is the pure angel of earlier nurture writers, but the world is now hell. Few people really love or understand Elsie. She is mistreated by everyone, especially her widower father, who has returned from Europe believing that she is an impossible child. Elsie's only friends are outcasts like herself—Negroes, a crippled boy and a lady religious fanatic.[4]

Elsie does not try to evade or soften her conscience. She is completely guileless and easily becomes an open target for pranks and teasing. She serves only the absolute but, unlike Rollo, has no power in a world of moral compromises, evasions of duty, and interest in money and power. Unlike her worldly father, she is a martyr for the cause of God's truth; yet her father's cruelty is not due to wickedness but to lack of understanding and confusion about his unusual child.

Having a pure will, Elsie never intentionally or consciously does anything wrong but somehow her innocent actions and motives are always misconstrued. They never bring the approval or rewards that earlier readers anticipated from serving virtuous ideals. She is warned by her father not to sit on the floor but, accidentally, one day she does so. Struck with horror (or with guilt for her unconsciously moti-

[4] Martha Finley, *Elsie Dinsmore* (New York, 1867).

vated rebellion), she rushes to her father and confesses her sin. But he scolds her and sends her to bed without supper instead of forgiving her or taking her good intentions into account.

The crisis comes when Mr. Dinsmore gives a dinner party on a Sunday, "apparently quite forgetful that it was the Lord's day." Adults and other children, are by now always making such mistakes and committing such sins. One of the guests wants to hear Elsie play the piano and sing. Mr. Dinsmore is happy to send for her but his step-mother warns him that Elsie will not obey him because it is Sunday.

> She will tell you she is wiser than her father, and that it would be a sin to obey him in this. Believe me, she will most assuredly defy your authority, so you had better take my advice and let her alone—thus sparing yourself the mortification of exhibiting before your guests your inability to govern your child.

Mr. Dinsmore is adamant. Although he knows Elsie's scruples, he is determined to make her play. Sensing this, Elsie prays for strength and appears to face the ordeal. A dreadful scene follows in which Elsie refuses her father and is made to sit at the piano until she decides to change her mind. She tells a guest, Mr. Travilla, who advises her to give in to her father, about offending Jesus' command and that there is no such thing as a little sin. Mr. Dinsmore says that it is nonsense for Travilla to say that no parent has a right to coerce a child into violating her conscience.

Elsie remains at the piano until well into the evening and then faints, falls, and seriously cuts her temple. "Dinsmore," says Travilla, "you're a brute." The father is now all remorse but angelic Elsie's first words are, "Dear Papa, are you angry with me?" Elsie is put to bed but, weak as she is, insists on her prayers, pleading especially that her father be made to love Jesus. Mr. Dinsmore asks her about this and Elsie answers that loving Jesus would make papa happy and send him to heaven. He asks why she thinks that he doesn't love Jesus. Elsie, tearfully answers, ". . . you know Jesus says, 'He that keepeth my commandments, he it is that loveth me.' " Dinsmore then asks if she loves her father. She makes it clear that she loves him deeply but when he asks, "Better than anyone else?" she answers, "No, papa, I love Jesus best, you next." He leaves the room after kissing her again but "not quite willing that she should love even her Saviour better than himself." The next day, Monday, Elsie plays for

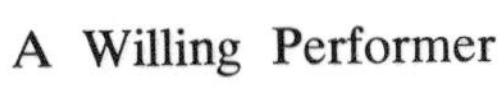

A Willing Performer

the company to her father's pride. "Thus the clouds which had so suddenly obscured little Elsie's sky, seemed to have vanished as speedily as they had arisen." Her father loved her more than he had for he thought of how he had nearly lost her through her fall. But not only has Elsie's "fall" been due to her virtue; the general harmony of the moral order now seems fundamentally disturbed. The child is still good and pure and true to the past but now the father, although in Dinsmore's case loving his daughter, is hard put to understand, let alone appreciate, her purity and innocence. On the contrary, he, his friends and other adults, now mislead, tempt, and punish the good child. The weight of the world against the Word is more onerous for loyalty to God and Christ is no guarantee of love and spiritual peace. Even at the end of the story when Elsie has largely won her father's love and, as the child redeemer, has affected his character for the better, dark clouds gather. Elsie's next test will be a new Mrs. Dinsmore but the reader can be certain that this model child will fervently cling to her simple faith, even at the cost of again embarrassing her father whose world of business, friends, and romance has no place for her purity and virtue.

In Louisa May Alcott's *Little Women*,[5] Beth closely resembles Elsie—she is all love and piety. In that respect she is unlike her more "real" sisters, Amy, Meg, and especially Jo, who are all conscious of their moral duties but are always practicing their particular faults; ". . . though we want to be good, it's hard work, and we forget, and don't do our best." The March girls are feminine versions of the lovable bad boy who made his first impression in America at this time in such books as Thomas B. Aldrich's *The Story of A Bad Boy* (1870). Both Tom the bad boy and the March sisters live in a world in which a moral life is difficult primarily because there is so much more to take into account in making one's decisions by the rules. But it is also a world like Harry Walton's in which it is possible to like people not only because they are virtuous but because they are clever, pretty, and sing or play well. More than any earlier writer for children L. M. Alcott deferred to her young reader's natural curiosity about how people look and live rather than stressing their moral qualities. Each of the girls can be admired despite small deficiencies of character. In fact, the heroine, Jo the tomboy, is the least virtuous of them all. But doing wrong does not bring loss of moral status, as much as worries that the girls will not be happy.

[5] Louisa May Alcott, *Little Women* (Boston, 1869).

All faults are forgiveable, however, through love and "trying to do better." More to the point, disobedience and willfulness are no longer always necessarily wrong. Jo, defying an order of her Aunt March, reads to her from the *Vicar of Wakefield.* Rather than the scolding, moralizing, and punishment one might have expected from a pious Christian lady, Aunt March likes the book and approves Jo's decision although it was made after she warned against reading to her from anyone but Belsham, a Bible commentator. Jo's general comment about stories with a moral that the girls enjoy hearing from their mother is, "I like to think about them afterwards if they are real and not too preachy."

Even more serious faults of character do not bring certain, complete ruin. One bad step does not imply all the rest to damnation. The worst fault is hurting the feelings of people who love you. Amy, for example, angers her teacher and is deeply troubled because she ". . . shall have to tell at home and they will be so disappointed in me." Mrs. March upholds the teacher because he does represent moral and intellectual authority. But after hearing Amy's story, she also says that he was a tyrant and not fit to teach. "Mr. Davis knew any quantity of Greek, Latin, Algebra and ologies of all sorts, so he was called a fine teacher; and manners, morals, feelings and examples were not considered of any particular importance." Mrs. March angrily withdraws Amy from the school but, nevertheless, she tells Amy ". . . you broke the rules, and deserved some punishment for disobedience."

Jo's struggle against her great fault, her temper, is a constant theme in the book. Even though she knows that her outbursts hurt other people, she can not curb them. Finally, after a particularly serious episode, Mrs. March makes a supreme effort and confides in Jo that she herself had to overcome a similar fault. This comes as a great surprise. "That her mother had a fault like hers, and tried to mend it made her own easier to bear and strengthened her resolution to cure it." Mrs. March tells Jo that she was helped by her husband's fine example and by the responsibilities of children. When all else failed she called on God. All goodness and happiness ultimately come from loving Him, but it is possible to desire them directly and for their own sake.

The emphasis on "character" is most obvious in those parts of *Little Women* based on Bunyan's *Pilgrim's Progress.* Several of the chapters have titles taken from the Bunyan book; its plot also enters the girls' conversation and affects their daily life. *Pilgrim's Progress* is not a formal text for meditation along with the Bible. It becomes, in proto-progressive fashion, a game in which a climb from the cellar to the attic imitates Christian's journey and meeting with temptations on the way. A the end of the trip the children receive cake and milk from mother at the top of the house, not intangible spiritual rewards in a lecture or lesson. Mrs. March does point out that the game is really ". . . a play we are playing all the time in one way or another . . . the longing for goodness and happiness is the guide that leads us through many troubles and mistakes to the place which is a true Celestial City." She asks her girls always to play the "game" in earnest.

Even after the girls' father returns from the Union Army Mrs. March remains the lawgiver in the home but somehow she must reconcile that role with her role as the source of permission and forgiveness. Although she wants her girls to learn moral principles, she does not believe in absolute application of unvarying rules. She thinks, for example, that all play and no work is as bad as all work and no play. When tempted to moralize she checks herself because she realizes the limits of preaching. Rather than catechize, she decides that rules can be learned only directly from experience. She will relax her authority and let the girls experiment for themselves, confident that "right living" will have a firmer basis in their daily experience than in her exhortation. When vacation comes, she relieves the girls of all duties for one week. The girls are free for day-dreaming, their favorite pastime, but the author makes clear her own preference for "reality." At the week's end the girls are bored, short-tempered, and unusually discontented. Mrs. March suddenly turns over all her duties to them on the last day and the girls botch everything. They quickly and happily agree when their mother, finally revealing her plan of education, says, "You think, then, that it is better to have a few duties, and live a little for others, do you?"

Still, although principles are now learned by direct experiment, conscience seems weak. Beth is the best-intentioned and best-behaved of the girls. Jo indicates Beth's place in the family and status in the story when she says "Beth is my conscience." The keeper of conscience, however, is frail and unimpressive as a personality. Her wishes for herself reveal a theme that will have growing importance in children's literature in the next generation, the rejection of adulthood and of mature responsibilities because of fears that the world's ways are too powerful and too dangerous for innocent moral beings to confront. In *Little Women,* Beth, the conscience, so in contrast with Rollo's eagerness to take on the world and test his manly powers, says "Let me be a little girl as long as I can." As the other girls grow older, despite their longing for wealth and travel, they sense and resent the fact that growing up inevitably involves the loss of the innocence and security of childhood. They wish to be women but only "little women." There are several hints of this. At one point Meg overhears someone comment about her approaching eligibility for marriage. "These foolish, yet well meant words had opened a new world to Meg, and much disturbed the peace of the old one, in which, till now she had lived so happily as a child." As Mr. Brooke, the tutor of Laurie, the boy next door, enters their lives, becomes a likely husband for one of the girls, and thus suggests the end of childhood, his relations with them are characterized as an "intrusion" on the family. Jo slowly gives up being a tomboy. But her ambivalence about womanliness and maturity is suggested when, instead of rearranging her long hair in the grown up fashion of the day, she cuts it short. She also resents Meg's engagement as another sign of approaching womanhood.

These three books published immediately after the war announce themes that were to be used extensively in the children's books of the next generation: the loveable, though erring child; the pure child whose good intentions are obscured or rejected by a corrupt world; the child whose spiritual or practical gifts can redeem the lives of adults but who sometimes senses his impotence.

These children live in a more open and dangerous world that makes maturity perilous. The boys and girls in earlier books never doubted that their decisions were clear; the consequences of their choice were equally unambiguous. Virtue would be victorious because it was virtue. After the Civil War, however, everything seems to intervene between the best will in the world and moral or material victory. There is still the "happy ending" but not without young people learning how much more life costs than their predecessors realized and how less often and more slowly the rewards of character and piety come. Above all, although the notion endured that only the pure and innocent could save the world, it was increasingly feared that the world might be too much for the pure and innocent.

10

Gentle Methods for a Harsher World

THE most striking quality of the most famous nurture book [1] in the decade just after the Civil War, is the way the promises it held out to parents contrasted with the possibilities we have just depicted in children's literature. New knowledge about human development made available between 1850 and 1870 increased Jacob Abbott's earlier confidence that an upright character and deeply pious faith could be achieved, and at little cost to the child's happiness and contentment. Abbott now made the most sweeping and optimistic deductions from the evidence of natural evolution. He showed no sensitivity to the bleak picture of man's struggle and death in a world without God, the vision that so many intellectuals derived from Darwin and that deepened the continuing "crisis of faith" of the mid-nineteenth century. Instead, Abbott adopted a conventional optimistic Christian compromise: evolution toward ever better forms of life was God's beneficent plan for man.

Even in a more sophisticated form this compromise cosmology was questionable on several grounds. As radicals on both sides of the great debate about evolution insisted, there was no possible compromise with the main claims and implications of Darwinism. Either evolutionary naturalism or the historic Christian view of man's special creation and God's continuing providence was the way to understand the origins and development of life; one could not really

[1] Jacob Abbott, *Gentle Measures in the Management and Training of the Young* (New York, 1871). This book will be examined as a transitional work exemplifying general changes in nurture books from 1860 to about 1880.

have both. Abbott, like many other writers, had already moved toward a more genial Christianity before Darwin. It was not, therefore, as difficult for him as for still-orthodox Protestants and Catholics to recast his faith to take account of the claims of evolution. His earlier turn from the old strenuous Christian axioms about God and man now also led on to growing optimism about the child in the light of evolutionary ideas.

There was intrinsically no connection, however, between the facts of biological evolution and priority for any specific morality for man or child. Nevertheless, in this first generation of Darwinism, progressive and meliorist views of man that had been developing in the West since at least the early eighteenth century were tacked onto the evidence for evolution. As Richard Hofstadter has observed,[2] the vastness and vagueness of Darwin's theories made them useful for a great variety of thinkers, ranging from authoritarian, militarist racists to humane, democratic socialists. The claims that evolution, inherently, was clearly headed in one direction or another or that one tendency of evolution had moral superiority over another, were not much more than pious personal preferences, since, in fact, evolution included the development of the idea and force of evils as well as virtues. That men preferred or practiced one or another ideal gave no intrinsic philosophic basis in evolution for recommending either.

By the 1870's, when Abbott published *Gentle Measures in the Management and Training of the Young,* the victory of the more optimistic nurture ideas of the two previous generations was almost completely assured. By uniting these views with what seemed the impressive evidence of evolution, Abbott helped move child study to much solider ground than supplied in previous debates about the child's eternal essence. However wrong Abbott and others may have been about the inherent moral of evolution, the shift to evolutionary studies of the child was immensely fruitful. Whatever life one wanted for the child, there was no doubt that he did develop and change in response to the possibilities of his native endowment playing against the limits of his surroundings.

Abbott cited no clue or authority for his new body of facts about child development, but he consciously and eagerly deferred to the latest knowledge about the origins and growth of the child's mind and body. He thus abandoned most of his older arguments from

[2] Richard Hofstadter, *Social Darwinism in American Thought* (Philadelphia, 1944).

abstract premises about the creation and destiny of the soul. He was less quick to use sweeping judgements about "sins" and faults, and adopted new "scientific" evidence for his older claim that the child's powers developed gradually and could not be forced. When compared with his earlier tone and ideas, *Gentle Measures* shows how much advice on the child had changed just in one lifetime.

Abbott's two principal themes were: authority "without violence or anger" and "right development . . . in harmony with the structure and characteristics of the juvenile mind." At every point Abbott emphasized that moral training must take into account physiological and neurological conditions.[3] At least half the book was filled with images and analogies drawn from mid-century science: "the laws of induction," the "hydrostatic paradox," "the persistence of force." He explained, for example, that children responded slowly to reading lessons because their "cerebral organization" was not sufficiently advanced. The mind at an early stage of growth could be influenced only by the immediate fact rather than by what was remote and general; this way of mental growth was now presented as "the design of Divine Providence."[4] A long, complex recapitulation of recent observations in physics and chemistry preceded the final explanation of why children were so active: eating food created energy; if the energy was not released, trouble would result. Play was thus a necessity because the child often took more pleasure in using excess energy in sheer action than in attaining the apparent object of his action. "Capriciousness" was thus only apparent; it had a cause and purpose that the mother should understand and respect.[5] The child's imagination was equally complex in origin; the more active it was, the better for the child. Parents could be pleased with both physical and mental exuberance and should not denounce and restrain them.[6] The imagination, when understood, could powerfully help both parents and teachers. As for the old question of innate depravity versus the effects of environment, "bad tendencies" in the child were blamed not on a supernatural essence, but on heredity; "bad habits of action" were not inevitable consequences of a partial spiritual corruption, but came from improper training.[7]

[3] Abbott, pp. 92-93.
[4] *Ibid.*, p. 87.
[5] *Ibid.*, Chap. 14.
[6] *Ibid.*, Chap. 15.
[7] *Ibid.*, p. 104.

Similar to this greater sophistication about physical and intellectual growth was Abbott's awareness of the difficulties moral questions created for both children and adults. To begin with, the child's judgments were simpler than the adult's because of physiological and neurological immaturity. But it was also important to recognize at any time that moral problems "are very complicated in their nature, and in their bearings and relations. They present many aspects which may vary according to the point of view from which they are regarded."[8] Such faults as boasting, wasting food, breaking a new knife, slowness in learning to spell, and stupidity were at least partly due to the difficulties immature children had in learning things, especially when what most affected them was "not the arguments that convinced but the person who led them."[9] As G. H. Mead and John Dewey were to argue a generation later in their famous work on ethics, Abbott recognized that the growth of a moral life was affected more by the person the child wished to resemble than by what the child is told or thinks he ought to do.[10] The parent should be tolerant, patient and, above all, sympathetic, not picking on seeming faults but waiting instead for virtues, commending them and encouraging their practice.

Among faults, Abbott gave special attention to the old problem of "Truth and Falsehood." What was now called a capacity for "truthtelling" was not inherent but learned from experience. Early "deviations" should be dealt with easily. The infant's powers of judgment were weak and should not be relied upon nor over-tested. Demand only what children can understand or accept. Call their powers "gently into action within the limits prescribed by the degree of maturity to which they have attained."[11] Instruction, not anger, was the ideal. Enlist the aid of a loving, not a vengeful God. Realize the distinction between deception and lying; not "by any means" were they the same.[12] A man's "sacred word" was far more important than the "mere action" of a deception, a "false appearance" far less blamable than a "false statement."[13] The truth need not be spoken at all times but "falsehood is to be spoken never." (Only some corrupt

[8] *Ibid.*, p. 127.
[9] *Ibid.*, p. 124.
[10] *Ibid.*, p. 123.
[11] *Ibid.*, p. 243.
[12] *Ibid.*, p. 225.
[13] *Ibid.*, p. 226.

Europeans believed that falsehood was permissible if it served a good end. On the contrary, Abbott insisted, it was never permissible.)

With each of the other specific problems of discipline Abbott stressed calm and gentle but inflexible firmness. For "Wishes and Requests,"[14] no reasons were to be given for essential commands. Obedience was to come after the first demand by the parent and the child was to take the first answer to any question. But for other than what the author vaguely called "essentials," the greatest freedom was to be allowed. Although inconvenient at times, children's questions were to be welcomed as a sign of "increasing mental activity" and as the best means of access to the mind and heart.[15] Short and simple answers, with as little information as possible were to be given so as not to "stuff" the child. Possibly no information at all needed to be given if, for example, the child was satisfied with so simple an explanation that stars shine because they are very bright.[16] "I don't know" should be used as an answer whenever it was appropriate.

Many problems were now fully discussed for the first time in nurture books. Money was to be used to develop judgment and wisdom.[17] A regular allowance was advised with no break in the system—and a real system was necessary for the child to prevent giving him money only as determined by "the frequency and importunity of his calls."[18] Such a system would also inculcate the business virtues of thrift and care that assured success in later life. "Money training" was not only a new subject but it now brought the commercial world directly into the home. The mother was to play banker and the child the businessman. To the objection that allowances would make the child believe that the money was owed him, Abbott answered that the parents' desire for the pleasure of giving money only when they wanted to was a "petty sentimental qualification"[19] that should be sacrificed for the greater good afforded by the allowance system.

An even more remarkable change in twenty years was Abbott's latest advice on religion. "Religious Training"[20] was now introduced with a denial that the author wished to touch on anything controversial! Just as he hoped he had avoided offending on any other matter, he promised to treat those aspects of religion that would arouse no dis-

[14] *Ibid.*, Chap. 18.
[15] *Ibid.*, p. 255.
[16] *Ibid.*, pp. 264-65.
[17] *Ibid.*, Chap. 20.
[18] *Ibid.*, p. 268.
[19] *Ibid.*, p. 271.
[20] *Ibid.*, Chap. 23.

sent, an indication of the extent to which religion was becoming a private matter that a popular moralist could no longer easily discuss in detail.

Indeed, Abbott's desire to find some broad middle ground on which all Christians could agree meant avoiding all those theological issues probably most worth debating. On the other hand, Abbott's "basic faith" is one of several indications after the Civil War of the decline of stringent sectarianism and the advances, alongside new waves of evangelism, of that broad common syncretist "American faith" that has by now become so familiar to us and often reaches at best, an intellectually vague emotional ethics.

Abbott started his advice on the child's religious life by stating that he believed there was universal agreement that piety meant a change in heart and that it consisted in "submission to the will of God and cordial, kind feelings toward every man."[21] Differences among Americans arose over means to these ends, over the meaning of the words of the Maker rather than the facts of human nature. Abbott thought there could be little argument with these propositions:

1. Religious training, like all training, takes time.
2. Trust in God's help.
3. Act as though your will counted even if it is really God's will that is needed.
4. Use only the appropriate means of influence.
5. Parents must set examples.
6. Avoid complex theology and read the Bible to touch the heart; emotions thus aroused will later blossom into right thoughts.
7. Avoid terror and distress.
8. Don't tell children they are sinners; it creates an unbridgeable gulf between them and ministers.
9. If used at all to stimulate piety, rewards and punishments should be employed sparingly.
10. Follow Jesus Christ in emphasizing future goodness and happiness rather than past errors.

One of the best tests of proper religious nurture, and of proper upbringing generally, continued to be the child's obedience to his parents.[22] Since the new "scientific" knowledge indicated that a fractious child could no longer be regarded simply as "a little viper" or

[21] *Ibid.*, p. 309.
[22] *Ibid.*, Chap. 21.

an example of depraved tendencies, the problem of discipline was much more complex. Abbott may have had greater realism about the child's development and natural needs so that he could now suggest a remarkably benign religious education but he was notably reluctant to compromise or qualify the parent's authority in any way. Advancing further from his enlightened views of the 1840's, he had even graver doubts about the propriety of using the rod. Many moral and psychological arguments were against it and with the future advance of knowledge of child behavior its use might completely disappear. For the present Abbott saw a case for it with savages, or when a situation was beyond the skill of a teacher, or with children hopelessly spoiled or mismanaged.

Corporal punishment, however, was the final and most forceful means to obtain "complete, absolute, unquestioned authority."[23] Two better and gentler means were "manoeuvre and artifice," and "reason and affection," while neither "tricks" nor soothing explanations in advance of a request were good bases for gaining obedience. These latter were "a sandy foundation" for establishing the parental authority that came from God and nature.[24]

It would still be splendid if the child could be trained to do the right for the right's sake, and merely because his mother or father asked something, but Abbott (and family life) had perhaps grown too soft to permit making the old authoritative and unrewarded demands. Parents should flatly state what they wanted and then, if they liked, follow compliance with reward, but long enough afterwards so that it would not seem an immediate result of obedience. If this bribe was not joining the devil's company it was at least fellow-traveling.

All his advice about gentler controls implied strengthened belief in the child's rationality or tractability. Not only could the child be saved from sin without harsh reproof, lectures, psychological disorders and frights (especially from nurses of "certain nationalities in Europe") but gentle methods would even increase his love for his parents. The mind would be calmed and "painful excitement" avoided. "Childish faults and foolishness" would be overcome and the child would take a positive pleasure in subduing wrong and doing what was right. Above all, however, all commands, if gently and firmly given, would establish that parental authority without which disrespect, contempt, and chaos would dominate family life. Used properly, Abbott

[23] *Ibid.*, p. 11.
[24] *Ibid.*, pp. 12-15.

said, his advice would make the mother a queen to her children, capable of maintaining control over them until their late 'teens when their own reason would be ready to assume command.

In beginning her work the mother had to recognize that the infant had at best only a capacity for the habit of obedience. The particular rules for creating the habit were few and simple. Above all, not severity but certainty of punishment must be the standard. Secondly, punishment should always be remedial, not vindictive. In school and family government there was "no question on this point." If "vengeance is the Lord's," the home was the first place to recognize that claim. Thirdly, the aim of all punishment should not be justice for past mistakes, for that would arouse the "anger, ill-will and ill temper" of the child, but wise provisions for his safety and happiness in the future.

These recommendations seem far more vague than the old system of nurture under which right was right and a violation was quickly and unambiguously punished. These latest methods for making discipline more rational and loving might eventually vitiate the very authority that parents sought for themselves, but Abbott maintained that if steadily used his methods would never degenerate into "trifling" with troubles. If, for example, the mother observed a fault she might calmly say "Prison." The well-trained culprit would then go into a special corner for a few moments of meditation after which the mother would smilingly say "Free!"[25] Supposedly such games and similar techniques would turn the child toward the right, but one wonders what a really shrewd recalcitrant would soon make of this sport or, for the less inventive child, what sort of feelings would really come from mother calmly sending her loved one to prison.

This drift toward excessively contrived discipline and over-optimism about the child's obedience were even more obvious in the many hypothetical situations Abbott conceived to illustrate his new ideals. These were, in fact, "case-studies" and attempted to tie theory to fact. They were to lead later to the question and answer exchanges in newspapers and magazines between "experts" and troubled parents.

In one of Abbott's "cases," a seventeen-year-old boy named George returned home to take care of his fractious brother, ten-year-old Egbert. Their mother is ill and her sickness gives young and knowledgeable George a chance to reform his spoiled younger brother. Egbert wants to go fishing and George agrees if Egbert promises to

[25] *Ibid.*, pp. 49-50.

obey him. They set out and soon come to a fork in the road. One spur leads directly to the fish pond, the other first crosses a stream over a log. Despite George's command, Egbert rushes off on the dangerous road and prances safely across the log. George follows and says nothing. On the other side he tells Egbert suddenly that he cannot go fishing, that they must go home for reasons that George will not reveal until that evening. Egbert refuses and starts to run off to play in the field. George responds by saying that is fine with him because he can relax under the trees. Ever-contrary, Egbert at once decides that he wants to go home. That evening George puts Egbert to bed without further fuss but he tells him a story of how some soldiers were killed because their leader did not follow orders. "In a manner adapted to Egbert's state of mental development," the events of the day were reviewed and Egbert sees his own errors and seriously resolves to correct them.[26] Abbott concluded with this summary:

> If the penalty annexed to the transgression is made as much as possible the necessary and natural consequence of it, and is insisted upon calmly, deliberately, and with inflexible decision, but without irritation, without reproaches, almost without any indications even of displeasure, but is, on the contrary, lightened as much as possible by sympathy and kindness, and by taking the most indulgent views and admitting the most palliating considerations in respect to the nature of the offense, the result will certainly be the establishment of the authority of the parent or guardian on a firm and permanent basis.[27]

This quotation by itself, let alone the rest of Abbott's book, prefigures some of the principal themes in child nurture advice after 1880. Essential and traditional ideals of moral conduct are not challenged in fact or compromised in theory. The latest scientific knowledge of child development replaces abstract arguments between humane claims about essential goodness and older Calvinist themes of innate depravity. The new knowledge is accepted as proof that the child can really have whatever future adults decide to give him. Although after 1870 a few men begin to study the child dispassionately, relatively free of conscious bias, the general public debate about the child continues to be colored more by ideas of what America needs than by what the child is or deserves. The arguments are more secular or, better, less

[26] *Ibid.*, pp. 53-57.
[27] *Ibid.*, p. 58.

Helping Mother

clearly religious, but the seeming assurance that so much in the child's nature is now within human control rather than in God's hand strengthens the belief that a near-perfect human nature can be created. Yet, such optimism about individual children plays against deepening fears. For one thing, a new natural limit on human possibility was raised by the claims of heredity, which countered the enthusiasm for using science to perfect the child so that he could save the nation or "the race." The optimism of the experts also has to be taken against the growing skepticism in fiction about the powers of the innocent child, the fear that the moral costs of life in America were growing too high for the pure to pay.

11

Grass-Roots Enlightenment

AFTER the 1870's and Abbott's book, the manuals and journals on home life and parenthood show how rapidly the study of the child came under professional scrutiny and control. Academic and scientific students of child behavior and development reached out to the general public through their own books and articles and popular writers following Abbott showed remarkable alertness to the usefulness of physiology, neurology, and physics in understanding the child. During the fifty years after American pediatrics had received a start with Dewee's treatise of 1826, writers for the parents were still deferring to "experts" largely by quoting the views of arm-chair philosophers or theologians. Within this same period, however, especially after the middle of the century, scientific and medical studies proliferated and deepened, gaining public prestige from their fight against disease, their seeming disinterestedness, and the hope they held out for longer and healthier lives. This reputation, along with the rapid accumulation of what seemed realistic indisputable facts about the child's development, obviously contrasted with advice on nurture cast in abstractions. After the publication of Abbott's *Gentle Measures* it seemed impossible to ignore "the claims of science."

The growth of *expertise* after 1870 was, however, eclectic, uncoordinated, and widely scattered over two continents. There were as yet no general "clearing houses," "institutes," or "conferences on values" to evaluate and "synthesize" the latest reports. Instead, the possibility of uniting many separate and special studies into a popularized general system of scientific nurture was encouraged by intellectual events themselves, principally by Darwinism and the great debates over evolution. We know that Darwin deepened and widened public curiosity about human origins and development but he also seemed to provide scientists with a fruitful basis for a systematic "unified understanding" of the vast disparate problems of the body and the mind that were under scientific investigation at mid-century. We have given so much attention to the ethical and religious consequences of Darwin's work that we tend to forget its equally extraordinary ramifications for biological studies and psychology. Darwinism was not, of course, revolutionary in proposing that disparate phenomena be studied in their development, for that idea had been used in the West since Aristotle, but in addition it suggested the possibility of a comprehensive naturalistic theory of life agreeing with all observable facts. Although Darwin's ideas were full of ambiguities and were in many respects tentative and incomplete, such phrases drawn from him and Spencer as "struggle for survival," "natural selection" and "survival of the fittest" seemed to point toward a definitive naturalistic cosmology, satisfying to both scientists and laymen looking for some viable model of "unified understanding." It was for this reason that Darwinism became the most serious challenge that idealist philosophy and religious orthodoxy had faced in a century of increasingly powerful opposition.

After 1859, however, pretensions to a radical naturalism, or, for that matter, on the other side, a thoroughgoing idealism or supernaturalism were only extreme positions in a highly variegated intellectual debate. And what scientists, philosophers, and theologians themselves claimed about evolution was more sophisticated than what the general public discussed, although there was a remarkably large lay interest in clashes of leading intellectuals as Spencer, Huxley, and others.

The principal names and events connected with evolutionary and scientific child study after 1870 alert us to these directions of expert opinion and popular understanding. Although diverse, "enlightenment" was reaching the grass roots of society and, increasingly, educated laymen were striving for the best scientific ideas. For the public at large, with the spread of literacy and publishing, and the force of ideologies our own familiar version of modernity was dawning; everything in life was becoming a "subject" or a "problem." The public also sensed the power and prestige to be gained from a more cultivated intellectual awareness, as exemplified by the life and work of leading contemporary scientists. It found most evidence of the potentialities of scientific ideas in their advances in controlling disease and death. Were there not, given such indications, definitive "solutions" and answers at last in sight about the child?

Between 1880 and 1900, among the European and American experts whose work became known to the public were Dewey, James, Thorndike, Tiedeman, Sigismund, Preyer, Sully, Pollock, Perez, Shinn, Winfield Hall, Tracy and, especially toward the end of the century, G. Stanley Hall. These men were publishing books and monographs and helping establish systematic studies of the child at universities. At Clark University, largely under Hall's aegis, a generation of child study was to culminate in the founding of the well-known Children's Institute in 1909, the year that Freud visited Clark to deliver his first lectures in America. Stimulated by Hall's famous pamphlet, *The Study of Children,* published in 1883, child-study clubs, including the Child Study Association, sprang up in several American communities, and these soon expanded into national groups like the National Congress of Mothers (1897). Many new, special journals of child study were begun, among them *The Pedagogical Seminary* in 1891 and *The Child Study Monthly* in 1895. They revealed an extraordinary degree of specialized research on the child. In just one issue of *The Pedagogical Seminary* (for October, 1895) there appeared an article on the fatigue of children during an ordinary recitation hour, a study of certain aspects of feeble-mindedness, and observations on manual flexibility in men and children.[1]

Within this mass of material published after 1880, replete as it was with so many conflicting ideas, it is difficult to isolate general trends let alone deduce "cultural tendencies." But a few outstanding problems preoccupied experts as well as popular pamphleteers and interested parents.

Chief among these was the question of nature *vs.* supernature in the understanding of child development, a question implicit in Darwinism itself. By 1860, many nurture writers had already come close to accepting the notion that at birth the child offered nearly limitless possibilities for moral and intellectual growth, but this assumption did not necessarily imply accepting a full naturalistic account of human

[1] *Pedagogical Seminary* 3 (October, 1895): M. E. Holmes, "Studies from the Psychological Laboratory of Leland Stanford Junior University," pp. 213-34; G. E. Johnson, "Contributions to the Psychology and Pedagogy of Feeble Minded Children," pp. 246-91; John A. Hancock, "The Relation of Strength to Flexibility in the Hands of Men and Children," pp. 308-13.

development. Rather, arguments for a more benign interpretation of childhood had preponderantly invoked some super-historical or supernatural wonderful "essence" in the infant. Paradoxically these claims were advanced against the dangers of a thoroughgoing naturalism principally by the "liberals" in child study of the generation after 1830.

Darwinism forced the issue.[2] If everything about life could be explained without referring to any entity or essence beyond or above nature, what then could be said about the child's possibilities? Was there any permanent "essence" at all within an evolving nature and history that endowed the child with the uniqueness the Christian soul or idealist "mind" had given him? However much more sound than substance was produced on this large question, by 1880 the older faith in "essences" probably remained, in William James' phrase, "vital options" for most Americans. Given this strong strain of idealism how could the nation avoid debating the contrasting general implications of evolution for understanding the child's character and assessing the weight nature and God had, respectively, in the evolutionary scheme? It is understandable how difficult it was to face fully and honestly the import of evolutionary naturalism that there was no permanent, transcendent "essence of man," that life in all respects was in ceaseless change, that morals had no sanction beyond their usefulness for a particular people, and that the fate even of mankind's best ideals was always in doubt.

Nevertheless, most experts on the child, as this revolution in philosophic and cultural mood moved on, were not pessimistic nor were many converted to moral relativism. Instead, the new major evolutionary premises about the child were accepted by professing Christians like Jacob Abbott and others in meliorist *mélanges* of science and faith that passed themselves off successfully as Christianity.

By 1900, the notion of infant depravity had been almost completely abandoned in theological debates about the child's "essence." An editorial in the *Reformed Church Review* summarizing theological changes in the nineteenth century stated that the doctrines of Calvinism and Arminian evangelicalism, the two leading systems around 1800, "are virtually dead." God was no longer conceived as an absolute being or power with little feeling or reason nor as an irate judge. He had become the rational and loving Father, in the world and caring

[2] See John Dewey, *The Influence of Darwinism on Philosophy* (New York, 1910).

for it.[3] The older anatgonism between the little viper and the stern God with his earthly surrogates, the parents, had disappeared.

Among the major Protestant sects the Presbyterians had remained among the most conservative in doctrine. In the late years of the nineteenth century, however, statements on infant election in the Westminster Confession were under constant attack. The more strict Presbyterian ministers saved the doctrine by enlarging God's calling: all dying infants would be saved.[4] In 1902 and 1903 a liberalized doctrine on infant salvation was again proposed and finally accepted by the General Assembly of the Presbyterian Church in the North, although the South did not follow until a few years later.[5] This revision of the doctrine of infant damnation amounted to accepting widely held liberal beliefs about the child's possibilities. But the Presbyterians' action also marked the end of really distinctive Christian premises about nurture and education. Although abandoning the notion of infant depravity, Protestants continued to believe that the child was made in the image of God, possessed a soul, and deserved an upbringing that recognized his "divine spark," but even the most ardent humanists and secularists accepted such axioms as valid metaphors. And as for whether metaphor or literal truth led the way, as Herbert Schneider has shown,[6] recent Protestant ideas have in general followed rather than resisted or led the secular tendencies of American thought. The Protestants have increasingly pursued moral and social rather than theological interests. Before it surrendered on the doctrine of infant election, Protestantism generally had also accepted a free, universal, and basically secular education, and had supported the strict separation of church and state. If there was any impulse to counter the threat of secularism in education, Protestants by their own logic could not use government to compel children to attend Sunday schools or use common schools for religious purposes. Any drift away from "really Christian education" could thus scarcely be corrected or stopped in the schools. By 1910 there was, in any case, little to distinguish the main ideas of American Protestants on the nature of the child from optimistic evolutionary notions.[7] Protestant thinkers became continuously

[3] *The Reformed Church Review* 4 (April, 1900), p. 264.

[4] L. A. Loetscher, *The Broadening Church* (Philadelphia, 1954), p. 41.

[5] *Ibid.*, pp. 87-88.

[6] Herbert W. Schneider, *Religion in Twentieth Century America* (Cambridge, 1952).

[7] For the typical rhetoric see A. D. Mayo, "The New Education—The Christian Education," *Education* 19 (May, 1897), pp. 546-55; and, nearly a generation earlier, "A Smattering of Things" (editorial) *New England Journal of Education* 11 (April 8, 1880), pp. 232-33.

more concerned with ethics and their theology ever more liberal. Their "reverence for the child" in the name of the glorious evolutionary future of the race was in no way remarkable.

The leading theological journals around 1900 did set themselves squarely against the crudities and inadequacies of early evolutionary naturalism but so had a host of American writers, notably William James,[8] who had abandoned supernaturalism. In reviewing a volume of letters of Pestalozzi, the great eighteenth-century educational theorist, *The Lutheran Church Review's* critic approved Pestalozzi's central idea that there was a spiritual principle in the child at birth which the mother was to cultivate.[9] He contrasted Pestalozzi with those many modern psychologists who taught that the child at birth was nothing except a selfish animal. He quoted Pestalozzi's own remark that if the child was only an animal ". . . would I cease forever to speak of the stamina of love in his heart, or of the antipast, however distinct, of faith."[10]

Yet, although ministers resisted what they thought were the premises of "modern psychologists", in dealing with practical problems they tended to give advice that even their caricatured enemies would approve. Not sin but cruelty, wrote an editor of the *Christian Intelligencer,* "is the basis of all crimes and the foundation of all wrongs, and if we can inculcate a spirit of mercy into the minds of our children we shall certainly do a great deal towards bringing about a better state, a finer race and brighter world."[11] Nowhere would one find any dissent from this opinion among leading naturalistic psychologists of the day. The fact was that by 1900 the first generation of crude formulations of evolutionary science had passed. Although evolution "from the simple to the complex" still seemed to many the Divine plan for the improvement of the race, the "plan" now went far beyond clumsy Spencerian notions of "survival of the fittest" as adapted to Christian theology.[12] Early Darwinism had left no room for what William James called "options," for significant choices to resist, tame, and direct the flow of the "cosmic process" as T. H. Huxley had called it. But by the turn of the century evolutionary naturalism had sufficiently broadened to recognize the importance of humane ideals, intelligent minds, and the stub-

[8] James' essay "Herbert Spencer's Autobiography" expresses most directly his discontent with the naturalism of the 1860's and 1870's.

[9] *Lutheran Church Review* 18 (January, 1899), pp. 174-75.

[10] *Ibid.,* p. 175.

[11] "Aunt Marjorie's Corner," *The Christian Intelligencer* 72 (January 16, 1901), p. 38.

[12] See Hofstadter, *Social Darwinism,* on the second-generation Darwinists.

born resisting will. In many ways this change made peace between science and religion easier and helped reconcile Christians and "modern psychologists."

It was a revised, non-fatalistic, more "spiritual" evolution that appeared in important books like Charlotte Perkins Gilman's popular work *Concerning Children.* Her initial theme was "The people must be steadily made better if the world is to move. The way to make people better is to have them born better. The way to have them born better is to make all possible improvements in the individual before parentage,"[13] since, she was certain, acquired characteristics could be inherited. The evolutionary improvement of the race depended not on chance or the blind inevitable forces of nature but on the child's desire to make himself better. Given the opportunity to develop their potentialities, by the age of fifteen the child's natural aspirations ". . . ought to be playing into the current of our racial life and lifting it higher and higher with each new generation."[14] W. B. Drummond, the well-known English writer, spoke with similar encouragement about the choices open to the child: "In the struggle for existence among the higher animals, brains have come to count for more and more."[15] In his seminal work, *Notes on Child Study,* E. L. Thorndike took special care to point out that what development is can never tell us what it ought to be. No word was a poorer synonym for "the good" than "the natural." Nature was neither to be condemned nor worshipped but to be used for moral ends. "We use the river for transport and power when we can; when it bothers us, we dam it up or divert its course."[16] So was the child to be trained in the light of what parents considered the best life for man.

The pre-Civil War nurture writers had already, if guardedly, granted greater neutrality or even dignity to natural impulses in the child. Largely, they wanted to capture these impulses, for the highest ideals and impulses were still viewed predominantly as intrinsically moral or immoral. By 1900, as Thorndike, Dewey, and James tried to demonstrate, will, instinct, interest, desire, energy, imagination, and temperament were to be taken as merely psychological phenomena without any moral connotations. Nor was the child's energy to be ro-

[13] Charlotte P. S. Gilman, *Concerning Children* (Boston, 1900), p. 21.

[14] *Ibid.,* p. 23.

[15] W. B. Drummond, *The Child, His Nature and Nurture* (London, 1901), p. 8.

[16] E. L. Thorndike, *Notes on Child Study* (New York, 1903), p. 142.

manticized as intrinsically divine or innocent. His raw powers were simply neutral and to be used to best advantage.

Enlightened Christians and scientific students thus arrived at intrinsic agreement on the child's possibilities regardless of old arguments about essences. For both, however, a second great problem had to be overcome in developing a voluntaristic evolutionary scheme of child nurture. What was the influence of heredity on human development?

As long as the debates about the child and evolution centered on observable behavior and external environment the wish for evidence of purposeful improvement of life fathered the thought that evolution was "open-ended" and for the best. While the question of purposive or non-purposive evolution was being bitterly debated in both Europe and America, in the 1880's renewed attention was given to the earlier experiments of Gregor Mendel. These seemed to some disputants to present disturbing evidence from nature itself, not mere religious, or moral, or esthetic claims, against the notion that man could control evolution and indefinitely improve himself. Mendel's experiments on the inheritance of peas seemed to show that there were inherent in nature biophysical limits which persisted from generation to generation. Variations occurred but originated deep and mysteriously within the organism.

The important and reliable experiments on heredity after Mendel, like the technical scientific work on general evolution, were far beyond the comprehension of the general public, which knew very little about all-important subtleties. It seized and exploited the sensational and facile. Within a generation after Mendel newspapers and magazines were filled with hopes and warnings about the "teachings of heredity." Pessimists charged that heredity proved that evolution was largely beyond man's control. Were there not biologically transferred characteristics that would appear or disappear whether men desired them or not? But what, others countered, were these resisting elements and in what degree were they immutable or beyond control? Were they specific traits of character, similar in father and son, or general tendencies sure to mature in a general pattern of appearance and behavior? Or were they vague dispositions whose strength would depend on their peculiar combination in the child together with the effects of his environment? Such questions came to be debated with almost as much urgency as the problem of God's place in the evolutionary scheme. Since each child was a new link in the continuous process of human evolution, if his nature could not be improved beyond the limits set by inherited endowment what were the specific implications for any individual or, generally, for "the race" (as Americans had become fond of saying)? And what, then, of the great plans and benign purposes of nurture reformers? However much the psychologists were emphasizing that the child's natural endowment was mere potentiality, was it true that all powers at birth could be turned to good account? Since the "improvement of the race" and the struggle to direct evolution to its highest goals now started at every American hearth, what dreadful news had the scientists brought parents eager to get on with their great work?

William J. Shearer, the author of a widely printed newspaper column on child care, symbolizes those who dealt with the problem. Drawing on these columns he published in 1904 a volume for parents called *The Management and Training of Children.* From the outset the habitual optimism and meliorism of the middlebrow nurture writer were obvious. He called the child "the tiny prophecy of future possibilities."[17] True, there was the power of heredity but against it were also "further possibilities," in the child. He stated, ". . . the most that can be claimed for heredity is a tendency to act as did the parents."[18] The child, consequently, could be trained only up to the limit of his natural powers. But Shearer's detailed advice suggests that, having made a proper bow to heredity, he felt free to assume that everything noble was still open to every child. This optimism was probably not the effect of stubbornness, ignorance, or *chic* (however much these may have influenced him). For, like earlier claims about innate depravity, what specifically could a parent know about his child's chances unless he tested him and gambled on the best possibilities? "Heredity" was an abstraction; what counted was not the hidden, erratically mutating "germ plasm" but the actual results of daily experience. As another nurture enthusiast expressed it "children can be trained in almost any direction."[19] Even though "child training does not change a child's nature . . . it does change his modes of giving expression to his nature."[20]

There was thus no clear and specific correlation possible between the biological inheritance of the child and presumptions about his

[17] William J. Shearer, *The Management and Training of Children* (New York, 1904), p. 13.

[18] *Ibid.*, p. 21.

[19] H. Clay Trumbull, *Hints on Child-Training* (New York, 1898), p. 19.

[20] *Ibid.*, p. 15.

potentialities or the direction he ought to go. The "laws of heredity" presumably proved whatever one was interested in proving, even the child's inherited natural desire for religious faith.[21] In her well-known *Home Manual,* Mrs. John A. Logan first paid respects to the power of heredity while saying nothing specific about how, or where, or why hereditary tendencies showed themselves: "Hereditary tendencies must not be ignored; for, alas, the children must suffer for the violations of nature's laws committed by parents and grandparents."[22] Previously, however, she had stressed the possibility of making all children "healthy, beautiful and graceful."[23] In other words, heredity had become a poorly understood catchword, used to strengthen intellectual credentials but without logical practical implications.

Mrs. Gilman, for whom the child was "The young of the human species, first a young animal . . . then a young human . . ."[24] and Shearer, who called him "an animal with certain advantages over other animals,"[25] were among the most insistent about the power of proper training despite heredity. Drummond similarly believed that however powerful inherited nature might be, it was weaker than nurture.[26] All efforts could still be made so that the "energy of growth may flow into the highest combinations."[27] Primarily because one could never know just what the child had inherited, it was possible for most popular writers on nurture to contribute to a growing optimistic activism and in effect, agree with Kate Douglas Wiggin that childhood somehow was "an eternal promise."[28]

---

[21] G. A. Hubbell, *Up Through Childhood* (New York, 1904), pp. vi-vii and Chap. 22, "Training a Child's Faith."

[22] Mrs. John A. Logan, *The Home Manual* (Boston, 1889), p. 162.

[23] *Ibid.,* p. iii.

[24] C. P. S. Gilman, *The Home, Its Work and Influence* (New York, 1903), p. 234.

[25] Shearer, *op. cit.,* p. 224.

[26] Drummond, *op. cit.,* pp. 6-7.

[27] *Ibid.,* p. 66.

[28] Kate Douglas Wiggin, *Children's Rights* (Boston, 1892), p. 15.

12

'Mid Pleasure and Principles

THE new knowledge from the scientists about the child's inherent activism and natural spontaneity had clear implications. It made parenthood ever more serious work, with mothers, fathers, and trained observers now working together to preserve or purify the race and speed the progress of evolution.

In 1888, at the suggestion of Felix Adler, the founder of the Ethical Culture movement, three New York mothers decided to meet "to discuss questions of interest in the education of children."[1] By 1890, what had been a small group, delighted with its work, had expanded to a membership of thirty-five. Judging by names and available biographical information, they were predominantly German-Jewish in background and from the upper middle class. In the autumn of 1890, "The Society for the Study of Child Nature" was adopted as an official name.[2]

Three principal themes run through the secretary's reports of the meetings of the early years. They confirm the growing importance to mothers of the theoretical themes in the nurture literature and chil-

---

[1] *Society for the Study of Child Nature, Reports 1890-95* (Pamphlet) (New York, 1895), p. 3; in files of Child Study Association, New York City.

I am deeply indebted to the former director of the Child Study Association of America, Dr. Gunnar Dybwad, for permitting me to use its papers without restriction. Although incomplete for the early years, these holographic records of actual mothers' meetings are primary materials of great interest for the social historian. They may be found on microfilm now in the Columbia University Library.

[2] *Ibid.*, p. 3.

dren's books of the time. The mothers were eager to defer as much as possible to the best ideas, but they now wanted their information directly from experts trained in child study rather than from popular writers.[3] They were still like earlier Americans in emphasizing general moral goals over specific techniques and in their lack of sensitivity to the vast range of individual differences among children. A truly moral nurture for "the child" was still the predominant motif.

The regular weekly meetings of these ladies from November to April or May, "filled with inspiration by the thoughts of the authors they studied,"[4] had a set order of business. Following the suggestions and plans of the executive committee, the mothers were to read specified authors who would then be discussed at the meetings. Papers based on the texts would also be delivered. These were generally "comments on such portions of the allotted text as appealed most forcibly to the attention of the writer of the paper."[5]

Scientific or philosophic authorities on the subject of the day would be cited in support or criticism of the members' opinions. The mothers soon became conscious of the importance of their work and prided themselves on breaking new ground.

> Even now the child is, as a rule, an object of scientific observation only; while we study it as a human being, giving attention to those manifestations of traits of character that are open to the observations of the mother, and of those about the child, whether, these persons have had the advantage of scientific training or not. Such traits, and dispositions, and tendencies are observed and discussed with a view to gaining a better understanding of the child's nature; and though scientific analysis is not the avowed attribute of the study, the work becomes scientific when conclusions and results are carefully noted and continued, consecutive work is pursued.[6]

Their moralistic conservatism and their intense old-fashioned American idea of life as a battle to make right prevail are everywhere obvious.

[3] See the Bibliography at the end of the *Summary of the Work for the Years 1896-1906,* as well as the weekly discussions of Locke, Rousseau, Herbart and contemporary authorities.

[4] *Reports 1890-95,* p. 3.

[5] *Ibid., p.* 4.

[6] *Ibid.,* p. 24.

> We do not aim to antagonize or overthrow the old in receiving the new, but merely to search for what is right and good. Whether those who have found enlightenment are too blind or too weak to profit by it—*that* is not our province to examine into. To define our own briefly would be to adopt the motto which once was proposed for our Society: *Altiora peto* (I seek the higher).[7]

During the 1890's the members did intensive reading in Rousseau, Stanley Hall, Preyer, Dr. Elizabeth Blackwell, Ueffelmann, Locke, Felix Adler, and many other authorities. They also subscribed to magazines and kept journals of observation on their child's development. Often experts like Professor Jerome Allen and D. Stanton Coit delivered special short lectures at meetings on such topics as "The Spiritual Discipline of Children.[8] Among the questions discussed between 1890 and 1900 were the following:

Should implicit obedience be enforced upon children?

How could the true idea of property be conveyed to the child?

Should the child see death in any form?

Does the time devoted to young children limit the mental growth of the mother? Does it detract from responsibilities to other members of the family, especially the father?

How much authority should older children have?

Is a child's imagination stunted if it is made to adhere strictly to the truth?

Should a desire for the right of franchise be inculcated in daughters?

Can music, *per se,* be demoralizing, especially when it is sensuous?

Is the feeling of self-esteem, which we experience when our children realize our expectations, a moral one?[9]

Obviously, the range of questions was very broad and it would be difficult to generalize about their conclusions. At least the general direction of argument can be inferred from the minutes of a few of their discussions.

The following arguments at a meeting on the question of allowances were reported in special fullness:[10]

"The physical and material wants of children are supplied by the parents; an allowance of money is, therefore, a luxury, and as such

[7] *Ibid.,* p. 19.
[8] *Ibid.,* p. 26.
[9] *Ibid.,* passim.
[10] "Minutes of Meeting, November 22, 1899," Ms. Child Study Association.

has a deteriorating influence. The luxuries of children are usually of the appetite and they will harm themselves in buying and eating candies and the like. Whenever parents give children a certain sum of money at stated intervals, children will very soon claim such an allowance as a right, whereas they should be permitted the use of money, not as a right, but as an indulgence on the parents' part."

"If you give children an allowance and supervise their spending it, they will consider your interference as a limitation of their rights, for if you hold the money in trust the child cannot consider it an allowance. If, however, you give a child an allowance with a philanthropic end to it, as it were, the child will feel that it is being dealt with unjustly."

"A regular allowance enables children to buy theatre tickets; many of them visit the matinees every Saturday. Aside from the fact that most plays are not meant and are unsuited for children, even in those that are, they are enjoying something which should be left for later mature life."

"A case was mentioned of a girl of fourteen, very musical and fond of opera, who begged that a subscription ticket to the Opera be given to her instead of other birthday presents. Aside from the fact that it would be well worth to give up one's birthday presents for such a continuous treat, Mrs. Hastings urged that for a child of that age the Opera, which usually depicts the strongest passions known to human nature, might have a harmful effect in a premature awakening of the child's emotional life. Fine concerts were recommended instead for their high ethical value."

"Mrs. Hastings advocated that children come to their parents for whatever money they wish to spend, for in this way you can control and teach them to spent [sic] money judiciously, not, however, to exclude children from pocket money for they will feel isolated from others who are supplied in that direction; only not make it a rule to give a fixed amount at a stated time."

"Robert Ingersoll made it a habit to leave a family purse on the table for the use of his children; he could depend entirely on their rectitude and sense in spending it. Mrs. Hastings said that such a plan could perhaps be carried out were our children always under our immediate care and attention and not subject to opposing outside influence."

"The pocket money which is at the disposal of children should always be spent under the supervision of the parent; however letting the child at times spend a little money in a way which to a grown person will not seem very judicious, [serves] merely to cultivate the child's judgment."

"In conclusion Mrs. Hastings advised that in as far as our city life will permit, children should earn their own spending money, thus teaching them the rewards of labor and the benefits of accumulation. To give no stated allowance as a right, to teach the child at an early age the value of money by doing acts of service in the household, not acts of love, however, which we do not wish to and cannot pay."

A meagrely recorded session on "Moral Education in Regard to Sex" concluded:

> The question being asked whether any of the mothers present had treated the question referred to, with the candor that was recommended, and if so, whether they would relate their experience. Mrs. Arnstein responded by reading an account of her own mode of procedure with her child, a little girl in her ninth year. In this account the radical view found a strong support, for while no part of the question was shirked, the explanation being given in full—the manner was so pure and natural that it was touching to the hearers, and seemed convincing of good results when applied to young listeners. Other experiences by members and visitors were also given, of a natural treatment of natural subjects, and the discussion branched off into a consideration of the question of decorum, as required to a mode of conduct in the family, the conclusion being, that while no distinction ought to be made between boys and girls in any manner that would direct attention to the differences of sex, tact should be used in maintaining that degree of decorum which is indicative of good breeding.

Whatever the differences of tone and context between our present notions and these and other discussions, that parents themselves were actually raising such questions in great detail shows that the child was no longer merely a beloved offspring or the nation's future in microcosm but a home-laboratory experiment as well. Close supervision of the child's development was not a new ideal but so high a degree of deference to scientific knowledge was. Already, the ideal was approaching our own: parents were to act as chiefs of staff of an organization,[11] patiently and devotedly watching and plotting the changes in the child's growth, ever quick to notice and analyze to the best possible advantage any opportunity that the child offered them. The seriousness of this work might even require both sexes "to present evidence of fitness" before marriage even at the risk of destroying "romance."[12] William Shearer claimed, "No parent can easily manage a child until he has made a very careful examination of himself."[13] Parents must be trained, cried Mrs. Birney. Mothers should join clubs or the Mother's Congress.[14] Mrs. Gilman warned that the maternal instinct was not all that was needed. "The mother, by virtue of being a mother, is supposed to know just what is right for her children."[15] When the right kind of children are created ". . . then we shall have some reason to honor motherhood, and it will be brain work and soul work we honor . . . not the uncertain rudiments of a brute instinct."[16]

By 1900, however, the "right kind of children" were to be as happy as they were dutiful. Did the new knowledge mean that parents could serve both high moral needs and the spontaneous pleasures of childhood? If anything, the sense of uneasiness about American morals that had so influenced the Jacksonians had deepened after 1880. The nation's freedom and energy, about which American consciences habitually had such ambiguous feelings, seemed to have escaped control or, as Henry Adams later emphasized, America's power seemed to have been dissociated from any moral limits.

In contrast with the Jacksonian era there was now recurring doubt that the old rules and mores could work. Against the strains of optimism and possibility just mentioned were irrepressible worries about the future. Great changes in American public life a generation after Sumter were felt throughout private society. Kate Douglas Wiggin spoke of the spirit of the age and asked, "how should parents hope to

[11] See the series of articles by various authors: "The Ideal and Practical Organization of the Home," *Cosmopolitan* 26-27 (April-July, 1899), pp. 659-64, 49-54, 167-71, 297-302. In the last of these, C. W. Eastman concluded that "a delightful home" could be had "on two dollars and fifty cents per day" (p. 302). See also J. B. Walker, "Motherhood as a Profession," *Cosmopolitan* 25 (May, 1898), pp. 88-93; P. Carus, "Parenthood," *Open Court* 13 (April, 1899), pp. 211-14; Ella Wheeler Wilcox, "Parenthood," *Cosmopolitan* 32 (December, 1901), pp. 175-78.

[12] M. A. Cassidy, "Home and School," *Education* 19 (May, 1899), p. 538.

[13] Shearer, *op. cit.*, p. 283.

[14] Mrs. T. Birney, *Childhood* (New York, 1904), Chap. 1.

[15] Gilman, *The Home*, p. 55.

[16] *Ibid.*, p. 61.

escape the universal interrogation point leveled at everything else?"[17] Mrs. Gilman went further:

> Our own personal lives, rich as they are today . . . are not happy. We are confused, bewildered. Life is complicated, duties conflict, we fly and fall like tethered birds, and our new powers beat against old restrictions like ships in dock, fast moored, yet with all sail set and steam up.[18]

The editor of *Childhood Magazine* noted the timidity and confusion of parents. She traced this to the clash of new ideas and old ideals.[19] Recommending that parents read an early book on child nurture that he was reprinting, another editor stated, ". . . in many sections of American society the home is in peril. Rapid growth of wealth, some unthinking imitation of supposed excellencies in other nations, social and other occupations of parents, and like causes, explain the discouraging symptom."[20] Gilman suggested that the cause for "this wearing unrest in life" lay not in the failure to use the old truths but in aspects of home life Americans should have peacefully outgrown. The essentials of home life were sound; the difficulty lay in peripheral matters which, if changed, could still leave "precious things unmolested." "We do small honor to nature's laws when we imagine their fulfllment rests on this or that petty local custom of our own.[21] Intelligent choice about what was to endure and what to be rejected was essential.

People had to get rid of unimaginative homes full of drudgery. "A good clean, healthy, modern home with free people living and loving in it, is no more sacred than a schoolhouse."[22] She challenged certain "domestic myths"—that women should stay at home, that homes were more secure and protective than other places, that the home was in fact a refuge for privacy.

All such general complaints found a specific objective in criticisms of unrealistic restrictions on the child. Mothers and fathers who loved their children and who tried to do everything possible to recognize their spontaneity might see the young child "contrast unfavorably in point of docility, with children reared after the old fashioned repressive

[17] Wiggin, *Children's Rights,* p. 20.
[18] Gilman, *The Home,* pp. 11-12.
[19] Florence H. Winterburn, *Nursery Ethics* (New York, 1895), pp. 11-13.
[20] John Hall, *Hints on Early Education* (New York, 1887), Prefatory note.
[21] Gilman, *The Home,* pp. 11-12.
[22] *Ibid.,* p. 49.

system."[23] One had to accept this "restlessness" as the early price for the good citizen with the self-discipline to face the modern world, "fraught with strange interest and importance to the future. . . ."[24] in which moral development might imply suffering."[25]

Parents had to face up to the facts of psychology. "You say to the child, 'Do Not,' and his whole nature says 'Do.' Every nerve and muscle within him calls for action, and yet you say, 'Sit still and be good,' but action is the law of life. . ."[26] "To be 'mamma's little lady' is to be a caricature of the real child, and bound with cords which will prevent the development of that wholesome and strong nature which the growing girl should have."[27] As Mrs. Birney understood the problem of parents it was to balance obedience to "universal," "relentless," and "impartial" law[28] with respect for individuality which "may not be just what you or I would choose . . . it is part of a plan and purpose too great for finite minds to criticize." [29]

Even Shearer, who could take cautious and conservative positions, warned parents to avoid excessive restraint, overtraining, not leaving the child to himself, too many direct issues, too many "don'ts," threats, nagging, excessive magnifying of faults, giving bribes and forbidding "temper." Instead, try with every child

> . . . to make out of each what the Almighty evidently intended him to be. What He intended is not always an easy matter to determine. The only way it can be determined is by carefully studying the peculiarities of each mind, heart and body with which every child is gifted.[30]

From every quarter, therefore, parents of 1900 were warned not to be too insistent about their standards and ideals in dealing with their children, those strange collections of "forces" and energies, but, at the same time, they were expected to raise children who did have clear ideals and the courage of their convictions. The parent was to use his authority and knowledge to balance what seemed essential in his world against what was novel and viable in the new world of the

[23] Winterburn, *op. cit.,* p. 82.
[24] *Ibid.,* p. 240.
[25] *Ibid.,* p. 235.
[26] Hubbell, *Up Through Childhood,* p. 274.
[27] *Ibid.,* p. 278.
[28] Birney, *Childhood,* p. 8.
[29] *Ibid.,* p. 66.
[30] Shearer, *op. cit.,* p. 269.

child. There were no absolute answers; every child was a gamble. As a writer in the *Delineator* commented

> Those who think, or who thought in the eighteenth century, that education might write its lessons equally upon the equally blank tablets of each young mind were hardly observers of the first days, the first weeks of life. Those weeks are all sufficient to show the implicit signs of the eternal differences of persons.[31]

Kate Douglas Wiggin's *Children's Rights* is an eminent and touching statement of the time of the hope of building character without crushing or depriving the child of the pleasures of childhood. Her general theme, that the child must have his own world and that the parent would have to make sacrifices to recognize what childhood rightly demanded, was a retreat from the moralism and righteousness of an earlier era. She urged the father to "Get down to the level of his boyhood, and bring him up to the level of your manhood."[32] Life was too hectic for the American child; he was always on edge, dressed for show like some pet animal and overclean. She warned that children should not be expected to be too good—"Beware of hothouse virtue."[33] Intellectual and moral precocity might cost too much in future character. The parent must build on the power of example, reassured, however, by the scientific knowledge of the child's strong tendency to imitation. Since Rousseau, reformers had been warning that the vague and abstract were ineffective in child training. Wiggin agreed: one must use the obvious and appeal to the child's actual interests. In time, and with the right examples, the child will ". . . pass from the concrete example of goodness to an abstract perfection."[34] But at the beginning physical impressions are ". . . the only possible medium for awakening the child's sensibility."[35] Her attitude toward old-fashioned "moralizing" was obvious in her remarks about a doll that spoke altruistic homilies: "Think of having to play—*to play,* forsooth, with a model of propriety, a high-minded monstrosity like that."[36] The

[31] Mrs. Alice Meynell, "The Boy and His Development," *Delineator* 53 (January, 1899), p. 114.

[32] Wiggin, *Children's Rights,* p. 18.

[33] *Ibid.,* p. 21.

[34] *Ibid.,* p. 22.

[35] *Ibid.,* p. 35.

[36] *Ibid.,* p. 61.

HAMPERED WITH A CONSCIENCE

child's faults and errors did not imply the end of the world as they had for the earlier children's author Mrs. Barbauld who had used eleven pages to deliver a sermon because a child had used the phrase "excessively pretty."[37]

Whatever the psychologists tried to teach about the "neutrality" of early endowment, did not such calls for more pleasure and less principles rest on an essentially benign assessment of the child's natural tendencies? Mrs. Wiggin did believe that most children "have a tolerably clear sense of right and wrong needing only gentle guidance to choose the right when it is put before them." They have "a natural sense of what is true and good" and will choose what is good if it is made comprehensible and attractive. The job is to "provide the right conditions of mental growth and then let the child do the growing."[38] Even those who believed that "character" required a more active role by the parents seemed to sense that there would be little resistance in the child if the right techniques were used. Mrs. Malleson put the case a little more strongly for active moral guidance than Mrs. Wiggin:

> What we have to do with it in early training is to direct it to desire what it ought to desire, to strengthen, and to develop it. . . . Make the daily routine of the child's life pleasant to him, its duties inevitable, and you will find obedience will follow your just demand of it . . . if you do not apportion his trial to his powers active or passive, you deserve defeat and run the risk of injuring the growing goodness of the little one.[39]

Parents could not be infallible, said the editor of *Childhood Magazine,* but love was. And true love, always unselfish, finds it possible to be inconsistent, because "being simple and frank it makes no pretenses, and being without egotism, it is not anxious to appear perfect, and is saved from the consequences of becoming absurd."[40] Let parents act with knowledge of the "higher and more enlightened modern methods" and they would be successful.

Shearer was more adamant: however gentle the methods, to get results parents had to have absolute authority. "A child should never be permitted to feel that he has a right to demand a reason of a

[37] *Ibid.,* p. 81.

[38] *Ibid.,* p. 119.

[39] Mrs. Frank Malleson, *Notes on the Early Training of Children* (Boston, 1892), pp. 38-40.

[40] Winterburn, *op. cit.,* p. 23.

parent."[41] But, at the same time, Shearer had also warned about excessive restraint and lack of realism about the child's energies. Apparently, then, "absolute authority" meant clear, inviolable moral rules strengthened by informed use of the child's curiosity and imagination. He said very little about actual repressive measures. The child was to be led, not driven into right ways, "by pleasant experiences and anticipations to prefer the correct paths."[42]

The most persistent criticism of the calls for more freedom for the child came from people deeply troubled by the weakening of religion in the nation's homes. Given the piety of such writers, their sense of what had happened in the home since the fervent Christian years a half-century earlier was probably correct. But the details of their analysis of the correct role of religion in the home shows how much less demanding piety had become since Dr. Humphrey's day.

"An American Mother" made the general complaint, "We Are Not Rearing Our Children as Christians." Character and benevolence were not enough. God was left out.

> I do not think that the average American parent knows how strange his attitude is toward his child. It is new—absolutely unique in the world. You will find nothing like it in any country. He no longer regards his child as an animal to be tamed by beating, or as a possible saint, but as the heir to all the good things of time. And the boy from his cradle knows his importance. There is no rawhide for him, no side-table, no snubbing, no discipline, not even a hint that he has sins, nor any effort made to convert him. The future is the kingdom of which these young people are taught that they will be the legitimate rulers. Is it their fault that they are vain, aggressive and ill-mannered? How, when they never have learned to obey, can they know how to command. In certain sections of the country, this universal homage to the coming generation has given birth to a singular theory of education. Boys are to be scrupulously left alone, freed from any restraint or fear of punishment, to grow as Nature chooses.
>
> I have not written of the finer Brahmin class among us, but rather of the majority of our homes and the general tendencies of American life. I can hear the eager protest

---

[41] Shearer, *op. cit.*, p. 43.
[42] *Ibid.*, p. 58.

> from the thousands of quiet homes where Christ is still an actual, live power. . . . The children of this class of Americans are kept in the background of the family life, and are treated at once with a tender care and a wholesome neglect eminently wise.[43]

This "American Mother" had asked in an earlier article, "Have Women Robbed Men of Their Religion?" She noted that the decline in the number of men who read the Bible was parallel to growing lack of concern about crime. It was the mother's fault that "the younger man now reads with indifference of a score of murders every morning puffing his cigarette the while." Grandsons didn't read the Bible; they had a vague idea that it was overthrown by the higher criticism. Very concerned with their physical well-being they never thought whether their souls were healthy. Mothers should teach their sons to read the Bible but they are too busy with humanity.

> What time has she to rock her baby to sleep with the Bible stories or hymns. . . . She belongs to a generation of busy mothers who have taken the world in hand to set it in order. They are too troubled to see the Master sitting in their midst; hence they do not lead husband or child to him.[44]

Another mother wrote that her children really belonged to God, not to her, and that they had to be trained on a lattice like ivy and not let alone to develop freely. A fast-growing German ivy she had purchased had worked itself through her curtains and was growing up their reverse side. She could not get it back without destroying the vine or the curtains.

> And as I looked I saw other vines that somehow slip through on the other side of the lattice from where the parents want them to grow. And I wondered whether the cause were not the same with my ivy—the proper early training had been neglected. Oh mothers, see to it that the little children do not get through on the wrong side. The children grow so fast—and sin is of such rapid insidious growth.[45]

---

[43] An American Mother, "The Modern Son and Daughter," *Ladies' Home Journal* 17 (March, 1900), p. 17.

[44] An American Mother, "Have Women Robbed Men of Their Religion?" *Ladies' Home Journal* 17 (February, 1900), p. 17.

[45] Margaret Bottome, "The King's Daughters," *Ladies' Home Journal* 17 (February, 1900), p. 36.

Although such warnings were, on the whole, sporadic, one cautionary word about them is necessary. However more humane and secular the nationally printed nurture advice had become, there were, of course, millions of homes it did not reach and countless hearths where more old-fashioned ideas were still powerful. The new ideas had replaced the older advice on the surface of national life and the evangelical and puritanical forces opposed to more modern and enlightened advice had been overshadowed or by-passed. But their greater anonymity should not make us think that they no longer had real power in American culture. As Prohibition, the revivals of the evolution controversy, and the resurgence of the K.K.K. were later to show, an older but increasingly frustrated America still had very large striking powers, especially when it felt itself forced into a corner.

A few case studies will serve to show how much more benign and rationalistic published advice on the child had become and how much more taxing and complicated parenthood was:

Shearer took up the old problem of lying children. Admitting the shock to the parent's ideals he nevertheless first asked, "But is it such an easy matter to tell the truth?"[46] What did a child know of duty? "Sad to relate, many parents make it very hard for their children to be truthful. . . The young child who tells an untruth should not be punished severely, if at all. What such a child needs is the right kind of instruction; not punishment in anger."[47] If not too young, the child should be explained the evils of telling lies. When a child tells the truth, and if it is difficult to do so, "too much approval cannot be given." Stories about truthful children and every other possible means should be used to create the habit of telling the truth.[48] Given Shearer's idea that "a child's imagination should be allowed great freedom in play and reading,"[49] it seemed unavoidable that immature children would not always know where stories ended and life began.

Often, however, the new subtler forms of controlling the child were probably much less effective and more objectionable than the simple "No!" or "Stop!" of earlier, less rationalistic times. Mrs. Birney, for example, thought that patience and sympathy would conquer every obstacle:

[46] Shearer, *op. cit.*, p. 160.
[47] *Ibid.*, p. 163.
[48] *Ibid.*, p. 165.
[49] *Ibid.*, p. 259.

> When any of the everyday problems of a nature to invite a conflict of wills present themselves, her mother considers for a moment and if there be nothing vital at stake, she allows the little girl to carry out her desires.

She considered the case of a girl who wanted to wear a special dress and advised the mother who opposed the child to say:

> Well, dear, of course you can wear that dress this afternoon, but mother thinks she would not, if she were you, for, you know, it is your very best white dress, and if you should be invited to a party or need it for some special occasion, you would be very sorry if it were soiled.

If the child persisted or cried, then

> Well, dear, it is *your* dress; mother only thought she should remind her dear little girl that there might be other afternoons when she would want it more, but mother is quite ready to fasten it for you.[50]

And, finally, the author's comment,

> I have never known that little girl to insist actively after that; she is usually silent and very thoughtful for a few moments; and then with a little sigh, before the victory is finally won, she says, "Never mind, mamma, I guess I'd better save it."[51]

In another case of a young boy who dawdled around the house before breakfast so that he was not ready when the food was on the table, Mrs. Birney advised the mother to talk to the child and ask him how he expected to grow up to be a great man if he was a tardy child. If the boy persisted in his habit, he should then have no breakfast.

H. Clay Trumbull, whose motto was, "Will Training Rather Than Will Breaking" cited the case of a father who was troubled by his child's resistance to his modern methods which Trumbull characterized as being carried on "by the operation of influences, inspirations, and inducements, in the direction of a right standard held persistently before the child without anything being said on the subject to the child at every step in his course of progress."[52]

---

[50] Mrs. Birney, *Childhood,* pp. 6-7.
[51] *Ibid.*
[52] Trumbull, *Hints on Child Training,* pp. 91-92.

At home one day the father was at his desk. His little girl entered and forgot to close the door as she had been taught to do. At first the father says, "Push the door to, darling." The child does nothing.

> The counsel of the morning came into the father's mind, and he said gently, "You needn't shut the door to, darling, if you don't want to. Papa will do it," and at once he stepped and closed the door, returning afterwards to his desk without a word of rebuke to his child.

The child, confused, came up to the father,

> "Dear Papa, I'm sorry I didn't shut that door. I will next time. Please forgive me, dear papa." And that was the beginning of a new state of things in that house.[53]

Julia M. Dewey in a well-known little book, *How to Teach Manners,* suggested that skillfully formulated questions would successfully drive home to the child her errors since she herself would help analyze them. Susie had just told the teacher and class that she could not read aloud part of the previous day's lesson.

> "Why not?"
> "I was not here yesterday, and I don't know the lesson."
> "Why were you not here?"
> "I did not wish to come."
> "What did you lose by not coming?"
> "My lessons."
> "Does that make any hard work for me Susie?"
> "Yes'm. You will have to teach the lesson again."
> "What will the rest of the class do while I am teaching you the lesson?"
> "They will have to wait for me."
> "What is thought of a school when the pupils do not come steadily?"
> "That it is not a good school."
> "Tell me, then why is it unfair for pupils to stay away from school, when they can come?"
> "It makes extra work for the teacher. It keeps the rest of the class waiting. It gives the school a bad name."
> "Yes, and all this is unkind, and if unkind?"
> "It is impolite."[54]

[53] *Ibid.,* pp. 88-89.

[54] Julia M. Dewey, *How to Teach Manners* (New York, 1888), p. 31.

None of these hypothetical cases touched the public as much as the actual histories of children that the police and the new social-workers like Jane Addams and Lillian Wald were uncovering in the burgeoning slums of American cities. There was no part of American society in which the belief in the salvation of every child was more tested than in the seeming startling increase in reports of juvenile crime and immorality. The basic problems of immigrant slum children had been a cause for concern for at least fifty years. However, like many problems endemic to industrialization and urbanism, the terrors of city life for poor children were increased in the last generation of the century as cities and immigration grew and as depressions, especially the disaster of 1893, hit first and hardest at the poor. The polite and comfortable public became more convinced by publicists and their consciences that disease, violence, and poverty were incompatible with humane standards as well as their own psychological comfort and political safety.

But nothing also reveals so clearly the moral stance of this audience and the deeper unarticulated assumptions of many of the popular nurture writers than their attitudes toward one of the social quandaries of the 'nineties, the "boy problem." The thick strain of old-fashioned moralism hidden in their work under the scientific language and pleas for a *real* childhood suddenly became clarified. The achieved rationality and comfort of the old American middle classes had helped their belief that much could be done for the child with willing enlightened parents like themselves. The rhetoric on the contrasting grave problems of the dispossessed child expressed the alarm and condescension of people who had assumed that the decencies of their world extended directly throughout mankind. On discovering how much misery and exploitation still existed among the mass of humanity they were confounded. Given the strong sense that they owned America and the likelihood that after a pleasant childhood of the best advantages their children would have little problem in finding a comfortable niche in society, the respectable classes' fright at what they read in the press is understandable.

F. H. Briggs argued that parents need not worry about their own natural boys, ". . . who come from the home where industry, intelligence and thrift prevail, where books and magazines abound, where the library table forms the center of an interested group, where refinement of thought and life prevail. . ." It is "the boy over the back fence in your alley" who needs watching for, among other things, "his vote will weigh just as heavily as your son's vote, and he will be able to run caucuses and pull votes by means that your son cannot use."[55] If the good citizens of the future were to inherit their birthright, these wild or immigrant boys must be saved. Before Mr. Briggs told how Americans could successfully counteract the effects of the bad homes, "the street," and "the law of transmitted tendencies," he used the piety and fervor so recurrent in the generation of progressive reformers after 1890.

Speaking of a destitute mulatto boy, he said,

> Think of the chains with which that human soul is bound. Think of it, ye whose mothers were chaste and pure as heaven, whose hearts and intellects were quickened by all the ennobling influence and agencies of the age.

Mentioning this boy's environment he went on ". . . can you find aught that will condemn this boy because he is a vagrant and a thief?"[56] He then cited offenses equalling those of our own thrill killers.

> The community is therefore responsible for the propagation of a race of paupers whose every hereditary tendency is to become criminals, a race of men and women who know not the meaning of *Father, Mother and Home,* who have no conception of honesty and truth, the *children of lust, the heirs of crime.*[57]

Writers like Briggs quickly invoked "hereditary tendencies" when dealing with the slum child, however much they discounted heredity as an influence on the character of the child in the "nice home." Goodness flowered from environment and training in the fine home but badness in the slums came from a flaw in human nature. Both the praise for the nice American home and the fears about slum homes were also usually touched by end-of-century racism, and intensity of language about race and innate criminality often revealed more than abstract argument about redeemability could cover. A common rhetoric even in the scientific journals was that delinquent children were "the product of a degenerative process at work in the drunken stock from which they were descended," augmented by bad environment; that they

[55] Franklin H. Briggs, *Boys as They are Made and How to Remake Them* (Syracuse, N. Y., 1894), pp. 5-7.
[56] *Ibid.*, p. 9.
[57] *Ibid.*, p. 11.

represented a "morbid" deviation from "their race and civilization."[58] A survey of people of "unquestionable moral standing" stated that delinquency was an easy reversion by the child to an older, instinctual level in the evolutionary process; from that level nothing more powerful remained than "race instincts." Children being younger were, naturally, closer to this level. It was because of this that "semi-criminal acts fill so large a part of boy-life." Parents and teachers should not arouse or use these "race instincts."[59]

The best reformers concerned about the problem of providing a substitute home for the slum child did not always express themselves as moralistically as had Briggs or use one-sided "explanations" of delinquency. Without referring to race or heredity and without conducting surveys, they said that "the home no longer influences the average boy as it did in the days when society had fewer claims upon us, and the problem of what is right is serious enough in the refined home."[60]

The new knowledge and awareness of the child's possibilities, they held, applied as much to the ruffian as to the little gentleman. Citizens and social workers should "study the tastes and talents of the boys and use them in reaching him."[61] The Boy's Club or special schools were auxiliaries to do the job that tenements and ordinary schools, being no substitutes for home, could not do. The Boy's Club was to be an island of refuge in a sea of immorality, a means, as Jacob Riis suggested in his classic *The Children of the Poor* (1892), of fighting gangs with their own weapon, organization.[62] Help was needed most by the outright bad boy but equally by the "tradeless boys who have been left to learn their manners and their morals in the streets of our great cities during their most impressionable years."[63] The enthusiasm of the social workers was directed to "taking them off the streets" and to assisting the boys in their "physical, mental and moral progress."[64] This work of reclamation had "for its supreme purpose the building of char-

[58] George Dawson, "A Study in Youthful Degeneracy," *Pedagogical Seminary* 4 (December, 1896), pp. 256-57.

[59] Edgar James Swift, "Some Criminal Tendencies of Boyhood; A Study in Adolescence," *Pedagogical Seminary* 8 (March, 1901), pp. 90-91.

[60] Charles Stelzle, *Boys of the Street, How to Win Them* (New York, 1904), p. 13.

[61] *Ibid.*, p. 88.

[62] Stelzle, *op. cit.*, p. 22.

[63] E. Paul Neuman, "Take Care of the Boys," *Living Age* (November, 1898), p. 507.

[64] *Ibid.*, p. 509.

acter;"[65] the alternatives for the bad boys were "the street or the saloon."[66] The best way of fighting crime was "not to cage it in the man, but to slay it in the boy."[67]

Judge Ben Lindsey of Denver was one of the leading American proponents of new juvenile courts for handling the special needs of young offenders. His introduction to Lilburn Merrill's book, *Winning the Boy,* is as revealing as Merrill's text of the lofty moralism, of the faith in "the right" and in "character" of even the more enlightened reformers.

> Society may be protected as long as they have to do right, but you have not a really safe citizen until there comes into the boy's heart the desire to do right because it is right. . . . I ask the boy why he will not steal again and he invariably replies, "Because I will get in jail." He is afraid of a jail; he is not afraid to do wrong. . . . Conscience is the moral director; without it character is impossible, and character is the greatest need, for it means that the pure in heart shall see and know and act the truth, as surely as they shall see God.[68]

Merrill himself pleaded for those "dirty kids" whom people call brats, for lighting the spark of essential goodness in the child. His inversion of the old tradition of intense Puritan concern with the world's ways was striking. The essentially good child, or the child corrupted by a harsh world, was to be converted or restored to his true innocent nature by the work of a dedicated group of "ministers" who followed the "calling" of social work. Through their labor the public would soon see ". . . the kingdom of heaven is not far from the common kid."[69]

Merrill dared to say about the "nice home" what has by now become our cliché:

> Ordinarily, the boy is all right. I cannot say as much for the big folk. If I could, there would be no boy problem. The trouble is with the adult. Boys are as good as the homes they

[65] Stelzle, *op. cit.,* p. 22.

[66] S. T. Arnold, "The Problem of the Bad Boy," *The Journal of Education* 41 (April 27, 1895), p. 242.

[67] Neuman, *op. cit.,* p. 513.

[68] Lilburn Merrill, *Winning the Boy* (New York, 1908), pp. 8-9. Compare also the similar tone and argument of John Spargo's *The Bitter Cry of the Children* (New York, 1906).

[69] Merrill, *op. cit.,* p. 31.

> come from, which is not saying that all boys are as good as their mothers. Sometimes fathers are not a credit to their sons.[70]

To us, accustomed to hearing that "there are no delinquent children, only delinquent parents," Merrill's statement is not shocking, but in an age which tried so hard to idealize the old American home and to teach respect for parents, it indicates that facts were harsh enough to wean people away from even the deepest pieties.

As substitute parents, the social workers were to save the slum child from the "degeneracy," ignorance, poverty, and foreign habits of the un-American home. By a new *expertise* in the old home and by "Americanizing" or by finding alternatives to the slum and immigrant home, the way would open again for the triumph of individualism and "character" in a world where they no longer seemed to matter. The world in the home would be made fit for the child so that the child need not fear to take on the world nor the world fear him.

---

[70] *Ibid.*, p. 11.

13

The "New Education" and the Old Ideals

In every generation after America began its system of free elementary education, the public bewailed the failures of the schools and debated the job teachers ought to be doing. "Fads and frills," specialization, "education for life," "rigor" or ease—by 1890, the topics on the agenda today were already recurrent in educational literature and were the stock-in-trade talk of cranks and critics of the schools. Although the schools had changed dramatically since 1830 the teacher's fears of the public and the public's fantasies about the teachers remained relatively constant, with teachers and parents often lapsing into cantankerousness and self-righteousness about each other.

Given the redemption that is supposed to take place in the American public school, teachers have gradually been loaded with superhuman responsibilities, certifying at graduation that their charges are bona-fide, literate practitioners of the democratic way of life, ready for college or a job, safe to entrust with a car, and primed with the best ideas about a happy sex-life. Yet despite this mission, the teacher ultimately serves at the pleasure of "the people," more concretely the taxpayers who, however pious about education, recurrently insist on a "practical and democratic" training and at the lowest possible cost.

Even without such public pressure the teacher, like the parent, has a difficult job. With the unpredictable future of the American child the same uncertainties beset the teacher as affect the parent when he tests the adequacy of today's mores and ideals against the likely demands of tomorrow. This insecurity about the present combined with resolve, nevertheless, to make the future ever better has bred great instability in American education, as it has in the home. In every generation of their history the American schools have been in a crisis.

The most recent emergency has tested in erratic and confusing ways the adequacy of "progressive education." Perhaps there is something new in the debates of increasingly well-educated parents today, a real concern that more academic and intellectual work be done in the schools. Whatever motivates the complaints, the one thing needful is now "excellence" or "rigor," and the *bête noire* "progressivism."

Our century-old educational melodrama's most recent phase, the attack on progressivism, involves a dramatic reversal in the attitude of the interested layman. What was most striking about the first moves toward "progressivism" after 1880 was the wide public enthusiasm the "new education," as it was called, evoked. Since, on the one hand, the new education was particularly involved with the extension of scientific research on the child and, on the other, promised expanded powers to the schools in saving traditional ideals, its welcome was not surprising. The "new education" invoked psychological realism a generation before its defenders became moral and social pluralists. As Morton White has put it, "one of the earliest problems for progressive education was how to preserve certain of the values of the earlier child's world in the urban society of the twentieth century," the problem of "restoring certain desirable elements of the previous situation . . . capitalism without fears," industry not business.[1] As the absolute and transcendent sanctions for the old Christian-republican code broke down under the twin blows of industrialism and science, the impressive scientific apparatus of the "new education" seemed to guarantee that the schools had found a way of saving traditional American ideals of character and faith.

After about 1880, as men and women in education came into touch with new ideas and sensed the conflict between the new republic and the old, they were conscious that they were breaking new ground, that they were shaping a new age.[2] Between 1880 and 1900 there occurred a conscious quickening of pace in the multifarious world of teaching.

---

[1] Morton G. White, *Social Thought in America* (New York, 1949), pp. 96-97.

[2] H. E. Winship, ed., "Twenty-Fifth Anniversary," *The Journal of Education* 50 (December 7, 1899), pp. 367-96. See also B. A. Hinsdale, "Education 1880-1900," *The Dial* 28 (May 1, 1900), pp. 352-56.

Older societies, like the National Education Association, founded in 1857, quickly expanded their membership and activities. Many new, more extensive, journals of education were started.[3] In 1880 there were eighty normal schools in the United States, by 1900, 264. A few experimental schools were already preparing for the future spread of the new subjects and methods advocated by young innovators like John Dewey. The kindergarten, a great enthusiasm of the period, became an established feature of American education and, at the same time as a rapid expansion of the high school started, the common school revolution ended with the establishment of a nation-wide system of local primary instruction.

John Dewey's early portrait of that generation still seems accurate. Dewey believed that these years put the school at the center of the education effort. Any "revolution" this implied seemed to him to be more in the role and idea of the teacher than in the generally held image of the child. The ideas of educational theorists, particularly Froebel and Herbart, about the pliable nature of the child and the necessity of following a natural evolutionary order in education, had become common among teachers by 1900. All educational theory since Mann and Pestalozzi, Dewey remarked, had been on the side of reform.[4] Actual changes of any significance in the schools had not come about because "conservatives" controlled the school system. With the advances made by the new subjects (drawing, music, nature study, gardening, shop, etc.) "natural principles" were at last coming to maturity, suggesting a new kind of school, new relations between teachers and students, and new conceptions of what the school was to do. In education, "the gospel of the emancipation of the child succeeded the gospel of the emancipation of the educational theorist."[5] The emancipation of the school was the next step.

Dewey thought that the reformers and conservatives had failed to agree because they had no basis for agreement; they needed a philosophy, which Dewey attempted to supply in his classic *The School and Society* (1899). The reformers suffered from too many means beyond their actual powers of use. There was no "old education" nor yet a "new education." There were only "vital tendencies . . . diverse and

[3] *The Educational Review* (1891); *Education* (1880); *The Child Study Monthly* (1895). Among the many state and regional journals, the *Michigan School Moderator* (1891) had a leading circulation as did the *Journal of Education* (Boston, 1875).

[4] John Dewey, *The Educational Situation* (Chicago, 1902).

[5] *Ibid.*, p. 11.

tangential."[6] Unnecessarily, newer and older studies conflicted. As G. Stanley Hall argued, the ideal school existed nowhere, its methods were valid everywhere.[7]

Although widespread practice of the innovations proposed by Dewey and used in his own school in Chicago did not come until later, in their essentials the ideals and methods of progressive education were already introduced before 1900. As long as they remained mere proposals, as they did far longer than today's opponents of progressivism realize, the ideas of the new education encountered little strenuous opposition that can be characterized as reactionary; perhaps doubts here and there, but on the whole, willing, even eager acceptance in the home magazines and newspapers.

If the new and the old did clash, it was in practice rather than theory. Dewey blamed the practical conflict on the powerful inertia of the old machinery, the formal conventions of classes, grades, curriculum planning, and choosing and assigning teachers. If the spadework of the generation of investigation before 1900 was to produce results, practicing teachers and administrators would have to recognize the supremacy of self-activity, the symmetrical development of all the powers of the individual, the priority of character over information, the necessity of putting the real before the symbol, the concrete before the abstract, and making only those demands that the individual child in the progressive stages of his own evolution[8] would be capable of comprehending and responding to. It is not coincidental that parents and ministers had been asked to adopt similar ideals since they, like teachers, were increasingly drawing on the same experts in pedagogy.

American parents and teachers might take common hope since the new methods were not associated with the claim that the old ideal of "character" was wrong. Vast changes in American life and the powerlessness of the old-fashioned schools against those conditions made fearful Americans eager for the best possible advice on saving traditional ideals. As G. E. Hardy, the influential New York educator announced, "our present system of public instruction during the last half century has proven itself over and over again incapable of teaching

---

[6] John Dewey, "The Situation as Regards the Course of Study for Schools," *Educational Review* 22 (June, 1901), p. 32.

[7] G. S. Hall, "The Ideal School as Based on Child Study," *Forum* 32 (September, 1901), p. 24.

[8] E. O. Mason, "Modern Education," *Education* 20 (December 1899), p. 235; N. M. Butler, "The Status of Education by the Close of the Century," *Educational Review* 19 (April, 1900), pp. 313-24.

morality, incapable of forming the character, incapable therefore of giving a true education."[9] In the great cities, in thousands of homes, "coarseness, dissipation, often cruelty and profanity" were making their ineradicable impression.[10] To save the individual from the perils of industrial society and the uncertainties of an evolutionary world without fixed moral rules and without God, American mothers subscribed enthusiastically to *Childhood Magazine,* or attended the Mothers' meeting, or slipped some enlightened pamphlets under their husband's eyes.[11] These were defensive, even conservative, actions, taken in a world where alien institutions seemed to be closing in and life shutting down on the old American middle classes and their ideals.

In the popular literature about education around 1900, one reads largely about the difficult job of the schools and teachers to form character and teach good citizenship or Americanism. The specific conflicts about pedagogical theory among the followers of Froebel, the students of Pestolozzi, and the Herbartians and Hegelians[12] are less impressive than the common determination to use any workable theory to enlist the child as painlessly as possible into the service of "the right" by correctly relating "the truth" to the "interests," the "faculties" or the "activity" of the child.

The most widely preached and adopted novelty of the times was the kindergarten.[13] The fervent faith of the kindergarten enthusiasts "that you have the truth as it is in Froebel,"[14] led to the most extravagant claims. Like Froebel its founder, full of hope and piety about the child, enthusiasts of the kindergarten made it the "one thing needful."[15]

---

[9] G. E. Hardy, *Literature for Children* (New York, 1892), p. 12, originally a speech delivered before the NEA.

[10] C. B. LeRow, "What It Means to be a Teacher," *Ladies' Home Journal* 16 (September, 1899), p. 16.

[11] Birney, *op. cit.,* p. 238.

[12] Frances B. Harmon, *The Social Philosophy of the St. Louis Hegelians* (New York, 1943), chap. 6. The views of their leading educational theorist, William T. Harris—for a time U.S. Commissioner of Education (1889-1906) and a power in the NEA—can be found in convenient summary in a printed speech by Harris titled *The World Educational Congress,* which was delivered before the Department of Superintendence of the NEA in Brooklyn, New York, February 1892. See also J. L. Hughes, "The Educational Theories of Froebel and Herbart," *Educational Review* 10 (October, 1895), pp. 239-47.

[13] See the series of articles by Nora A. Smith, "The Kindergarten Made Possible to Every Home, Village or Small Neighbourhood" (with slightly varying titles) in *Ladies' Home Journal* 15-16 (November, 1898-March, 1899).

[14] Elizabeth P. Peabody, "The Art of Training Kindergarteners," *Journal of Education* 15 (June 22, 1882), pp. 393-94.

[15] See the eulogistic poem "Froebel" by Justine Sterns, *Child Study Monthly* 3 (April, 1898).

The kindergarten promised everything from the prevention of juvenile delinquency[16] to the salvation of man[17] and the regeneration of society.[18] By 1900 Frederick Eby, the influential educator, was alarmed enough about the effects of the campaign to warn that "the spirit of Froebel's utterances may be smothered beneath the letter of his methods."[19] Kindergartens were becoming "unnaturally and unhealthily" dominated by the interests and viewpoint of the adult.[20] The arguments for the kindergarten recapitulated many of the basic ideas and certainly the mood of the new education as a whole. The kindergarten literature was constantly concerned with the personality and training of teachers, the relation between teacher and parent or school and home, what children are and how children learn or ought to learn, the nature of morality and moral growth, the demands that a child could be expected to make and respond to, the nature of individualism and social responsibility, and the roles of spontaneity and discipline.[21]

Kate Douglas Wiggin's *Children's Rights* expertly summarized the case for the kindergarten for the lay audience. When the child left home for school, great care was to be taken that the teacher be a fit person. She must be a surrogate parent in every respect, loving, fair, and expert in her knowledge of the child's nature. Starting in kindergarten, the schoolchild was to be kept busy at all sorts of things that interested him, in order to find out, as Herbart had taught, what he could do and what could be expected of him. Nevertheless, "the

[16] F. H. Briggs' answer to the problem of "the children of lust, the heirs of crime" was first to substitute the kindergarten for the home and the street. Briggs, *op. cit.*

[17] See Kate L. Brown, "The Moral Influence of the Kindergarten," *Journal of Education* 15 (March 16, 1882), pp. 166-67.

[18] Mrs. Mary Mann, "The Kindergarten or the New Education," *Journal of Education* 15 (April 20, 1887), pp. 249-51.

[19] Frederick Eby, "The Reconstruction of the Kindergarten," *Pedagogical Seminary* 7 (July, 1900), p. 263.

[20] *Ibid.*, p. 282.

[21] Other than the articles cited above, see C. C. Van Liew, "Relation of the Kindergarten to the Public School," *Educational Review* 10 (February, 1895), pp. 172-86; Nicholas Murray Butler, "Some Criticism of the Kindergarten," *Educational Review* 18 (October, 1899), pp. 285-91; Thomas Tash, "Kindergarten," *Journal of Education* 22 (September 3, 1885), pp. 156-57; Bertha Payne, "Kindergarten Theory and Practice," *The Elementary School Teacher* 2 (July, 1901), pp. 27-29; Mrs. Louise Pollock, "Is the American Kindergarten Adapted to American Wants," *New England Journal of Education* 14 (August 19, 1880), p. 133; John Ogden, "Some Hindrances to Kindergartening," *Journal of Education* 19 (February 14, 1884), pp. 99-100; C. B. LeRow, "What It Means to be A Teacher," *Ladies' Home Journal* 16 (September, 1899), p. 16; M. M. Glidden, "Kindergarten Methods in Education," *Education* 18 (October, 1897), pp. 83-94.

kindergarten starts out plainly with the assumption that the moral aim in education is the absolute one, and that all others are purely relative."[22] The greatest job of the teacher was to reach "the creative instinct" and to this everything else was to be secondary.[23] Starting in the kindergarten, "moral culture" was to be made "a little less immoral."

The kindergarten also recognized the "practical virtues" (temperance, self-reliance, frugality), creative activity (manual training), the sense of beauty, harmony, and order, and the cultivation of the social nature and a sound, healthy body.[24] The primary objectives of all this liberality about the child's needs were conscience and right for right's sake:

> We appoint more and more monitors instead of training the inward monitor in each child, make truthtelling difficult instead of easy, punish trivial and grave offenses about in same way, practice open bribery by promising children a few cents a day to behave themselves and weaken their sense of right by giving them picture cards for telling the truth and credits for doing the most obvious duty.[25]

But—a small new note, later to din in American ears—righteousness and self-sacrifice were to be learned through "the magic of together."

> There comes a time in the child's development when he begins to realize his own individuality, and longs to see it recognized by others. The views of life, the sentiments of the people about him, are clearly noted, and he desires to so shape his conduct as to be in harmony with them.[26]

This seeking sanctions on one's conduct from society rather than an autonomous conscience hints of what were to become two recurrent implications in later progressive ideas of the interplay of individual and society and in Dewey's words that ". . . the school itself shall be made a genuine form of active community life, instead of a place set apart in which to learn lessons."[27] However, Mrs. Wiggin's description of enlightened discipline in the kindergarten might

[22] Wiggin, *op. cit.,* p. 115.
[23] *Ibid.,* p. 127.
[24] *Ibid.,* pp. 136-37.
[25] *Ibid.,* p. 120.
[26] *Ibid.,* p. 158.
[27] John Dewey, *The School and Society,* revised ed. (Chicago, 1915), p. 11.

scarcely appeal to today's teacher, whatever her sympathy for "democratic living":

> If the child is unruly in play, he leaves the circle and sits or stands by himself, a miserable, lonely unit until he feels again in sympathy with the community. . . . If he does not work in harmony with his companions, a time is chosen when he will feel the sense of isolation that comes from not living in unity with the prevailing spirit of good will.[28]

She backed away from authoritarian implications by adding that this kind of relation to the group must not destroy personal responsibility or common sense. "Our task is to train responsible, self-directing agents, not to make soldiers."[29]

Mrs. Wiggin's classic sentiments about the kindergarten help refute the cranky notion that progressive educators were from the outset bent on destroying traditional American moral ideals. Similarly, John Dewey's early program, *The School and Society* shows that the first progressives in education were on the side of older angels. Dewey's ties with a humanistic individualism and the traditional moral virtues of the old American character were always deep and continuing, although his early enthusiasms in education tended to underestimate, in building character, the value of the formal aspects of study and the cultural worth of the humanities.

In educational theory at about 1900 Dewey had not yet become the full-fledged pluralist and instrumentalist. He had traveled some distance from his earlier Hegelian idealism and had largely accepted only naturalistic premises about experience and "value." Despite his naturalism, few liberal Christians or philosophic idealists would have challenged his educational standard of "saturating [the child] with the spirit of service and providing him with the instruments of effective self-direction."[30]

Dewey's reiterated early theme was that education for citizenship in an industrial age would be effective only when teachers learned to inculcate discipline and nourish individual talents through using the child's actual experience. Whatever the child learned best he learned from real problems and from real people, not from abstract maxims

---

[28] Wiggin, *op. cit.*, p. 121.

[29] *Ibid.*, p. 122. Cf. C. W. French, "Problem of School Government," *School Review* 8 (April, 1900), pp. 201-12; L. R. Harley, "The Family as the Standard of School Government," *Education* 17 (June, 1897), pp. 622-24.

[30] Dewey, *School and Society*, pp. 27-28.

Each child "shall have had the education which enables him to see within his daily work all there is in it of large and human significance."[31] The child weaving wool in class, he believed, could be easily led to learn about where wool came from, how it was gathered, what the customs of shepherds and sheep-raising countries were, the geography and botany of pasture lands, how wool was weighed and marketed (and thus how important numbers, measurement, and arithmetic were to civilized life), the care with which sheep must be watched and thus the necessity of loyalty, kindness, and diligence in one's job and in life in general.

> The occupation supplies the child with a genuine motive; it gives him experience at first hand; it brings him into contact with realities. It does all this but in addition, it is liberalized throughout by translation into its historic and social values and scientific equivalencies. With the growth of the child's mind in power and knowledge, it ceases to be a pleasant occupation merely, and becomes more and more a medium, an instrument, an organ of understanding—and is thereby transformed.[32]

The old education, the going formalistic system of 1900 was highly specialized, over-intellectualized, and narrow; it was made for listening, not making, doing, creating, producing. It was built on a conception that the same predetermined results were valid for all, to be achieved in a measured period of time. "It may be summed up by stating that the center of gravity is outside the child. It is in the teacher, the textbook, anywhere and everywhere you please except in the immediate instincts and activities of the child himself."[33] What was in the raw child—energy, will, desire, ebullience, a ceaseless push for life and pleasure—formed "the natural resources, the uninvested capital, upon the exercise of which depends the active growth of the child."[34]

What does the child need *now,* what can he enjoy *now* should be the recurring questions. It was Dewey's generous belief that "if we identify ourselves with the real instincts and needs of childhood, and ask only after its fullest assertion and growth, that discipline and culture of adult life shall all come in their due season."[35] Above all, the

[31] *Ibid.,* p. 22.
[32] *Ibid.,* p. 20.
[33] *Ibid.,* p. 35.
[34] *Ibid.,* p. 45.
[35] *Ibid.,* p. 55.

teacher must appeal to the imagination, which was not just one "faculty" of the child, to be satisfied with fairy tales and adventure stories. The imagination was, rather, everywhere in his inner life. "To him there is everywhere and in everything which occupies his mind and activity at all a surplusage of value and significance."[36] This imagination, properly cultivated, would gain in flexibility, in scope, and in sympathy until "the life which the individual lives is informed with the life of nature and society."[37]

The humane beliefs in the individual possibilities of the child, and, at the same time, in the limitless powers of the right kind of education to move him "in the direction of social capacity and service,"[38] the emphasis on the need for expert advice, intelligence, patience, and love in handling the impressionable creature—all are ideas that united Dewey with the large body of writers on child nurture and still linked him with the Hegelians[39] in these years of a radically altering America.

Was it not logical, given the weakening of the churches and the seeming inexpertness in the home, that the schools should become ever more concerned with the building of character? If home, church, and press would not spontaneously help the school in this work, the school would have to go to them.[40] The old problem of the proper relation between school and home as influences on the child was implicit from the first year of his acquaintance with the new education. In the kindergarten, the child found "a large group of equals," at home "a small group of superiors."[41] W. T. Harris realistically emphasized the "isolation of the school"—that it made unique demands on the child which of necessity involved a break in the continuity with home life and the life of society. At school came "the emancipation of the youth from the immediate sway of what is near and the bringing

---

[36] *Ibid.*

[37] *Ibid.*, p. 56.

[38] *Ibid.*, p. 81.

[39] See Dewey's favorable comments on William T. Harris (the leading St. Louis Hegelian) in "Psychologic Foundations of Education," *Educational Review* 16 (June, 1898), pp. 1-4. Cf. Harris' praise for Dewey in "Herbart's Doctrine of Interest," *Educational Review* 10 (June, 1895), pp. 71-80. See also Morton White, *The Origins of Dewey's Instrumentalism* (New York, 1943).

[40] C. McKinney, "Co-Relation of Educational Forces," *Michigan School Moderator* 20 (January 18, 1900), pp. 303-05.

[41] Bertha Payne, "Kindergarten Theory and Practice," *Elementary School Teacher* 2 (July, 1901), pp. 27-28.

of his mind into an appreciation of what is far off in time and space . . ."[42]

The enthusiasts of the new education, claiming much for the school and their expertness, were eager to spread their word and their cause. For them the school was "the holy of holies of democracy . . ."[43] Yet even the most modern parent of the time must still have found it difficult to resist the power of the traditional belief that "the true school of morals is at home."[44]

This war between school and hearth had been raging for three generations but now, unlike 1830, public schools were everywhere a fact in American society. Many states had passed laws requiring attendance and teachers sensed a power and exhilaration in the size of the education system and their newly acquired professionalism. Still, the tendency was to deny the need for conflict. "The home and the school seem to be at cross purposes," said one writer,[45] but cooperation between the intelligent parent and trained teacher was both natural and advisable. Not only should the teacher cooperate with the home, but he should "participate in all endeavors to elevate the moral tone of the community."[46] Such cooperation was possible through intelligent interest by parents and teachers in each other's problems and jobs, through mutual discussion and thus, logically, through the work of parent and teacher associations. Who could "estimate the result of sympathetic mothers and teachers clubs upon the future of American citizenship?"[47]

But there were new notes of sharpness as well. Many writers were aware of the friction to be expected when the new teachers "intruded" on the home or when the parent expressed his ideas to the "professional" or trained teacher on school matters. "Laymen's interfer-

[42] W. T. Harris, "The Isolation of the School; Its Educational Function," *Independent* 53 (August, 1901), p. 1786; cf. however, with M. R. Alling's view a generation earlier in "The New Movement in Education," *New England Journal of Education* 12 (June, 1880), pp. 4-5.

[43] M. Strickland, "The School and the Home," *American Mother* 13 (March, 1901), p. 13.

[44] J. C. Browne, "Parental Responsibilities," *American Mother* 12 (October, 1900), p. 27.

[45] W. B. Jacobs, "The People and the Schools," *Educational Review* 21 (May, 1901), pp. 457-58.

[46] "The True Teaching Spirit" an extract from M. P. E. Groszmann, "The Teacher and His Duties" which appeared originally in *The Forum* for September, 1899 and is here cited from *Michigan School Moderator* 20 (October 5, 1899), p. 71.

[47] J. L. Richard, "Cooperation in Education," *Education* 19 (September, 1898), p. 46.

GOD BLESS OUR SCHOOL.
HISTORY OF AMERICA
N. AMERICA
AMERICA

ence in professional matters," said one critic ". . . is not helpful to operation but obstruction."[48]

Another writer was even bolder, "The school is made to usurp the rights of the home. . . . Let school superintendents . . . demand more of the home, not less. . . ."[49] At least, went one plea, "let the parent be patient with the teacher."[50]

The *Child Study Monthly* printed a survey entitled "Conflict of Authority" in which two thousand parents and teachers were asked for an opinion about a little girl who had been forbidden by her parents to sit on the floor, but was told by her teacher to do so in a kindergarten play. The survey asked whom should Mary have obeyed, and why. The answers were tabulated according to age, sex, and reasons given. The author concluded:

> If a large majority of children in early and many in later years, regard home authority as final, the school will do well on the ground of discipline alone to make an effort to win the approval and cooperation of parents and a fair-minded teacher will see that abstract recognition of the righteousness of school discipline as opposed to home discipline is not to be expected till toward the later years of school life.[51]

The controversy rapidly reached the large popular magazines. Edward Bok repeatedly tried to bridge the gap by calling for more cooperation between teachers and parents from his editorial page in the *Ladies' Home Journal*.[52] A speaker before the NEA observed that if the public school was supplanting the home it was because the home itself demanded it.[53] Similarly, Frederick Eby thought that the kindergarten was a compensation for the loss of the private nursery "which the present social conditions have rendered impractical,"[54] and a

[48] P. A. Hanus, "The School and the Home," *International Monthly* 2 (December, 1900), p. 669; cf. "The Old and the New Education," *Woman's Journal* 31 (April 28, 1900), p. 130.

[49] W. N. Ferris, "The Home and the School," *Michigan School Moderator* 18 (April 7, 1898), p. 437.

[50] M. M. Strickland, "The School and the Home," *The American Mother* 13 (March 1901), p. 13.

[51] E. Mansfield, "Conflict of Authority," *Child Study Monthly* 3 (March, 1898), p. 539.

[52] Edward Bok, "How We Are Harming Our Children," *Ladies' Home Journal* 15 (September, 1898), p. 14.

[53] A. Gove, "The School is Supplanting the Home," *Journal of Education* 50 (August, 1899), pp. 141-42. See another protest about the school supplanting rather than supplementing the home in M. A. Cassidy, "Home and School," *Education* 19 (May, 1899), p. 535-43.

[54] Eby, "The Reconstruction of the Kindergarten," *op. cit.,* p. 282.

devotee of manual training justified its inclusion in the school curriculum in part because it had disappeared from the home.[55]

Whatever fears parents felt and whatever superiority teachers claimed, a peace treaty was needed in the interests of the child.

> Is it not about time that the traditional schism between parent and teacher be bridged over? Should we be contented with the relation of armed neutrality which so often exists? The importance of the issue at stake demands mutual sympathy and cooperation. The teacher greatly needs the respect, the confidence and the esteem of the parent. He needs information concerning the child's home life, his tastes, habits, etc. The parent on the other hand should have the frankest statements from the teacher concerning the child's interests as displayed in the school room. Through such conferences, teacher and parent are able to supplement the efforts of each other.[56]

Concern for the child should make for a "wise cooperation" between parents and the schools.[57] The drift of events was producing a blank check from the parents to the state and the teachers; the parent must make his voice heard. "If our present school system must continue to disintegrate the home life, it will be a curse to mankind."[58] Nicholas Murray Butler, however, expressed his certainty that the kindergarten, for example, did not threaten the home and was not disorderly. It inspired an individualism that all parents prized.[59]

Kindergarten teachers should not hesitate, it was said, to take an interest in bringing Froebel's message of enlightenment from the schoolroom to the mother. Many positive arguments "urge the young kindergartner forward and embolden her to start her mothers' class, however presumptuous her actions may be considered."[60]

While parents and teachers were thus being bombarded with advice on what attitudes to take towards each other, news of actual

[55] G. Stoker, "A New Feature in Manual Training," *Pedagogical Seminary* 5 (October, 1897), p. 282.

[56] S. T. Dutton, "The Correlation of Educational Forces in the Community," *Educational Review* 13 (April, 1897), p. 338.

[57] I. F. Bellows, "Modern Hindrances to Culture," *Education* 20 (November, 1899), p. 166.

[58] A. C. Ellis, "Suggestions for a Philosophy of Education," *Pedagogical Seminary* 5 (October, 1897), p. 193.

[59] Nicholas Murray Butler, "Some Criticisms of the Kindergarten," *Educational Review* 18 (October, 1899), pp. 285-91.

[60] Emilie Poulsson, *Love and Law in Child Training* (Springfield, Mass., 1899), p. 6.

"radical" innovations in schools raised some doubts about where the new education would end and helped aggravate the conflict between the school and the home. Spurred by her interests and fears one "doubting mother" visited Dewey's University Elementary School in Chicago to spend "A Day With the New Education." Among other things, the astonished woman saw no books, a live alligator, an Indian blanket, and fruit and sandwiches in the classroom! There were ten students to each teacher and continuing conversation rather than silence was the rule. Student leaders played important roles. The children sang songs they had written for themselves. A ten-year-old was engaged in setting up electric bills, younger children were removing wool from a sheep skin. Others were spinning yarn on spindles they had made or using looms located in the classroom. Several children were allegedly speaking Latin.[61]

Amazed and confused, yet fascinated, this mother reported her questions and Dewey's answers. Did he believe in teaching reading or using books? Was the new education a preparation for "Tolstoy's socialism?" Dewey's answers pleased her, for he assured her that traditional subjects should be learned but through practical activity which interested a child more than a formal approach to those subjects could. The mother noted, however, that none of the children in the class could write; instead they dictated a report on primitive life to their teacher. Dewey's final remark to the mother, quite taken by her experience, was, "The process is the valuable part."[62]

Even education's confessed conservatives would often praise the more modest proposals in the new education, especially those aimed at undoing empty formal discipline.[63] "What can the formal routine of fact-teaching offer to call out anybody's deepest interest and resources?" was a good question.[64] Still, for all its liberality, wasn't the new education too easy, and too entertaining? Public schools were becoming "intellectual Strasburg goose farms"[65] from which children were emerging without being "permeated with the ideals of the founders

[61] Laura Runyon, "A Day With the New Education," *Chatauquan* 30 (March, 1900), pp. 589-95.

[62] *Ibid.*, p. 592.

[63] C. DeGarmo, "The Economic Idea in Education," *Gunton's Magazine* 17 (September, 1899), pp. 199-211.

[64] "For Character Not Cleverness," *Gunton's Magazine* 18 (March, 1900), p. 251.

[65] Lys d'Aimée, "The Menace of Present Educational Methods," *Gunton's Magazine* 19 (September, 1900), p. 257.

of the republic."[66] Where were the successors of Clay, Webster, Grant and Lincoln? Why weren't the immigrants learning English? Citizenship training with songs and salutes was insufficient; training in taxation was essential. Students were learning dribs and drabs even though we know that "It is of the half educated that agitators are made. . . . And if we do not raise up preservors we raise up destroyers of the republic."[67]

Some attacks on what small changes in the school system did take place were intellectually relevant but weakened by crankiness about indoctrination and ignorance about "intellectual discipline." Setting herself against "frills and fads," the author of "Disillusioned Daughters" in *Living Age* asked for a simpler curriculum than that found in modern schools. It would "allow young women to go back to domestic matters" and "restore to domestic pursuits the honor that was theirs in the eighteenth century."[68] The growth of so many subjects was traceable to "ambitious school men."[69] Another plea for a simpler curriculum attacked the formula that everything could be taught. Even if it could, what would become of the Daniel Boone tradition of individual pioneering in the face of the power of the new pedagogy imported from Germany with its smell of state socialism?[70]

When critics attacked the new curriculum for frills and fads, or its "paraphernalia" and for neglecting what the practical American people needed and ought to get in the schools, they were overestimating the actual advances of their opponents. Very few experimental schools like Dewey's existed in the country. The curriculum continued almost universally to be built on formal subjects whose content was set out in advance for each student to master at each grade. F. W. Parker's famous *Talks on Pedagogics,*[71] which stressed new courses of study adjusted as much as possible to the needs and interests of the individual child rather than to age groups, was a manifesto for the future, not the proclamation of forces in control of a nation. It is estimated that, at about 1890, eighty per cent of

[66] *Ibid.,* p. 264.

[67] *Ibid.,* p. 267.

[68] P. Unite, "Disillusioned Daughters," *Living Age* 227 (December 29, 1900), p. 806.

[69] "The Schools for the People," *Child Study Monthly* 6 (March, 1901), p. 355.

[70] H. T. Peck, "Some Phases of Education in the United States," *Cosmopolitan* 23 (July, 1897), pp. 263-71.

[71] F. W. Parker, *Talks on Pedagogics* (New York, 1894).

the time of American students was still spent on the three R's.[72] New subjects had certainly appeared. Music, for example, had been widely introduced in schools even before the Civil War. But even by 1900, like other seeming novelties, it took up far less time than critics understood. Few better proofs existed of the truth of Dewey's claim about the conservative control of the "machinery" of education than the famous NEA report of 1895. A two-year study of a special committee on elementary school curricula approved the retention of the formal eight-year plan for mastering five chief branches of knowledge and for training "the faculties."[73] Dewey, in contrast, attempted to reconcile the alleged alternatives of the child's interests *or* the set subject matter in *The Child and the Curriculum,* but like most of his ideas and his practical innovations, his revolution had to wait for another generation to begin to come to fruit. Later, the charges of frills and fancies and "spoonfeeding," might have had more relevance than in fact they had to the practices of 1900.

Most criticisms of what novelties were practiced in 1900 avoided crankiness about matters like taxation, and made clear at least some sympathy with the broader aims of the theory of the new pedagogy. Fears about foreigners, "socialistic tendencies," or the threat to American individualism were not frequently expressed in the mass journals. The most serious and most persistent criticism was similar to what we have heard, with some justice, in our own times—that certain "disciplines" could not be learned without some disagreeable effort, that "self activity" could not always be directed to or "interest" aroused in subjects which, however difficult, ought to be learned. The early emphasis on the practical and immediate in education dismissed too quickly, or even ignored, certain humanistic studies[74] that did not seem to have pertinence to daily life, as Dewey himself later agreed they did.

The kindergarten, claimed one opponent of "spoonfeeding," followed the line of least resistance in the child and did not enforce the lesson of personal effort. "In laying itself out to make things pleasant for the learner, it makes them too easy, and does not make

[72] Butts and Cremin, *op. cit.,* p. 435.

[73] *Ibid.,* p. 384. For the report and the beginnings of a famous debate it stimulated see W. T. Harris, "Report of the Fifteen" in *Journal of Education* 41 (March 7, 1895), pp. 155-67. N. B. its curious mixture of older schools of thought, notably "faculty psychology," with the rhetoric of the new education.

[74] For an expression of concern for "the great books" see H. E. Starrett, "The Golden Mean in Educational Methods," *Education* 20 (February, 1900), pp. 334-39.

sufficient demand upon attention."[75] He called the kindergarten "the mud pie theory of education."[76] We are misled in assuming that such criticisms were reactionary. This same critic, for example, asked that the child be taught to read early so that he could improve his mind by himself and that he be left alone without the constant interference of overconscientious parents and without unnecessary, harmful "perpetual moral prescriptions."

When "interest" did not appear spontaneously, however

> . . . the child should face the fact that some things must be, because they are required, and are for their good. When a course of action is obviously the best, and inclination does not lead the way, duty must come to the rescue . . . the pleasure theory . . . will make a generation of weaklings.[77]

Along the same lines, Hugo Münsterberg of Harvard said that while the desire to make concessions to individual differences was the essence of recent reforms, many people failed to see the conflict between "what may best suit the taste and liking of Peter, the darling" and "what Peter the man will need for the battle of life in which nobody asks what he likes, but where the question is how he is liked, and how he suits the tastes of his neighbours."[78] The old schools were bad; now children were happier and their parents were glad; their drudgery was over but "To do what we like to do,—that needs no pedagogical encouragement: water always runs downhill."[79] Duty could not be taught on the basis of whim and fancy.

The favorite phrases and words of critics—whim, laziness, lines of least resistance, all appeared in an *Atlantic Monthly* article by L. B. R. Briggs, well-titled "Some Old Fashioned Doubts About New Fashioned Education." In speaking of the necessity, even the beauty, of drudgery and of conquering what was difficult, the writer tried to characterize the new education with words of the modern pupil, "Mind, you must not be dull, or I will go to sleep; you must attract me, or I shall not get on an inch; you must rivet my attention, or my

[75] S. Gwynn, "The Modern Parent," *Living Age* 226 (July 7, 1900), p. 47.

[76] *Ibid.*, p. 45.

[77] J. H. Baker, "Educational Values," *Educational Review* 10 (October, 1895), p. 216.

[78] Hugo Münsterberg, "School Reform," *Atlantic Monthly* 85 (May, 1900), p. 662.

[79] *Ibid.*, p. 665.

thoughts will wander."[80] This new education turns out to be "a sort of bluff at general education." What we must try to do is to keep in the student mind "not pleasure only, but the stern Lawgiver who wears the Godhead's most benignant grace."[81]

In the *North American Review* another critic warned that to eliminate difficulty from study was dishonesty.[82] It was a pedagogical crime for a teacher to think for a student. The coddled youngster "has no more chance of winning in the race than a jellyfish matched against a pike."[83] All our progress came through conflict as Ranke said, and "an element of resistance is required to incite mental effort of the best kind."[84]

C. W. Porter, in a quasi-prophetic article, spoke of the "twentieth century character," the result of a new spirit everywhere. Speaking with the voice of the past with the Puritan idea that what is easy can't be good, what is pleasant can't be pure, she claimed that there was no check on "the spirit of independence." The sense of virtue was enfeebled as were obedience and discipline. Everywhere there was a readiness "to question and resent the exercise of authority," because of the lack of discipline in the family. "Untutored impulses," laziness, "drones," "weakening of the moral fiber," lowered public school standards, restlessness, ennui were the problems ahead. It was the job of the private school, wrote this lady, "to turn the current" and for dedicated teachers to hold back "every pleasure that unfits them [the children] for the performance of duty."[85]

The criticism of the new education for its neglect of difficult and demanding tasks contrasted with the continuing concern of the end-of-century reformers about the weight of studies and homework.[86] Mrs. Wiggin joined a rebellion, but one whose battle lines were less clear than the critics of the new education implied.

Even with the precocious child, said Mrs. Wiggin, the weight of formal drills and memorized facts would interfere with the formation of "character"; "if information cannot be gained in the right way,

---

[80] L. B. R. Briggs, "Some Old Fashioned Doubts About New Fashioned Education," *Atlantic Monthly* 86 (October, 1900), p. 467.

[81] *Ibid.*, p. 470.

[82] P. T. Austen, "The Educational Value of Resistance," *North American Review* 166 (May, 1898), pp. 631-34.

[83] *Ibid.*, p. 633.

[84] *Ibid.*, p. 634.

[85] C. W. Porter, "The Opportunity of the Girl's Private School," *North American Review* 165 (August, 1897), pp. 252-56.

[86] See below.

it would be better not to be gained at all."[87] The child could become right only by doing right, not by memory work or by catechisms. Thus excessive demands on the child were still attacked for enlightened reasons. Her argument was supported by a host of the most respectable popular authorities.

Mrs. Birney was asked if a seven-year-old child who went to school four hours a day should have home study. Her answer was: "It is not only unwise but positively cruel."[88] Shearer was concerned with the complaint against "brain fag" but disagreed that it was due to pressures at school: "Probably not one case out of twenty reported can be shown to be the result of too much school work."[89] Mrs. Scovil, editor of the "Mother's Corner" in the *Ladies' Home Journal* spoke of "our pernicious system of education, which obliges lessons to be learned at home." The child might well be so exhausted by an hour's study in the evening that the tired brain would not quiet down and allow the child to sleep. "If this outrage on nature cannot be stopped" the parent should try a glass of warm milk.[90]

An article in *Popular Science Monthly* entitled "Should Children Under Ten Learn To Read and Write?" advised that reading and writing before that age were too abstract for the child and that the physical and mental strain would harm his health.[91]

Edward Bok called the increasing load of school studies "A National Crime at the Feet of American Parents." He suggested that up to the age of fifteen the child needed only one to four hours of school a day. About homework, he commented: "To rob a child of the play time which belongs to him is a rank injustice."[92] Mrs. Lew Wallace was even more vehement in her special guest editorial, "The Murder of the Modern Innocents." Directed against "over-education" and particularly against too many formal disciplines at school, she complained, "School is never out." She quoted a conversation between a mother and her little boy. The mother asked the child, "Two and two are what?" The boy did not answer. "Surely you know that two and two make four." The child said, "Yes, mamma, but I am trying to remember the process."

[87] Wiggin, *op. cit.*, p. 116.
[88] Birney, *op. cit.*, p. 243.
[89] Shearer, *op. cit.*, p. 278.
[90] Elizabeth R. Scovil, *The Care of Children* (Philadelphia, 1895), p. 67.
[91] G. Partick, "Should Children Under Ten Learn to Read and Write?" *Popular Science Monthly* 54 (January, 1899), pp. 382-92.
[92] Edward Bok, "A National Crime at the Feet of American Parents," *Ladies' Home Journal* 17 (January, 1900), p. 16.

Other cases cited by Mrs. Wallace included the story of a girl who came home sick from school after the class had dissected a cat. The indignant question was, "Are our daughters being trained for surgeons?" Her conclusion was even more angry:

> Constantly the question is being brought up, "Shall this and that be added to our public schools?" But who asks, "Can the scholars endure any more?" They have no protest or petition; they must stand like human vessels ready to be filled to the brim with mixtures of facts. I plead for a childhood of the soul as well as of the body, for the free air, the blessed sunshine, the moderate task ended at the schoolhouse. This night young heads are leaning against their mothers, tired as no young things should ever be and it is a sorrowful sound to hear a child waking from what might be the sunny slumber of a light heart beating to healthful music to ask in a troubled voice, "Do you think I can make the pass grade."[93]

None of the criticisms or defenses of the effects of the new education matched the balance and appropriateness of William James' remarks in *Talks to Teachers*.[94] As the foremost American psychologist and a leading critic of all "closed systems," his liberal credentials were above reproach. He delighted in the freedom suggested for the child and welcomed the new activity and innovation implicit in the enthusiasms which he himself helped to stimulate. It was typical of the man that James' warnings about the new education were based more on fears of what most took to be its virtues or achievements than on its more obvious vices or practical failures. A brief catalogue of his caveats, expressed as they are in his superb style, serves better than any paraphrased analysis.

On teachers as child study experts:

> The best teacher may be the poorest contributor of child study material, and the best contributor may be the poorest teacher.[95]

---

[93] Mrs. Lew Wallace, "The Murder of the Modern Innocents," *Ladies' Home Journal* 16 (February, 1899), p. 14.

[94] William James, *Talks to Teachers* (New York, 1899). These lectures were delivered in Cambridge in 1892 and in other places subsequently.

[95] *Ibid.*, p. 14.

On memory work, rote recitation, and the prosaic:

> The extreme value of verbal recitation as an element of complete training may nowadays be too much forgotten. . . .[96] There is however in all schoolroom work a large mass of material that must be dull and unexciting and to which it is impossible in any continuous way to contribute an interest associatively derived . . .[97] learning things by heart is now probably somewhat too much despised.[98]

On competition and grades, James remarked that marks and standing in the class were rewards without which effort became positively frustrating to the student:[99]

> . . . to veto and taboo all possible rivalry of one youth with another, because such rivalry may degenerate . . . does seem to savor somewhat of sentimentality, or even of fanaticism. The feeling of rivalry lies at the very basis of our being, all social improvement being largely due to it.[100]

On decreasing the difficulty of study:

> We have of late been hearing much of the philosophy of tenderness in education; "interest" must be assiduously awakened in everything, difficulties must be smoothed away. "Soft" pedagogics have taken the place of the old steep and rocky path to learning. But from this lukewarm air the bracing oxygen of effort is left out. It is nonsense to suppose that every step in education can be interesting; the fighting impulse must often be appealed to. Make the pupil feel ashamed at being scared at fractions, of being downed by the law of falling bodies; rouse his pugnacity and pride, and he will rush at the difficult places with a sort of inner wrath at himself that is one of his best moral faculties. A victory scored under such conditions becomes a turning point and crisis of his character. It represents the high water mark of his powers, and serves thereafter as an ideal pattern for his self-limitation.[101] . . . Be systematically heroic in little unnecessary points, do every day or two something for no other reason than its difficulty . . .[102]

[96] *Ibid.*, p. 34.
[97] *Ibid.*, pp. 104-05.
[98] *Ibid.*, p. 131.
[99] *Ibid.*, p. 36.
[100] *Ibid.*, p. 52.
[101] *Ibid.*, pp. 54-55.
[102] *Ibid.*, p. 75.

On the need for scientific techniques in teaching:

> . . . the total impression which a perceptive teacher will get of the pupil's condition . . . will be of much more value than those unreal experimental tests, those pedantic elementary measurements of fatigue, memory, association, and attention, etc., which are urged upon us as the only basis of a genuinely scientific pedagogy.[103]

On cultivating the childs' sense of security and on removing his anxiety:

> The highest form of character, however abstractly considered, must be full of scruples and inhibitions. But action in such a character, far from being paralyzed, will succeed in energetically keeping on its way, sometimes overpowering the resistances, sometimes steering along the line where they lie thinnest.[104]

On the formalistic dangers of antiformalism:

> The need of feeling responsible all the livelong day has been preached long enough in our New England. Long enough, exclusively, at any rate. . . . Even now I fear that some of my fair hearers may be making an undying resolve to become strenuously relaxed, cost what it will, for the remainder of her life. The way to do it . . . is genuinely not to care. . . . Then . . . you may all at once find that you are doing it. . . .[105]

No more appropriate criticisms can be found about ideals which, in a few generations, would become the dominant ideology of the American school leadership.

[103] *Ibid.*, p. 136.
[104] *Ibid.*, p. 179.
[105] *Ibid.*, pp. 227-28.

14

A God Fit for Children

Most nurture writers around 1900 paid very little attention to the possibility of conflict between what science and "progress" dictated for the child and what God wanted for him. Those ministers who were disturbed about the growth of indifference and secularism in the home found their task difficult. If they really resisted the trends to create a more carefree childhood and pressed the claims of orthodoxy against evolutionary and scientific ideas of child development they might well lose what audience they still had. But, even for the dwindling numbers of articulate, deeply orthodox ministers, ignoring the new knowledge might surrender the powerful weapons of science to the liberal and secularist enemies.

The great question of the day for the ministry was no longer whether the child was ready for God but, as Mrs. Gilman put it, whether worship of the God of our fathers ignored the God of our children.[1] Only after settling the question of what religion was fit for children could one know what the aims of religious training ought to be. In a speech delivered before the National Council of Congregational Churches a prominent minister expressed many of the common ideas of the time.[2]

Reverend Richards began by saying, "Our age has awakened to the new realization of the value of the child. He is not a plaything

[1] Gilman, *The Home,* p. 51.

[2] Rev. Charles H. Richards, "The Spiritual Nurture of Children," Speech at the meeting of National Council of Congregational Churches, Portland, Maine, October, 1901.

to be petted and admired; he is a mystery to be solved, a seedling to be developed." He went on to notice the great interest and growing activity in the field of child study and asked why they had arisen. Fascinating in itself, the "deeper reason for the new enthusiasm in child-study lies in the genetic relations of childhood to the future. The boy of today is the citizen of tomorrow."[3] The child is an "undeveloped germ," neither angel nor devil but on his way to becoming one or the other. He cited the importance of evolutionary ideas in forcing Americans to consider the future of "the race." Quoting John Fiske, the popular Darwinian historian and would-be cosmologist, and G. Stanley Hall, Richards spoke of the "splendid possibility of every child," of each child's individual and social value in the great evolutionary scheme. "At this very hour there are nestling in many cradles, and hushed by the lullabies of mothers who little dream of their responsibilities," the great and the wicked people of the future. Which would any child become? Americans could reduce the growing peril to society and assure the safety and success of the individual child "by a wise and thorough spiritual nurture."[4]

The aim had to be "character," which meant the child must acquire ideals, principles, discipline and something called "the spirit of the life."[5] Dr. Richards analyzed the influences at work on the child: heredity, environment, free will, and training. Of these the child's free will was most important. The home and the church would determine the child's fate, i.e. how he would use his will. The state was specifically excluded because, since true nurture must be Christian nurture or spiritual nurture, the religiously neutral state could have no concern with character. No further mention was made of the schools—a startling omission, given the wide concern of the age about the schools and character training.

In the home there had to be a new awakening to "the job to be done." All parents should become acquainted with the broader truths and ideas that the child-study experts had discovered. Mothers and fathers must maintain the proper atmosphere, set good examples, establish steady and affectionate control, strive for wider family fellowship and, finally, inculcate early religious truth (which Richards did not make explicit) adapted to the child's understanding. They should take the child to church, simply, when he is "ready." The job of the

[3] *Ibid.*, p. 1.
[4] *Ibid.*, p. 2.
[5] *Ibid.*, p. 3.

church will be to arouse the "interest" of the child. "Social worship," as exemplified in Junior Endeavor, and Sunday School should be encouraged. The speaker closed with an extra emphasis on the need for all to learn from the new pedagogy.

What is noteworthy is how long it took Rev. Richards to get to "the church," how little of his time he devoted to it, and how vague and general his actual remarks on religion were in comparison with his interest in an upright character fit for a perilous world. What the public of 1850 would have expected from a talk entitled "The Spiritual Nurture of Children," delivered to a national conference of ministers and what the emphasis had become by 1900 were radically different.

Something a little more explicit, if equally liberal and secularized, emerges in an article, "The Religion of Childhood," dealing with the problem "how to present Christ to the wonderful child-mind, not full of atrophies and monstrosities, but normal, healthy, receptive, and religious, preoccupied and ensphered by the Spirit of God.[6] The child is understood as being born with mere tendencies to good and evil; however, evil now implied no inherited guilt or conscious rebellion. Children were specially protected by God and Christ. "Christ saves the children though they know him not."[7]

The core of the argument in this essay was that "there must be somewhere discoverable what we call natural laws for the spiritual growth of a child."[8] One could start with certain facts: that the child was receptive to religion because he had a soul, and that its existence was proven by his early and exalting religious impressions, his horror of evil, his aspirations for goodness, and his sense of the unseen world.[9] How then to touch the soul? The abandonment of the old formalistic religious life for an emphasis on the individual case and practical needs was apparent in the writer's remark:

> In our study of the problem we must not frame a system of theology first, and afterward look to see whether the children are taken in or left out; we must not pinch and squeeze the child till his experience takes the shape of our theology; but we must simply look at all the facts of child-life and at all the facts of Christ's life, and ask what we

[6] John A. Story, "The Religion of Childhood," *Methodist Review* 82 (July, 1900), pp. 524.

[7] *Ibid.*, p. 527.

[8] *Ibid.*, p. 528.

[9] *Ibid.*, p. 526.

> can do to get the child acquainted with Christ and to keep up the acquaintance.[10]

Conversion was now dismissed because it was too dangerous a shock, too formal a procedure, too far beyond the child's possibilities; besides, it was too much "a moment to be met, not a life of love and joy to be led."[11] Precept and example were better than evangelists and revival scenes for children.[12] Then, without any apparent consciousness that he had shifted from theological considerations to moral purposes, the writer asked that the creation of good people by "habit, examples, ideals," be made the religious ideal of parents and teachers. He commented on the lack of knowledge limiting the church's work:

> The intelligent kindergartener of today who is an earnest Christian comes nearer to finding the natural laws of the Christian life for childhood than all the Sunday preaching and teaching of our fathers. . . . Whatever associates the highest life with common everyday experiences helps to make the spiritual life natural. . . . Whatever teaches the child to subordinate the senses to the intellect and conscience . . . helps the religious life.[13]

The religious life was defined as "the community idea," responsibility for others, self-mastery and liberty through law. The child's natural instincts would mature into a genuine devotion to principles if parents avoided "prosy practical handling" that hurt the child's spiritual nature. The great range of child studies, while seeming to go far afield and producing much confusion for some people, will eventually reveal a "natural entrance" for Christ.[14]

What mattered most was to be a good man and a good citizen, dedicated to serving one's fellow men and thus following Christ's law of love. Natural impulses in the child, properly trained, made for such righteousness. The new pedagogy was welcome because it gave more knowledge about these impulses and thus made for more effective training in virtue. *The Christian Advocate* commented on W. L. Tomlins' widely publicized efforts to use music in schools:

> These little hearts are to be taken, while still fresh with the dew of heaven, and set to beating in harmony with the

[10] *Ibid.*, p. 524.
[11] *Ibid.*, p. 528.
[12] *Ibid.*, p. 531.
[13] *Ibid.*, pp. 529-30.
[14] *Ibid.*, p. 532.

> highest laws. So shall the little feet be kept from stumbling and the little hands from reaching after evil. . . . Children . . . from depraved homes . . . began to develop in gentler ways. They were taught that the outer self must be subdued, and the inner, better self, must become supreme. . . . A new pathway was opened to right impulses.[15]

With family worship and attendance at church given increasingly smaller importance, the chief religious observances recommended for children were prayers and Sunday School. But even Sunday School literature seems to have been devoted almost entirely to moral development. Christ, for example, was conceived as the manly, truth-seeking son of God who scorns worldliness. Failure to emulate Christ was taken as evidence of weakness of character which could be "corrected" if only one would try. The old interests in meditation and introspection, speculation on God's nature, and Biblical guidance are never featured, if they appear at all.[16] Similarly, the decline of sectarianism had become precipitous even in denominational journals and magazines.[17] For the child as well as the adult of 1900 the "American religion[18] with a common faith in social action as expressed by various "branches" was already well developed. This faith acknowledged the fatherhood of God and the brotherhood of man through the example or sacrifice (according to one's tastes) of that great and good man Jesus Christ. To a large extent, the child's religion was like clean underwear; necessary and kept out of sight. No nice boy or girl would be caught without it.

The many prayer books specially prepared for children presented no real burdens or taxing theological distinctions. Blandina S. Babcock's *The Children's Daily Service,* for example, gives no indication of any denominational bias.[19] No more precise classification of the book is possible than to say it seems Christian and Protestant. In

[15] *The Christian Advocate* 73 (July 7, 1898), p. 1100.

[16] See the objections in M. C. Brown, *Sunday School Movements in America* (New York, 1901), Chap. VI.

[17] The two leading denominational Sunday school publications in 1899 were both Methodist: the *Berean Intermediate Lesson Quarterly* (New York), 670,000 copies; and the *Sunday School Journal* (New York), 103,000. Among the nondenominational leaders were the *Sunday School Times* (Philadelphia), 155,000; and the *American Sunday School Union Quarterly* (Philadelphia), 71,000. These figures are drawn from N. W. Ayer, *Directory of Newspapers and Periodicals* (Philadelphia, 1899), pp. 1334-42.

[18] The phrase is used by Will Herberg in *Protestant, Catholic, Jew* (New York, 1955).

[19] Blandina S. Babcock, *The Children's Daily Service* (New York, 1908).

the foreword to parents the author warned that to make a child love Christ and his religion, one must be a lover of children; the first seven years of life were all-important in training. Judging by the contents of the book, about three minutes a day, for slow readers, would complete the formalities necessary to bring the child to Christ. For every day in the year there was a separate page on which appeared a very short selection from the Bible of two or three lines, a little poem, and a short prayer. Many of the poems were moralistic and hortatory and stressed love, mercy, faith, and that preoccupation of the age of the slum and the rise of mass hygiene programs—cleanliness. The prayers are to Christ and God for their care and help in becoming worthy of their love.

The demands that this new light-touch Christianity were likely to make on the child are also obvious in a story written by Mrs. G. R. Alden. A young boy, Joseph, promises to take a verse from the Bible to live by every month. The author commented that it was much too difficult and excessive to expect the hero to choose one a day. "Joseph would never make so close a promise as that."[20] Although at first onerous, this discipline eventually brings him the happiness that comes only from such exemplary reverence and benevolence.

One great recurring temptation for the eager religionist of 1900 was somehow to use the public schools to save the child for Christ. Given the growing power of the schools in American society and the increasing likelihood that they might employ the new knowledge about child development for only vaguely Christian or even secular purposes should not some way be found to influence the new education directly? Or perhaps, if the new education was already too radical shouldn't Christian citizens prevent its theories from being put into practice? Recurrently, as the new education gained strength, critics complained about its "real slight to religion." "Our educational panacea," complained Judge C. E. Grant, "is no longer compounded from the pharmacopoeia of religion."[21] The materialism of education "comports with the mercantile tendencies of the time. . . A successful swindle . . . needs trained and disciplined powers of mind. . .[22] Morality alone, he said, could not mould character as the French Revolution showed. To say that religion and public education could not be combined would

[20] Mrs. G. R. Alden ("Pansy"), *A Dozen of Them* (Boston, 1888), p. 9.

[21] Judge C. E. Grant, "Religious Teaching and the Moral Life," *Arena* 17 (June, 1897), p. 1026.

[22] *Ibid.*, p. 1027.

be an "impeachment" that we should resent and deny.[23] *The American Mother* voiced a claim that the final object of education was the first in value; "that which must knit and consolidate all the rest, is the timely instilling of conscientious principles and seeds of religion."[24] A survey of opinions about the basis of moral education in *The Pedagogical Seminary* reported, among other things, that "for the evolution of the ethical consciousness nothing is perhaps better than the arousing of the religious sentiments."[25] Still another complaint was that though "our scheme of life includes good toward our neighbour . . . we do leave God out of it. How many of us teach our boys and girls when they go out into the world, that God is the only reality in it—its being and its end."[26]

Those who still wished to bring religion into public education faced the great constitutional barrier between church and state as well as the fact that the battle for religious use of the public schools had already been fought out between 1830 and 1860. Ever since about 1870 most public schools had been officially closed to any substantial religious teaching. What had remained in the school curriculum was probably only a general acknowledgement of God the father and the importance given Christian ethics.

There was still one attractive possibility. The ardent believers who hoped to use the schools to fight irreligion could and did rest their case on Bible reading. There was nothing approaching a "movement" to do this, but sporadic statements prefaced, by implication, with "wouldn't it be a good thing if . . ." If the fires of traditional faith had burned higher, this call back to the word of God would have been more urgent and louder than it was. But there was no longer any wide, enduring effective call away from the world and back to God.

One study of children's interest in the Bible, for example, concluded that the Old Testament ought to be given to children from eight to fourteen so that they could learn about heroes, moral principles, history, and geography.[27] Adolescents should study the Bible, concentrating their attention on Jesus as an adult. "The spontaneous interest

[23] *Ibid.*, p. 1033.

[24] "What Education Comprises," quoted from Sir Henry Walton, *American Mother* 12 (September, 1900), p. 7.

[25] J. R. Street, "A Study in Moral Education," *Pedagogical Seminary* 5 (July, 1897), p. 40.

[26] An American Mother, "The Modern Son and Daughter," *Ladies' Home Journal* 17 (March, 1900), p. 17.

[27] G. Dawson, "Children's Interest in the Bible," *Pedagogical Seminary* 7 (July, 1900), p. 178.

in Jesus should be seized upon to bring the adolescent lives into harmony with Him, and to make His teaching effective in establishing a correct reminder of conduct as it affects the child and others." But again, as in what ministers had suggested for spiritual nurture, history, and ethics, where was God?

Most proponents of some sort of religious instruction in the public schools did not in fact favor a revived orthodoxy but rather, as one plea expressed the doctrine, "the growth of the individual paralleling that of the race."[28] The history of mankind enroute to emotional and religious enlightenment was doctrinally the obvious point of departure. As for the psychological basis for beginning, the child must never be permitted to lose his early animistic conception of the universe. Above all, teachers must follow the order dictated by science and observation:

> Get back to the Pestalozzian principle of making self-activity the basis for religious instruction as well as for the secular. What is actually needed is an analysis of the religious environment and an orderly consecutive arrangement of the material that it may lead to positive definite ends and an adaptation of this material to the stages of sound development.[29]

In other words, whatever might be said about the need for religion in education, on the whole—except for Catholics[30]—there was little proposed that was radically doctrinal or even distinctly theological. Religion had an important place—it was "a good thing"—but exactly what it was and what its place was were unclear. When clergymen actually called for Bible-reading in the public schools,[31] several serious objections beyond the legal difficulties were raised. Elizabeth Cady Stanton, interested perennially in equal rights for women as the key to America's redemption, said that the time had come to study religion as a science, essential to all people but differing according to climate and civilization. The Bible itself should not be read in public schools because, as Andrew White had shown, "the Bible has been the greatest

---

[28] "A Genetic Study of Immortality," *Pedagogical Seminary* 6 (September, 1899), p. 311.

[29] *Ibid.*, p. 312.

[30] W. Poland, "Pedagogics, The Ethical Movement in Education," *American Catholic Quarterly* 24 (April, 1899), pp. 18-40.

[31] "Clerical Ideas of Education," *The Nation* 69 (November 1899), p. 405.

block in the way of progress."[32] It was, furthermore, not fit for the child. A good lesson for those wishing to use the Bible in schools was cited in the report that children in a school in New York City had stampeded when someone said the devil was present: the Old Testament was too frightening for children. She continued by remarking that there were no books in English literature "more unfit reading for young people than those of the Old Testament."[33] Since she did not believe that Jesus was divine but only the most moral man who ever lived, the New Testament's portrait of him would "unfit them for our present civilization of selfish competition."[34] Reading the Bible in school would also lead to the unrest and discontent of special groups: Jews, Catholics, millionaires, and women would object. Children would want to know if the poor were blessed, why weren't they loved; why were they suffering? Was it not a corollary to belief in the Bible that the Puritans should seem heroes—yet they were really religious bigots. It is, she concluded, "this life" that really counts. True religion is the faith in equal rights. It is this that we ought to teach. "Such will be the triumph of true religion, and such the solution of the problems of just government."[35]

A less special and the most typical position was sketched by A. D. Mayo in his article, "The New Education—The Christian Education." In trying to reconcile Christianity and the new pedagogy, Mayo in fact translated the latter into the language of Christianity, Christian education, for example, was "the training of the vast majority of American children for an American citizenship that includes the noblest ideals of a practical, moral and religious manhood and womanhood."[36] After showing what was new in the new education, and contrasting its views of the child favorably with American education fifty years earlier, Mayo claimed that the American school system had become

> the people's university for training young America in that Christian civilization which contemplates the union of all the elements of our cosmopolitan population in the common American life; the great achievement of 100,000,000 people

[32] E. C. Stanton, "Reading the Bible in the Public Schools," *Arena* 17 (June, 1897), p. 1034.

[33] *Ibid.*, p. 1037.

[34] *Ibid.*, p. 1035.

[35] *Ibid.*, p. 1038.

[36] A. D. Mayo, "The New Education—The Christian Education," *Education* 19 (May, 1899), p. 547.

> living together according to the ideals and methods of human intercourse set forth in the Gospel of Jesus Christ.[37]

Character training involved applying this religion to the world in the form of "the Common Christianity of the American People." The new education itself embodied true Christian education: "It may without irreverence and with perfect fitness, be named—'The Gospel of the New Education.'[38] Its essentials were that the child is of God, possesses freedom, and is thus capable of moral obligation, which makes "character" possible. He is in touch with the infinite and his perfection lies in his obedience to perfect law; thus, "no family can rightly give to society an enemy in the form of a neglected or perverted child."[39] After eighteen centuries, "the absolute religion of Jesus Christ . . . has won its greatest victory in the acceptance of the new education by the American people as the last and best organization of the gospel of love for God and man, for the training of American childhood and youth for sovereign American citizenship."[40] Mayo simply denied any conflict between the new education and the word of God by demonstrating that novelties in the schools were, after all, only better attempts at what God really wanted. By teaching the gospel law of love with a realistic assessment of the child's peculiar needs, the new education was doing what every good Christian wanted. Mayo's article again showed how preferable it was for the American moralist to avoid disturbing issues and to seek instead a broad and comfortable, if intellectually thin, middle ground. What Mayo had said would have gained wide assent from the respectable public at the turn of the century. What mattered, after all, was the right kind of American, and where—except among radicals, atheists or fundamentalist fanatics—was there real debate on that? Christians and educational reformers could all agree on the old goal, now so threatened, of the disciplined moral man who made his own way in life in free cooperation with his fellow citizens. If the new education made this traditional individualism possible, so much the better, for as another seeming "conservative" put it:

> . . . through the ferment and even the wild license of this New Education will have been secured to every child his birthright of individual development, of self-expression, of

[37] *Ibid.*, p. 548.
[38] *Ibid.*, pp. 548-49.
[39] *Ibid.*, p. 550.
[40] *Ibid.*, p. 555.

sympathetic understanding and helpfulness from others. These would not have been attained without a reaction, often an excessive reaction, against the old methods of compulsion symbolized by the rod, but the final result will, I feel certain, amply justify even that present extravagance of laissez-faire and foolish mollycoddling which brings so much modern teaching into deserved contempt.[41]

[41] J. P. Munroe, "Sparing the Rod," *Educational Review* 22 (December, 1901), p. 520.

15

Resisting the Tide of Pluralism

ABOUT 1880, a golden age of children's books began. The child could then enter what was probably a wonderfully appealing fantasy world with tales and stories drawn from all of Europe as well as America. The generation after 1880 was the era of Robert Louis Stevenson and Howard Pyle, of L. Frank Baum, Beatrix Potter, and Laura E. Richards. A list of the famous authors who first began to publish at that time at once establishes the contrast between books deeply engaging the child's imagination and those earlier tract-like or "preachy" books that irritated Jo March and that are now largely forgotten.

These later books carry on and embellish themes that had appeared earlier, such as the need for "character" or moral righteousness. Their most notable characteristic, however, is the increasing variety of settings they supplied for fantasy encounters with the world. One of the great literary achievements of the period was the modern adventure story for children.

The adventure stories included the exciting melodramas of the dime novels, mythology and "in the olden days" tales like *Ben Hur,* the E. E. Hale editions of Bulfinch's *Age of Chivalry* and *Age of Fable,* and the equally famous Howard Pyle editions of the stories of King Arthur and Robin Hood. There were also the adventures of young people such as Jim Hawkins, Tom Canty, Mowgli, and Kim, the stories of the lives of famous animals such as Black Beauty and the little animals of Beatrix Potter's world, and tales of children "just like us," faced with the problems of growing up either in foreign lands, in such favorites as *Hans Brinker* or in America, as in *Rebecca of Sunnybrook Farm.* The popular scientific fantasies of Jules Verne about people with "missions" helped prepare the way for the interest in the Tom Swift and Rover Boy stories later in the twentieth century. Smaller in size but no less ingenious were such little magical creatures as Palmer Cox's *The Brownies.* Even children with distorted natures, as in Gelett Burgess' *Goops,* achieved great popularity.

Collectively, as implied earlier, these stories have one unifying theme. They all concern children confronted with an astonishing variety of situations in which each child must deal with problems like finding his true self, testing his character, and exploring the possibilities of the world. As the child finds or vindicates the principles that constitute "character," his standard is usually taken as morally authoritative or as a safe but welcome novelty. In the world after 1880 in which so many adult writers sensed a decline of "principles" and the open use of any means to secure an end, the child loyal to high ideals also served as a center of sanity and as a rebuke to corrupt adults. Often the child had near-magical powers to do what adults had failed to do or to put right what adults had bungled.

The growing literature about "little folk" (Brownies, imps, elves, sprites, etc.) established a secret compact between the reader and these meta-children. The child could vicariously participate in all sorts of marvelous acts and share many mysteries. The Brownies perform "harmless pranks and helpful deeds,"[1] but only at night when wishes fill the child's mind with dream fantasies. The Brownies are a special child nature; their world is a child's fantasy of Utopia which, however, is not so subversive that it cannot be approved by parents. Brownies, for example, like to learn geography because at their school:

> The rod looks better on the tree
> Than resting by the master's knee.

Almost all energy, they spill over into excusable mischief:

> Now Brownies seldom idle stand
> When there is a chance for fun at hand.

Without the author's disapproval they steal a cart and horse for a ride. Their powers go beyond anything that is recognizable in grown-ups. Unlike adults, the little folk can penetrate locked doors to a world of what in real life are usually forbidden joys and pleasures; they can

[1] Palmer Cox, *The Brownies, Their Book* (New York, 1887), Preface.

also deal with the world better than others because of their special talents:

> . . . we by exercising skill
> May travel in and out at will.

They are beyond ordinary law:

> But we, who laugh at locks or law
> Designed to keep mankind in awe,
> May praise the keeper's cautious mind
> But all the same an entrance find.

They help adults like the sick farmer whose work they perform to save him from the local miser:

> So wrapped in self some men can be
> Beyond their purse they seldom see.

They can "steal" things which, through their magic powers will never seem taken:

> And little danger could they see
> In what would trouble you or me . . . .
> And in the main, as history shows,
> Succeed in aught they do propose.

Yet, on Washington's Birthday, like all good children, they revere the man who never told a lie and who served the cause:

> Until he shook the country free
> From grasps of kings beyond the sea.

Not all writers were enthusiastic about the child who possessed great powers of ingenuity and inventiveness. In one of the popular stories of the 'nineties, Frank R. Stockton's *The Clocks of Rondaine,*[2] a little girl lives in a town famous for its many clocks whose chiming, however, is uncoordinated. Determined not to lose the joys of Christmas day because of the difference between the town's time and what she thinks is the true time of her own clock, Aila sets out on a reform campaign; she visits the clock owners of Rondaine and urges them to coordinate their clocks for the sake of more rational time and the child's pleasure on Christmas day. Everywhere she is rejected and scolded. She is told:

[2] New York, 1892.

> Of all things that one hundred and fifty seven years ago were able to life an arm to strike, they alone are left. And now you, a child of thirteen, or perhaps fourteen years, come to me and ask me to change that which has not been changed for a century and a half and seven years.

Elsewhere she hears, "Never ask persons as old as I am to alter the principles which have always made clear to them what they should do, or the clocks which have always told them when they should do it. Aila fails in her mission but her character profits for she learns that her own clock was wrong and that her desires for perfection and pleasure are wrong-headed.

In contrast with this type of story, skeptical about the freshness and inventiveness of the child, were the many books of Laura E. Richards. Her recurrent theme was expressed in a line of one of her poems:

> Then the whole wide earth doth wait
> On each little child.

Her book *Melody,* epitomized, as much as Rollo had for his era, many of the recurrent sentiments and thoughts of the 1890's about the child and the world:[3]

Melody is a foundling, a beautiful little girl who has been adopted by two spinster sisters. Her coming into their lives is described as a "miracle." She transforms the lives of all the adults in the small village in which they live. She sets an irresistible example; her sweetness and kindness touch everyone. Her special gift, an exquisite voice, can soften the most quarrelsome with songs. It is said: "She is a child of God who has never forgotten her Father." This angel's perfection and powers come from both heaven and nature. "Who taught Melody to dance? Surely it was the wind, the swaying birch tree, the slender grasses that nod and wave by the brookside." Rather than being corrupted by nature or alienated from God, the child is now morally perfect and exemplifies the harmony of the natural and the Divine. Childhood and the adult world that remains in touch with its magic become essentially the Garden of Eden, a world of blissful innocence and universal trust and love. Unlike heavenly angels, however, Melody has two "flaws." She is blind, which means that she is not able to make her way everywhere (but her blindness has compensations in her magical powers of insight). Unknown to the sisters, she also has a

[3] Laura E. Richards, *Melody* (Boston, 1896).

weak heart which could not stand the shocks of the cruelties beyond the blissful village where her blindness does not incapacitate her and in which her magic can work.

The theme of the garden is set off against the theme of "the world outside," represented in *Melody* by the city—selfish, impious, sordid, hot, dominated by the business spirit, and above all, greed. Two promoters from the city who are passing through the hamlet hear Melody sing and make her guardians an offer to take Melody on a singing tour so that she can really profit from her gifts. She will make her own way in the world, have a more adventurous life, and return some of her earnings to help her loved ones in the town. Adamantly, the sisters reject the crooked impresario's offer with remarks like "It's inside that one has to be happy; one can't be happy from the outside ever." They also call the showmen's offer "the serpent,"—understandably, since it is a temptation to end the state of innocence, to venture outside the garden and lead a life whose risks and costs are too great.

Having been refused, the men kidnap Melody and take her to the city. As in the earlier case of Elsie Dinsmore, her fall, or expulsion from the garden, is really due to virtues and talents which the world wishes to pervert or exploit for selfish purposes. Village life collapses as though something has gone wrong with human nature: the sisters quarrel, husbands and wives and lovers have spats, gloom and despair touch everyone. "The light of our life . . . is gone out . . ."

The possibilities of a "deal" with the kidnappers are dismissed with expressions about the impossibility of sacrificing a child for others: ". . . you would rather die ten times over than have luxuries bought with the child's happy innocent life . . ." Only the Doctor knows that outside the garden, in the fallen world, Melody will probably die because of her weak heart. One of the sisters is confident that God will protect and return Melody. The other complains about taking God's aid for granted, given the nature of the world.

In the big city Melody thinks about Milton's *Paradise Lost* and persistently refuses to sing for her captors. This completely frustrates the impresario, who is not a totally corrupt man. He pleads with Melody. "You belong to the world, I tell you," he cried again. "The world has a right to you." He wants her to bring her remarkable gifts to the world so that what has happened in the village will happen everywhere: Melody's song will replace evil and suffering with love and happiness. But Melody knows his other motives and the only life appropriate for an innocent. She again refuses and shortly after is rescued by an old Negro fiddler from the village who plays Melody's favorite song through the streets of the city, hoping to attract her attention. Melody returns to the garden and all that was wrong in the village at once becomes right. Happy and secure, innocence has rejected the world for the simple pastoral life of love and morality but one understands what Melody really has in mind when, after returning, she says, "I don't want to grow up, ever, at all."

Many of the most famous stories about 1900 use these themes of the innocent garden of childhood and the wicked or ferocious world outside. In Beatrix Potter's *Peter Rabbit* (1904), Peter and his brothers and sisters, Flopsy, Mopsy, and Cottontail, are safe enough when they stay close to mother. When Peter ignores her warnings and jauntily visits the outside world, Mr. McGregor's cabbage patch, he is nearly caught and killed before making home by a hair's breadth.

At the beginning of *Little Black Sambo* (1900) the little Hindu hero, secure at home, is being dressed in the fine clothes his loving mother has made for him. Venturing out into the jungle, however, Sambo meets several vengeful tigers in succession, against whom he has so little power that he has to placate them by giving each one of the symbols of his mother's love.

He is nearly stripped naked and helpless when, fortunately, the tigers quarrel and chase each other in order to capture all the fancy clothes. Competition among the evil creatures of the jungle is the child's only hope; the enemies may destroy themselves if only the child can hold on. The tigers go so fast that they turn into a pool of butter. Sambo, now safe, ladles up the butter and puts on his clothes and returns home in triumph to a dinner of pancakes in which he eats far more than his father. Only luck in the outside world has enabled him to survive the tigers. At dinner, eating the threatening "tigers" on his, the largest portion of pancakes, makes him even a bigger man than his father. But in "the world outside" he was essentially powerless.

Similarly, in *Black Beauty* (1897), the old horse, after dreadful beatings, wounds, and brushes with death finds peace and security only when she returns to the home of those who love her. Jim Hawkins in *Treasure Island* (1892), learns the full horror and greed of man's world but he also succeeds in redeeming the pirate Long John, if only temporarily. Despite Jim's betrayal of him, Silver cannot bear to harm the boy. Jim, in turn, frees Silver. Yet, although Jim is affectionate and grateful to this "father," Silver is really irredeemable and fit only for the world of gold and blood. Jim, however, returns home and writes off the "outside world" of Treasure Island. In *Peter Pan* (1911), the child does stay a child forever because in every generation the daughter will relive the delights of the mother's childhood, while Peter himself never does grow up. The world of childhood, although filled with trouble and threats, keeps death and destruction at bay. In Never-Never land Tinker Bell doesn't die but is saved by the wishes of children, and the threats of the crocodile, Captain Hook, and the Indians are overcome or turn out to be harmless.

Alongside these tender innocents, so limited in their power to battle the world, a number of more resourceful heroes were appearing in children's books. Their world was equally perilous and without moral certainty or steady divine guidance. It was a world in which there was no once-and-for-all order but only a constant changing multiplicity of options and possibilities for good and for evil. Death, tragedy, suffering, and struggle had perhaps more weight in this universe than progress or rationality but there was at least the choice to make one's life as one chose. The resourceful child, in stories with this setting, differs from earlier heroes in several respects, principally because he has greater freedom since society is less cohesive against him; the world is already more "open." Consequently, he can manipulate it or more easily slip through the web that law and convention set for him. He searches for a new kind of order against the pat certainties or canons of culture, and substitutes a personal code to replace "the law." This child seems instinctively moral and yet undogmatic. Unlike Rollo or the children of the garden, he can meet a world where anything can happen on its own terms. In the alien "world outside" he gets on successfully and maintains his robustness and integrity. Despite his apparent disregard or scorn for "civilization," he is often more civilized than the adult culture he rejects or ignores. Unlike Rollo or Melody he often has to break the accepted morality or the rules, but he does so because of a willingness to honor a wider range of human experience than encompassed by existing morality and the conventional decencies.

Mowgli in *The Jungle Book* (1899) has lost his father and mother. The animals of the jungle have become his nearest kin and in their world sheer necessity is the only code. One lies or kills only when hunger or safety demand it and then without false pieties about why it was done. ". . . the Law of the Jungle . . . never orders anything without a reason." All the pretense and falseness of civilization have disappeared. Honest dealings between creatures and elaborate rituals and rites honoring the varied rhythms of nature make the dangerous jungle preferable to the village-life in which "men must always be making traps for men . . ." Appealing to a child's natural resentment against limits, the jungle frees much of the instinctual life that society represses. Its lore gives the quick child a primitive wisdom about the mystery of creatures and things, enabling him to survive the dreadful struggles that take place around him. The jungle is not morally damned as "savage." It is taken as given, but played on its own terms, it can be transcended. Mowgli can overcome dangers that would kill uninitiated, "soft," and too-quick-to-categorize adults. His escape from the law as a boy enables him to learn a code by which, we are told, he lives better as a man when he returns to human society. The jungle ultimately is abandoned but its freedom for instinct and its realism have given Mowgli a sophistication about life that he might never have otherwise acquired.

Kim (1901) learns in the world of men what Mowgli learns from the animals. Like Mowgli and many other resourceful boys and girls in the fiction of the time, he has lost his parents, his connection with the past, and the traditional roots of authority and behaviour.

Kim's claims on life are not satisfied by the Lama with his reverence for truth, by the world of the bazaars, by the school of Lucknow, or by the ways of the soldier. His talents have their greatest success in the Secret Service, where his boyish ingenuity and simulation, his disarming air of innocence, enable him to capture the spy who had eluded the adults. Kim is able to learn from all men, from life everywhere and from many "fathers." His talent for coping with a diverse world gives him powers that no one of India's styles of life or callings could have provided.

Huck Finn and Tom Sawyer[4] represent variants of both types of heroes I have been discussing. Huck is the spirit of pragmatic innovation; Tom's strongest tendency is to systematize, to organize, to try to encompass all possibilities within one consistent system and then to clothe it in humdrum pieties. He is trapped by the conventional morality and ideals of civilization largely because of his inability to look fact in the face and take life as it comes. His desire for the abstract and "gold-lead distinctions" drawn from books rather than life, intrigues and irritates Huck. Although he is one of the "natural" or bad boys he is, under everything, the heir of Rollo. His moralism and the-

[4] Mark Twain, *Huckleberry Finn* (New York, 1885).

orizing nearly prevent freeing Jim and constantly interfere with Huck's directness, activism, and intellectual honesty.

Law and order and most things that men live by on the River are shown to be as cynical and corrupt as Huck's father, however much the worthy citizens believe themselves his superiors. Huck's conduct and intense concern with justice and truth are always reminders of better possibilities than those of the civilization he rejects: kindness, decency, fellow-feeling, tolerance, forgiveness, and a sense of responsibility. Like all the resourceful boys, his conduct—instinctive rather than abstractly reasoned—really involves no break at all with civility. He learns that for all a culture's pretenses to finality the world is almost infinite in its possibilities; virtue has no precise outer form. Indeed, Huck assumes many "identities" and "roles" on his journey but he is always, irrepressibly, himself—moral and humane. However much the men on the River abuse and trick each other and Huck, he is always ready to trust, to believe, to let the situation reveal itself, to reject any of the claims of culture on the river banks. As Leslie Fiedler has said of the frontiersman, he is the noble savage in a world of original sin. Deceit and knavery are usually his undeserved rewards, nothing in life seems fixed or certain, and he must often fall back on his own self-reliance.

His code is most severely tested in his relations with "nigger Jim." Huck helps free Jim, he protects his freedom, he even apologizes to Jim for hurting his feelings despite his strong patina of Southern Missouri town prejudices about slaves and abolitionists. When he has offended Jim something instinctive and beyond "the law" intervenes and brings them together again. Much has been written in this respect about the ambiguities at the end of Huckleberry Finn.[5] Despite the lessons of a common humanity on the river, Huck toys with helping to return Jim to his owner and slavery. Twain's problem was to show how powerfully conventional life could affect Huck without at the same time destroying the relevance of what happened "outside" of civilization on the river—without reducing the love between Huck and Jim to a mere trick of fate, a whim or something morally meaningless. Despite his hint that Huck might again "light out," no one knew better than Samuel Clemens how the lures of conventional life could claim a boy; yet Huck could not be a boy or resist all the proprieties indefinitely. Huck's and Jim's idyll on the raft was a rare exception to all

[5] See a summary of critical opinion in Barry Marks, ed., *Mark Twain's Huckleberry Finn* (pamphlet), Boston, 1959.

the rules of their civilization. Huck's threat to Jim seems contradictory but given Twain's knowledge of the pull of life to which most boys succumb, Huck's inclination is understandable. It is Twain's attempt to show the impermanence of those moments when we overcome the obstacles life puts between men. Captivated by the possibilities offered by the river we naturally resent Twain's final irony that Huck Finn might capitulate to civilization as Clemens thought he had.

In adult fiction of 1900 about the child, Henry James' *What Maisie Knew* (1897) exposed even more deeply than *Huckleberry Finn* the challenges faced by the resourceful child in an alien world. In *What Maisie Knew,* we find many portents of childhood in our age of marital and sexual freedom, and of the bewildering other changes in family life of the twentieth century.

Pearl in *The Scarlet Letter* is the best contrast to Maisie from earlier in the century. However, although Pearl is used to dramatize the tendencies of the moral life of her parents to the point of being the touchstone of the story, her parents are the central characters. In James' book, not only is Maisie almost constantly in view, but most of what we know about the adult world comes to us through the record of her experiences and responses. *What Maisie Knew* is almost unique, in a century of great poems and novels about children, for its concentrated portrait of the inner life and development of a child. At the same time, the book is more a harbinger of the transformation of traditional family life than we can find elsewhere.

The resourceful child of the fiction of 1900, and the earlier little servants of orthodoxies, lived in a world in which adults defined conventional good and evil. However hypocritical or lax in their own behavior, the adults in *Huckleberry Finn* stated moral ideals that the child was to accept. But in the world heralded by *What Maisie Knew,* the adults have scarcely any consciousness of traditional morality. They have passed beyond not merely Victorianism but all familiar customs and ideals about sex, marriage, parenthood, and family. They know only the world of the pleasure principle. Their rules are only strategems for sensual gratification tempered, infrequently at best, by vestiges of sentimental propriety about a child's place and upbringing. Under these conditions it is almost impossible to believe that any child could find her way to morally responsible adulthood. Even the one voice of conscience in *What Maisie Knew,* Mrs. Wix, the governess, has her own quota of temptation to impropriety, and seems most often merely fussy about right and wrong.

We have been assured by James himself and most of the best critics of *What Maisie Knew* that Maisie is triumphantly innocent. It may, of course, be difficult now to accept any such extravagant notion of innocence, given what we have had to learn about a child's constant sexual awareness and pleasure. Although we violate James' own terms, it is difficult to resist interpreting Maisie's recurrent insistence that she "really knew" as a signal that her vivid imagination is erotically involved in the sensual ties and strategies in the lives of her parents and their *amours*. The truth about the post-moral world of the adults among whom she is shunted is inescapable at every turn, and Maisie in that world has no choice but to see, hear, and "know."

Deprived then by her parents of every source of moral stability and serenity traditionally posited for childhood, and given as counterweight only the moral clacking of Mrs. Wix, Maisie nevertheless finally rejects the pleasure principle. She seems to have made an extraordinary choice of discipline and propriety over the freedom the other adults offer her. What finally brings Maisie firmly into the moral world, however weakly represented by Mrs. Wix, is her knowledge that grows from the first pages of the novel: she has meant scarcely anything to any of the adults except as a means to their pleasure, their power, or their revenge. However cloying, the world of Mrs. Wix does represent, at its best, concern for the child for her own sake; above all, love for her and care for her wellbeing and happiness.

In most of Maisie's life, not only morals but even the moral pretensions of Huck's world have disappeared. We are in a new age with the old middle-class "family school of morals" collapsed, and neither "holy precept" nor "shining example" held before the child as they once were. Even the child's idols who show kindness and concern for Maisie turn to clay. Reason as justification has become mere rationalization of desire, failing not only to delineate morality but cloaking private, as it will later in the century, social exploitation.

By 1900 the child's search for a rule of life in a perilous world unresponsive to inherited beliefs had involved endowing some children with miraculous powers of self preservation and the ability to better or even redeem the lives of adults. But along with this investment in the child there was a profound uneasiness about the adequacy of their gifts in a world hostile to innocence. By 1900 Americans were creating a powerful fantasy that they might reject the corrupt complexity of their new polyglot civilization because its moral cost to "character" and "faith" were too high. In fact, this revolt against pluralism in American society after 1890 is just as remarkable as the so-called "revolt against formalism" of the progressive intellectuals of the same period. Very little in the nation changed for all the promise of a redeemed republic and talk of a return to a golden age. Despite strong recurrent fantasies of innocence, Americans for generations had made their decision. They had followed the lures of the world and, given additional temptation, the promised powers of the twentieth century were too large to resist. Their fantasy was no less real, however, than the tempting power, the old Word no weaker than the new will. The innocent child, properly raised, was to redeem the republic. But if "character" and "faith" were still possible how were they to be created in so radically different a world? Hope was still invested in what reason said or what revelation commanded. A few seers were only groping toward the heresies that the child's self-interest and instincts could be nourished to pass beyond the chaos of infantile omnipotence and to resist, at the same time, being withered by the crushing claims of "Reason" of the twentieth century. The "character" and "faith" so anxiously sought by the decent parent of 1900 might thus still be possible, but not without a far more radical alteration of family and society than most parents a half-century ago—or today—even dreamed necessary.

Bibliography

GENERAL WORKS

Ariès, P., *Centuries of Childhood,* New York, Knopf, 1962.

Barry, F. V., *A Century of Children's Books,* New York, Doran, 1923.

Bettelheim, B., *Dialogues with Mothers,* Glencoe, Free Press, 1962.

———, *Love Is Not Enough,* Glencoe, Free Press, 1950.

Blanck, J., *Peter Parley to Penrod,* New York, Bowker, 1938.

Brown, N. O., *Life Against Death,* Middletown, Wesleyan University Press, 1959.

Bruner, J. S., *The Process of Education,* Cambridge, Harvard University Press, 1960.

Butts, R. F. and Cremin, L. A., *A History of Education in American Culture,* New York, Holt, 1955.

Calhoun, A. W., *A Social History of the American Family,* Cleveland, A. H. Clark, 1918.

Chase, R., *The American Novel and Its Tradition,* New York, Doubleday, 1957.

———, "Neo Conservatism and American Literature," *Commentary,* 23 (March 1957).

Children's Aid Society of New York, *Annual Reports.*

Child Study Association of the United States, *Our Children Today,* New York, Viking, 1952.

Chrisman, O., *The Historical Child,* Boston, Badger, 1920.

Curti, M., *The Growth of American Thought,* 2nd ed., New York, Harper, 1951.

———, *Probing Our Past,* New York, Harper, 1955.

———, *Social Ideas of American Educators,* New York, Scribners, 1935.

Davis, S. E., *Educational Periodicals in the Nineteenth Century,* U. S. Office of Education Bulletin #28, 1919.

Dinkel, R. M., "The Influence of Nursery Literature on Child Development," *Sociology and Social Research* 31 (March, April, 1947).

Eby, F., *The Development of Modern Education,* New York, Prentice Hall, 1952.

Erikson, E., *Childhood and Society,* rev. ed., New York, Norton, 1964.

Frazier, E. F., *The Negro Family in the United States,* Chicago, University of Chicago Press, 1939.

Friedenberg, E. Z., *The Vanishing Adolescent,* Boston, Beacon, 1962.

———, *Coming of Age in America,* New York, Random House, 1965.

Freud, A., *Psychoanalysis for Teachers and Parents,* New York, Emerson, 1935.

Freud, S., *The Standard Edition of the Complete Psychological Works of Sigmund Freud,* London, Hogarth, 1954.

Gardner, E., *A Handbook of Children's Literature,* Chicago, Scott Foresman, 1927.

Gesell, A. et al., *The Child from Five to Ten,* New York, Harper, 1946.

———, *The First Five Years of Life,* New York, Harper, 1940.

Glover, E., *Freud or Jung,* London, Allen and Unwin, 1950.

Goldman, E., ed., *Historiography and Urbanization,* Baltimore, Johns Hopkins University Press, 1951.

Goodman, P., *Growing Up Absurd,* New York, Knopf, 1962.

Goodsell, W., *A History of the Family as a Social and Educational Institution,* New York, Macmillan, 1915.

Gruenberg, S. M., *The Encyclopedia of Child Care and Guidance,* New York, Doubleday, 1954.

Halsey, R., *Forgotten Books of the American Nursery,* Boston, Goodspeed, 1911.

Jordan, A. M., *From Rollo to Tom Sawyer,* Boston, Horn Book, 1948.

Key, E., *The Century of the Child,* New York, G. P. Putnam's Sons, 1909.

Malinowski, B., *Sex and Repression in Savage Society,* New York, Meridian, 1959.

Meigs, C., et al., *A Critical History of Children's Literature,* New York, Macmillan, 1953.

Monroe, P., *A Cyclopedia of Education,* New York, Macmillan, 1911-19.

Mott, F. L., *Golden Multitudes,* New York, Macmillan, 1947.

———, *A History of American Magazines,* Cambridge, Harvard University Press, 1938-57.

Piaget, J., *The Child's Conception of the World,* Totowa, N. J., Littlefield, 1960.

Reed, R., *The Modern Family,* New York, Knopf, 1929.

Ribble, M., *The Rights of Infants,* New York, Columbia University Press, 1943.
Ruhrah, J., *Pediatrics of the Past,* New York, Hoeber, 1925.
Spock, Dr. B., *The Pocket Book of Baby and Child Care,* New York, Pocket Books, 1946.
Sullivan, M., *Our Times,* New York, Scribners, 1927.
Weekes, B. E., *Literature and the Child,* New York, Silver Burdett, 1935.
White, M. G., *Social Thought in America, The Revolt Against Formalism,* New York, Viking, 1948.
———, *The Origins of Dewey's Instrumentalism,* New York, Columbia University Press, 1943.
Woody, T., *A History of Women's Education in the United States,* New York, Science Press, 1929.
U. S. Children's Bureau, *Your Child from 1-6,* Washington, Gov't. Printing Office, 1956.
———, *Your Child from 6-12,* Washington, Gov't. Printing Office, 1949.
American Journal of Sociology.
American Sociological Review.
Journal of Educational Sociology.
Marriage and Family Living.
Monographs of the Society for Research in Child Development.
The Psychoanalytic Study of the Child.

COLONIAL DEVELOPMENTS

Boorstin, D., *The Genius of American Politics,* Chicago, University of Chicago Press, 1953.
Brewer, C. H., *A History of Religious Education in the Episcopal Church to 1835,* New Haven, Yale University Press, 1924.
Bridenbaugh, C., *Cities in the Wilderness,* New York, Ronald, 1938.
Caulfield, E., *The Infant Welfare Movement of the Eighteenth Century,* New York, Hoeber, 1931.
Earle, A. M., *Child Life in Colonial Days,* New York, Macmillan, 1899.
———, *Home Life in Colonial Days,* New York, Macmillan, 1899.
Edwards, J., *Works,* 4 vols., New York, Leavill, Trow, 1849.
Fleming, S., *Children and Puritanism,* New Haven, Yale University Press, 1933.
Ford, P. L., *The New England Primer,* New York, Dodd Mead, 1897.
Fox, D. R., "The Protestant Counter-Reformation," *New York History,* XVI (Jan., 1935).

Holme, C. G., *Children's Toys of Yesterday,* New York, Studio Publications, 1932.
Homan, W. J., *Children and Quakerism,* Berkeley, University of California Press, 1939.
Jordan, A. M., "Early Children's Books," *Bulletin of the Boston Public Library* XV (April, 1940).
Kiefer, M., *American Children Through Their Books,* Philadelphia, University of Pennsylvania Press, 1948.
Mather, C., *A Family Well Ordered,* Boston, 1699 (Columbia University microfilm).
Morgan, E. S., *The Puritan Family,* Boston, Boston Public Library, 1944.
Miller, P., *Jonathan Edwards,* New York, Sloane Associates, 1949.
———, *The New England Mind, The Seventeenth Century,* New York, Macmillan, 1939.
———, *The New England Mind, From Colony to Province,* Cambridge, Harvard University Press, 1953.
———, "From Edwards to Emerson," *New England Quarterly* XIII (Dec., 1940).
Palmer, R. R., *Catholics and Unbelievers in Eighteenth Century France,* Princeton, Princeton University Press, 1939.
Rosenbach, A. S. W., *Early American Children's Books,* Portland, Maine, Southworth Press, 1933.
Selbie, W. B., *The Psychology of Religion,* Oxford, Clarendon, 1926.
Watts, I., *Divine and Moral Songs for the Use of Children,* London, 1715, Reprinted 1848.
Wigglesworth, M., *The Day of Doom,* Boston, 1662, Reprinted New York, Spiral, 1929.
Wright, L. B., *The Cultural Life of the American Colonies,* New York, Harper, 1957.

1830 - 1860

GENERAL SECONDARY WORKS

Aaron, D., ed., *America in Crisis,* New York, Knopf, 1952.
Berger, M., *The British Traveler in America, 1836-1860,* New York, Columbia University Press, 1943.
Branch, E. D., *The Sentimental Years,* New York, Appleton Century, 1934.
Davies, J. D., *Phrenology, Fad and Science,* New Haven, Yale University Press, 1955.

Furness, C., ed., *The Genteel Female,* New York, Knopf, 1931.
Guernsey, L. E., *School Days in 1800,* Philadelphia, Union Press, 1875.
Jacoby, G. P., *Catholic Child Care in the Nineteenth Century,* Washington, Catholic University of America Press, 1941.
Pierson, G. W., *Tocqueville and Beaumont in America,* New York, Oxford, 1938.
Tyler, A. F., *Freedom's Ferment,* Minneapolis, University of Minnesota Press, 1944.
Weinberg, A., *Manifest Destiny,* Baltimore, Johns Hopkins University Press, 1935.

GENERAL PRIMARY SOURCES

Bremer, F., *America of the Fifties,* New York, American Scandinavian Foundation, 1924.
———, *The Homes of the New World,* 2 vols., New York, Harper, 1853.
Duncan, M. G. L., *America As I Found It,* New York, Carter and Bros., 1852.
Martineau, H., *Society in America,* 2 vols., New York, Saunders and Otley (1837).
Tocqueville, A. de, *Democracy in America,* 2 vols., New York, Knopf, 1945.

GENERAL PRIMARY PERIODICALS

Atlantic Monthly.
DeBow's Review.
Democratic Review.
Godey's Lady's Book.
Harper's Monthly.
Knickerbocker.
The Man.
New York Review.
North American Review.
Putnam's Monthly.
Southern Literary Messenger.
Southern Quarterly Review.
Southern Review (new series).
Western Journal and Civilian.
Westminster Review.

MORAL AND RELIGIOUS IDEALS

SECONDARY SOURCES

Bates, E. S., *American Faith,* New York, Norton, 1940.
Niebuhr, H. R., *The Social Sources of Denominationalism,* New York, Holt, 1929.
Sweet, W. W., *The Story of Religions in America,* New York, Harper, 1930.

PRIMARY SOURCES

Abbott, J. S. C., *The Child at Home,* New York, 1833.
Alcott, A. B., *Conversations with Children on the Gospels,* Boston, Monroe, 1836.
American Sunday School Union, *The Better Home,* Philadelphia, American Sunday School Union, 1836.
Arthur, T. S., *The Mother,* Boston, Colman, 1846.
———, *The Mother's Rule,* Philadelphia, Peck and Bliss, 1856.
Beecher, C., *The Evils Suffered By American Women and Children,* New York, Harper, 1846.
Bushnell, H., *Views of Christian Nurture,* Hartford, Hunt, 1847.
Child, L. M., *The Mother's Book*, 2nd ed., Boston, Carter, Hendee, and Babcock, 1831.
Cobb, L., *The Evil Tendencies of Corporal Punishment,* New York, Newman, 1847.
Dwight, T., *The Father's Book,* Springfield, Merriam, 1834.
Fuller, Margaret, *Woman in the Nineteenth Century,* New York, Sheldon, Lamport, 1855.
Gallaudet, T. H., *The Child's Book on the Soul,* Hartford, Cooke, 1831.
Graves, Mrs. A. J., *Woman in America,* New York, Harper, 1843.
Goodrich, S. G., *Fireside Education,* New York, Huntington, 1838.
Hale, Sarah J., *Woman's Record,* New York, Harper, 1853.
Humphrey, H., *Domestic Education,* Amherst, Adams, 1840.
Hyde, A., *Essay on the State of Infants,* New York, Davis, 1830.
Muzzey, A. B., *The Fireside,* Boston, Crosby, Nichols, 1856.
The Parent's Assistant, New Haven, 1849.
Sedgwick, C. M., *Home,* Boston, Monroe, 1835.

Sigourney, L., *Letters to Mothers,* Hartford, Hudson and Skinner, 1838.
Thayer, W., *Life at the Fireside,* Boston, Congregational Board of Publications, 1857.
Waterston, R. C., *Thoughts on Moral and Spiritual Culture,* Boston, Cocker and Ruggles, 1842.

PRIMARY PERIODICALS

Bibliotheca Sacra.
Christian Disciple and Theological Review.
Christian Examiner.
Literary and Theological Review.
Mercersberg Review.
Monthly Religious Magazine.
New Jerusalem.
Princeton Review.
Spirit of the Pilgrims.
Youth's Companion.

DAILY CARE

SECONDARY SOURCES

Kuhn, A. L., *The Mother's Role in Childhood Education,* New Haven, Yale University Press, 1947.
Mead, M. and Wolfenstein, M., *Childhood in Contemporary Culture,* Chicago, University of Chicago Press, 1955.
Shyrock, R. H., *The Development of Modern Medicine,* Philadelphia, University of Pennsylvania Press, 1936.
Wilson, E. A., *Hygienic Care and Management of the Child in the American Family Prior to 1860,* unpublished M.S. ms., Duke University, 1940.

PRIMARY SOURCES

Ackerley, G., *On the Management of Children in Sickness and Health,* New York, Bancroft and Holley, 1836.
Alcott, W. A., *The Laws of Health,* Boston, Jewett, 1857.

———, *The Mother's Medical Guide in Children's Diseases,* Boston, Marvin, 1842.

———, *The Young Housekeeper,* 4th ed., Boston, Light, 1839.

———, *The Young Mother,* Boston, Light and Stearns, 1836.

———, *The Young Wife,* Boston, Light, 1837.

Bakewell, Mrs. J., *The Mother's Practical Guide in the Early Training of Her Children,* New York, Lowe and Sandford, 1843.

Beecher, C., *Letters to the People on Sickness and Happiness,* New York, Harper, 1855.

———, *A Treatise on Domestic Economy,* revised, Boston, Webb, 1842.

Chavasse, P. H., *Advice to Mothers on the Management of Their Off-Spring,* New York, Appleton, 1844.

Child, L. M., *The American Frugal Housewife,* Boston, American Stationers, 1836.

———, *The Family Nurse,* Boston, Hendee, 1837.

Combe, A., *A Treatise on the Physiological and Moral Management of Infancy,* 2nd ed., Edinburgh, Machlachlan, Stewart, 1841.

Combe, G., *The Constitution of Man,* Boston, Ticknor, 1838.

DeBow, J. D. B., *Mortality Statistics of the Seventh Census of the United States,* 1850, Washington, Nicholson, 1855.

Dewees, W., *A Treatise on the Physical and Medical Treatment of Children, Philadelphia,* Carey and Lea, 1826.

Donne, A., *Mothers and Infants, Nurses and Nursing,* Boston, Phillips, Sampson, 1859.

Fern, F., *Fresh Leaves,* New York, Mason, 1857.

Fowler, O. S., *Education and Self Improvement,* 2nd ed., New York, Fowler, 1844.

———, *Love and Parentage Applied to the Improvement of Offspring,* New York, Fowler and Wells, 1844.

Hoare, L., *Hints for the Improvement of Early Education and Nursery Discipline,* Salem, Buffum, 1826.

Hough, L., *The Science of Man,* Boston, Marsh, 1849.

Ladies' Annual Register, Boston, Carter, 1839.

Leslie, E., *Miss Leslie's Complete Cookery,* 38th ed., Philadelphia, Baird, 1851.

Martineau, H., *Household Education,* Philadelphia, Lea and Blanchard, 1849.

Nichols, T. L., *Esoteric Anthropology,* New York, 1853.

Searle, T., *Companion to Seasons of Maternal Solicitude,* New York, Moore and Payne, 1834.

Warrington, J., *The Nurse's Guide,* 1839.

PRIMARY PERIODICALS

The Family Magazine.
Ladies' Magazine.
Mother's Assistant.
Parent's Magazine.

EDUCATION

SECONDARY SOURCES

Brown, S. W., *The Secularization of American Education,* New York, Teacher's College, 1912.

American Book Co., *A Brief Outline of the Evolution of the American Text Book,* New York, American Book Co., 1935.

Cremin, L. A., *The American Common School,* New York, Teacher's College, 1951.

Jackson, S., *America's Struggle for Free Schools,* Washington, American Council on Education, 1941.

Knight, E., *A Documentary History of Education in the South,* Chapel Hill, University of North Carolina Press, 1949-53.

McCuskey, D., *Bronson Alcott, Teacher,* New York, Macmillan, 1940.

Mead, M., *The School in American Culture,* Cambridge, Harvard University Press, 1951.

Miller, R. V., *Nationalism in Elementary School Books Used in United States History from 1776-1865,* unpublished PhD dissertation, Columbia University, 1952.

Monroe, P., *The Founding of the American Public School System,* New York, Macmillan, 1940.

Monroe, W. S., *The History of the Pestalozzian Movement in the United States,* Syracuse, Bardeen, 1907.

Mosier, R. D., *Making the American Mind,* New York, Kings Crown Press, 1947.

Johnson, C., *Old Time Schools and School Books,* New York, Macmillan, 1904.

PRIMARY SOURCES

Alcott, A. B., *Observations on the Principles and Methods of Infant Instruction,* Boston, Carter and Hendee, 1830.

Alcott, W. A., *A Word to Teachers,* Boston, Allen and Ticknor, 1833.
Association of Masters of the Boston Public Schools, *Remarks on the Seventh Annual Report of the Honorable Horace Mann,* Boston, Little and Brown, 1844.
Beecher, C., *Suggestions Respecting Improvements in Education,* Hartford, Packard and Butler, 1829.
Hall, J., *On the Education of Children,* New York, Haven, 1835.
Hall, S. R., *Lectures in School Keeping,* Boston, Ricardson, Lord, and Holbrook, 1829.
Mann, H., *Lectures on Education,* Boston, Ide, 1848.
Massachusetts Board of Education, *Annual Reports,* Boston, Dutton and Wentworth, 1838-1847.
Packard, F. A., *Thoughts on Popular Education,* Philadelphia, Waldie, 1836.
Page, D., *Theory and Practice of Teaching,* New York, Barnes, 1853.
Peabody, E., *Record of A School,* 2nd ed., Boston, Russell, Shattuck, 1836.
Saussure, Mme. N. de, *Progressive Education,* Boston, Ticknor, 1835.
Smith, M. H., *The Bible, The Rod and Religion in Common Schools,* Boston, Redding, 1847.

PRIMARY PERIODICALS

American Institute of Instruction.
American Annals of Education and Instruction.
American Journal of Education.
Common School Journal.

CHILDREN'S LITERATURE

PRIMARY SOURCES

Abbott, J., *Cousin Lucy at Play,* Boston, Mussey, 1842.
———, *Harper's Monthly Story Book,* New York, Harper, 1854.
———, *The Little Philosopher,* Boston, Carter and Hendee, 1830.
———, *The Rollo Code,* Boston, Crocker and Brewster, 1841.
———, *Rollo on the Atlantic,* New York, Anderson, 1858.
———, *The Young Christian,* New York, Harpers, 1851.
Abbott, J. S. C., *The School Boy,* Boston, Crocker and Brewster, 1839.
Aimwell, W., *Clinton,* Boston, Gould and Lincoln, 1858.

Alexander, Dr. A., *Advice to A Young Christian,* New York, American Tract Society, 1843.

American Sunday School Union, *Bosses and Their Boys,* Philadelphia, American Sunday School Union, 1853.

———, *Hymn Book,* Philadelphia, American Sunday School Union, 1832.

American Tract Society, *Memoir of Henry Obookiah,* New York, American Tract Society, circa 1835.

Association for the Improvement of Juvenile Books, *First Reading Lessons for Children,* Philadelphia, Grigg and Elliot, 1830.

Arthur, T. S., *Advice to Young Ladies,* Boston, Phillips, Sampson, 1850.

———, *Advice to Young Men,* Boston, Phillips, Sampson, 1853.

Aunt Fanny's Story Book, New York, 1852.

Barbauld, A. L., *Hymns in Prose for the Use of Children,* Philadelphia, Carson, 1824.

———, *Lessons for Children,* New York, Francis, circa 1856.

Belcher, J., *Facts for Boys,* New York, Lewes Colby, 1853.

Bentley, R., *Pictorial Primer,* New York, Cooledge, 1842.

Berquin, A., *The Children's Friend,* Boston, Marsh, Capen, Lyon, and Webb, 1840.

———, *An Introduction to the Study of Nature,* Philadelphia, Crissy, 1841.

———, *The Looking Glass for the Mind,* New York, Appleton, 1849.

Bonner, J., *A Child's History of the United States,* New York, Harper, 1855.

Child, L. M., *Flowers for Children,* New York, Francis, 1846.

———, *The Girl's Own Book,* New York, Austin, 1833.

———, *The Little Girl's Own Book,* Boston, Carter and Hendee, 1834.

The Child's Annual, Boston, Allen and Ticknor, 1834.

Cobb, Mrs. C. S., *Cobb's Toys,* Sandy Hill, New York, Griffen, Mabbett, 1836.

Cobb, L., *Juvenile Reader #2,* Philadelphia, Bonsal, 1832.

Craik, D. M. M., *John Halifax, Gentleman,* London, Hurst and Blackett, 1857.

Edgeworth, M., *The Fireside Story Book,* New York, Appleton, 1853.

Elliott, M., *The Bird's Nest,* New York, McLoughlin, 1856.

Goodrich, C. A., *A History of the United States of America,* Hartford, 1833.

Goodrich, S. G., *The Child's Botany,* Boston, 1833.

———, *The First Book of History,* Richardson, Lord and Holbrook, 1831.

———, *The Young American,* New York, Robinson, 1842.

Howitt, M., *The Child's Picture and Verse Book,* New York, Appleton, 1850.

Marryat, F., *Jacob Faithful,* New York, circa 1845.

Martineau, H., *Life in the Wilds,* Boston, Bowles, 1832.
"Parley, P.", *Juvenile Tales,* Philadelphia, Desilver and Thomas, 1833.
———, *The Parent's Present,* Boston, Light and Horton, W. Pierce, 1835.
Phelps, A., *Beauties of Nature,* Greenfield, Mass., 1846.
Sherwood, M. M., *The Youth's Casket,* Boston, Loring, 1827.
Sigourney, L. H., *The Boy's Book,* New York, Turner, Hughes, and Hayden, 1845.
———, *Tales and Essays for Children,* Hartford, Huntington, 1835.
———, *The Young Ladies' Offering,* Boston, Phillips and Sampson, 1848.
———, *The Young Man's Offering,* Boston, Phillips and Sampson, 1852.
Simmons, J., *The Juvenile Class Book,* Philadelphia, Pugh, 1832.
Smiles, S., *Self Help,* New York, Harper, 1860.
Smith, Rev. D., *Natural History for Sunday Schools,* New York, Mason and Lane, 1838.
Taylor, Mrs. J., *Primary Lessons in Physiology for Children,* New York, Cooledge, 1848.
Thayer, William M., *The Bobbin Boy,* Boston, Tulton, 1860.
The True Mother Goose, New York, Francis, 1842.
Truman, William T., *Two Peacocks,* Cincinnati, 1844.

1860-1900

GENERAL SECONDARY WORKS

Dewey, J., *The Influence of Darwin on Philosophy,* New York, Holt, 1910.
Eliot, T. S., *Selected Essays,* London, Faber and Faber, 1949.
Goldman, E., *Rendezvous With Destiny,* New York, Knopf, 1953.
Gruenberg, S. M., *Our Children Today,* New York, Viking, 1951.
Herberg, W., *Protestant, Catholic, Jew,* New York, Doubleday, 1955.
Harmon, F. B., *The Social Philosophy of the St. Louis Hegelians,* New York, Columbia University Press, 1943.
Hofstadter, R., *Social Darwinism in American Thought,* Philadelphia, University of Pennsylvania Press, 1944.
Key, E., *The Century of the Child,* New York, Putnams, 1909.
Loetscher, L. A., *The Broadening Church,* Philadelphia, University of Pennsylvania Press, 1954.
Niebuhr, R., *Faith and History,* London, Nisbet, 1949.
Schneider, H. W., *Religion in Twentieth Century America,* Cambridge, Harvard University Press, 1952.

GENERAL PRIMARY PERIODICALS

American Catholic Quarterly.
American Quarterly Review.
The Arena.
The Book Buyer.
The Chautauquan.
The Dial.
The Forum.
Gunton's Magazine.
International Monthly.
Ladies' Home Journal.
Land We Love.
Living Age.
Monthly Review.
Munsey's Magazine.
The Nation.
Nature.
The New England Magazine.
The New Englander.
New World.
Open Court.
Popular Science Monthly.
Portfolio.
Review of Reviews.
Science.
World's Work.

CHILDREN'S LITERATURE

SECONDARY SOURCES

Cheney, E. D., *Louisa May Alcott, Her Life, Letters and Journals,* Boston, Roberts, 1890.

Field, Mrs. E. M., *The Child and His Book,* London, Gardner and Daron, 1895.

Hardy, G. E. P., *Literature for Children,* New York, Scribners, 1892.

Johannsen, A., *The House of Beadle and Adams,* Norman, Oklahoma, University of Oklahoma Press, 1952.

Linengood, W. W., *Our Heritage,* Speech to agents of American Book Co., January 4, 1947, Cincinnati, Ohio.

Mayes, H. R., *Alger, A Biography Without A Hero,* New York, Macy Masius, 1928.

Moore, A. C., *Roads to Childhood,* New York, Doran, 1920.

———, *The Three Owls,* Vol. 1, New York, Macmillan, 1925.

Newell, W. W., *Games and Songs of American Children,* New York, Harper, 1884.

Pearson, E. L., *Dime Novels,* Boston, Little Brown, 1929.

Scudder, H. E., *Childhood in Literature and Art,* New York, Houghton, Mifflin, 1894.

Welsh, C., *The Right Reading for Children,* Boston, Heath, 1902.

Wiltse, S. E., *The Place of the Story in Early Education,* Boston, Ginn, 1892.

PRIMARY SOURCES

Alcott, L. M., *Little Women,* Boston, Roberts, 1868.

Alger, H., *Bound to Rise,* Philadelphia, Loring, 1873.

Aldrich, T. B., *The Story of a Bad Boy,* Boston, Fields and Osgood, 1870.

Bannerman, H., *The Story of Little Black Sambo,* New York, Stokes, 1900.

Barrie, J. M., *Peter Pan and Wendy,* New York, Scribners, 1911.

Boy Scouts of America, *Handbook,* 1911.

Brooks, E. S., *The Century Book of Famous Americans,* New York, Century, 1896.

Burgess, G., *Goops and How to Be Them,* New York, Stokes, 1900.

Burnett, F. H., *Little Lord Fauntleroy,* New York, Scribners, 1886.

Collodi, C., *Pinocchio,* Boston, Ginn, 1904.

Cox, P., *The Brownies, Their Book,* New York, Century, 1887.

Diaz, A. M., *The William Henry Letters,* Chicago, Interstate Publishing Co., 1870.

Dodge, M. M., *Hans Brinker,* New York, O'Kane, 1866.

Eggleston, E., *A History of the United States and Its People for the Use of Schools,* New York, American Book Co., 1888.

———, *The Hoosier Schoolboy,* New York, Scribners, 1883.

Field, E., *Love Songs of Childhood,* New York, Scribners, 1894.

———, *With Trumpet and Drum,* New York, Scribners, 1892.

Finley, M., *Elsie Dinsmore,* New York, Dodd, Mead, 1867.

Hale, L. P., *The Peterkin Papers,* New York, Houghton Mifflin, 1891.

Dewey, J. M., *How to Teach Manners,* New York, Kellogg, 1888.

Hale, E. E., ed., *The Age of Chivalry,* Boston, Tilton, 1884.

———, *The Age of Fable,* Boston, Tilton, 1881.

Howells, W. D., *Boy Life,* New York, Harper, 1909.
Kipling, R., *The Jungle Book,* New York, Century, 1899.
———, *The Second Jungle Book,* New York, Century, 1899.
Lang, A., *The Blue Fairy Book,* New York, Longmans Green, 1890.
Larcom, L., *A New England Girlhood,* Boston, Houghton Mifflin, 1889.
Macdonald, G., *Robert Falconer,* Boston, Loring, 1876.
"Pansy" (Mrs. G. R. Alden), *A Dozen of Them,* Boston, Lathrop, 1888.
Potter, B., *Peter Rabbitt,* Philadelphia, Altemus, 1904.
Pyle, H., *Men of Iron,* New York, Harper, 1891.
———, *Some Merry Adventures of Robin Hood,* New York, Scribners, 1883.
———, *The Story of King Arthur and His Knights,* New York, Scribners, 1903.
———, *The Wonder Clock,* New York, Harper, 1887.
Richards, L. E., *Five Minute Stories,* Boston, Page, 1895.
———, *Melody,* Boston, Estes and Lauriat, 1896.
Riley, J. W., *The Book of Joyous Children,* New York, Scribners, 1902.
Scudder, H. E., *Children's Book,* Boston, Houghton Mifflin, 1900.
Sewell, A., *Black Beauty,* Philadelphia, Altemus, 1897.
Sidney, M., *Five Little Peppers and How They Grew,* Boston, Lothrop, 1881.
Spyri, J., *Heidi,* New York, Burt, 1901.
Stevenson, R. L., *A Child's Garden of Verses,* New York, Scribners, 1885.
———, *Treasure Island,* Boston, Roberts, 1892.
Stockton, F. R., *The Clocks of Rondaine,* New York, Scribners, 1892.
Thayer, W. M., *The Poor Boy and Merchant Prince,* Boston, Gould and Lincoln, 1857.
Twain, M., *Huckleberry Finn,* New York, Webster, 1885.
———, *The Prince and the Pauper,* Boston, Isgood, 1882.
Wallace, L., *Ben Hur,* New York, Harper, 1880.
Wiggin, K. D., *The Bird's Christmas Carol,* Boston, Houghton Mifflin, 1893.
———, *The Posy Ring,* New York, McClure Phillips, 1903.
———, *Rebecca of Sunnyboook Farm,* Boston, Houghton Mifflin, 1903.

PRIMARY PERIODICALS

St. Nicholas.
Our Young Folks.
The Youth's Companion.

RELIGIOUS TRAINING

PRIMARY SOURCES

Babcock, B. S., *The Children's Daily Service,* New York, Whittaker, 1908.
Brown, M. C., *Sunday School Movements in America,* New York, Revell, 1901.
Richards, Rev. C. H., *The Spiritual Nurture of Children,* National Council of Congregational Churches, 1901.
Religious Education Association, *Proceedings.*

PRIMARY PERIODICALS

Berean Intermediate Lesson Quarterly.
The Christian Advocate.
The Christian Intelligencer.
The Christian Observor.
The Christian Review.
Evangelical Review.
The Independent.
The Intermediate Quarterly.
The Junior Quarterly.
Lutheran Church Review.
Methodist Quarterly.
Methodist Review.
Outlook.
Reformed Church Review.
The Senior Quarterly.
Sunday School Times.

CHILD DEVELOPMENT AND CARE

PRIMARY SOURCES

Abbott, J., *Gentle Measures in the Management and Training of the Young,* New York, Harper, 1871.
Adler, F., *The Moral Instruction of Children,* New York, Appleton, 1895.

Birney, Mrs. T., *Childhood,* New York, Stokes, 1904.

Blackwell, Dr. E., *Counsel to Parents on the Moral Education of Their Children in Relation to Sex,* 7th ed., revised, London, Hatchard, 1884.

Briggs, F. H., *Boys As They Are Made and How To Remake Them,* Syracuse, Bardeen, 1894.

Chamberlain, A. F., *The Child, A Study in the Evolution of Man,* London, Scott, 1900.

Compayre, G., *The Development of the Child in Later Infancy,* New York, Appleton, 1902.

———, *The Intellectual and Moral Development of the Child,* New York, Appleton, 1896.

Drummond, W. B., *The Child, His Nature and Nurture,* London, Dent, 1901.

Fletcher, H., *That Last Waif,* Chicago, Kindergarten Literature Co., 1898.

Fowler, J. A., *A Manual of Mental Science,* New York, Fowler Wells, 1897.

Gilman, C. P. S., *Concerning Children,* Boston, Small Maynard, 1900.

———, *The Home, Its Work and Influence,* New York, McClure Phillips, 1903.

Girardey, F., *Popular Instructions to Parents on the Bringing Up of Children,* New York, Benziger Bros., 1897.

Hall, G. S., *Adolescence,* 2 vols., New York, Appleton, 1904.

Hogan, L., *How to Feed Children,* 3rd ed., Philadelphia, Lippincott, 1899.

Holt, L. E., *The Care and Feeding of Children,* 2nd ed., New York, Appleton, 1900; Revised and Enlarged edition, Garden City, New York, Garden City Publishing Co., 1943.

Hubbell, G. A., *Up Through Childhood,* New York, Putnam's, 1904.

King, H. C., *The Appeal of the Child,* Oberlin, Ohio, Harkness, 1900.

Kirkpatrick, E. A., *Fundamentals of Child Study,* New York, Macmillan, 1904.

Logan, Mrs. J. A., *The Home Manual,* Boston, Thayer, 1889.

Malleson, Mrs. F., *Notes on the Early Training of Youth,* Boston, Heath, 1892.

Major, D. R., *First Steps in Mental Growth,* New York, Macmillan, 1906.

Merrill, L., *Winning the Boy,* New York, Revell, 1908.

Meynell, A., *The Children,* New York, Lane, 1897.

Moore, K. C., *The Mental Development of a Child,* New York, Macmillan, 1896.

National Congress of Mothers, *Proceedings of the First Annual Conference,* Washington, 1897.

Oppenheim, N., *The Development of the Child,* New York, Macmillan, 1899.

Perez, B., *The First Three Years of Childhood,* Syracuse, N. Y., Bardeen, 1894.

Proudfoot, A. H., *A Mother's Ideals,* Chicago, Flanagan, 1897.

Poulsson, E., *Love and Law in Child Training,* Springfield, Mass., Bradley, 1899.

Riis, J., *The Children of the Poor,* New York, Scribners, 1892.

Rowe, S. H., *The Physical Nature of the Child,* New York, Macmillan, 1899.

Scovil, E. R., *The Care of the Child,* Philadelphia, Altemus, 1895.

Shearer, W. J., *The Management and Training of Children,* New York, Richardson Smith, 1904.

Shinn, M. W., *The Biography of a Baby,* New York, Houghton Mifflin, 1900.

Smith, N. A., *The Children of the Future,* Boston, Houghton Mifflin, 1898.

Spargo, J., *The Bitter Cry of the Children,* New York, Macmillan, 1906.

Stelzle, C., *Boys of the Street, How to Win Them,* New York, Revell, 1904.

Sully, J., *Studies of Childhood,* New York, Appleton, 1896.

Thorndike, E. L., *Notes on Child Study,* New York, Macmillan, 1903.

Trumbull, H. C., *Hints on Child Training,* New York, Scribners, 1898.

Warner, F., *The Study of Children,* New York, Macmillan, 1897.

Wiggin, K. D., *Children's Rights,* Boston, Houghton Mifflin, 1892.

Wiggin, K. D. and Smith, N. A., *The Republic of Childhood,* 3 vols., Boston, Houghton Mifflin, 1896.

Willcox, S. M., *The Legal Rights of Children,* Washington, Government Printing Office, 1880.

Winterburn, F. H., *Nursery Ethics,* New York, Merriam, 1895.

PRIMARY PERIODICALS

American Childhood.

The American Mother.

The Child Study Monthly.

Childhood.

Cosmopolitan.

The Delineator.

Ladies' Home Journal.

McCall's Magazine.

The Mother's Journal.

The Woman's Journal.

SCHOOL LIFE AND EDUCATION

PRIMARY SOURCES

Barnes, E., *Studies in Education,* 2 vols., Stanford University and Philadelphia, 1896-97 and 1902.

Claparede, E., *Experimental Pedagogy,* New York, Longmans Green, 1911.

Dewey, J., *The Child and the Curriculum,* Chicago, University of Chicago Press, 1902.

———, *The Educational Situation,* Chicago, University of Chicago Press, 1902.

———, *The School and Society,* Chicago, University of Chicago Press, 1899.

Eliot, C. W., *Educational Reform,* New York, Century, 1898.

Hall, J., *Hints on Early Education,* New York, Funk and Wagnalls, 1887.

Hanus, P., *Educational Aims and Educational Values,* New York, Macmillan, 1899.

Herbart, J. F., *Outlines of Educational Doctrine,* New York, Macmillan, 1901.

James, W., *Talks to Teachers,* New York, Holt, 1899.

Larned, J. N., *Primer of Right and Wrong; for Young People in Schools and Families,* Boston, Houghton Mifflin, 1902.

Nelson, M. F., *Index to the Publications of the N.E.A., 1857-1906,* National Education Association, 1907.

Parker, F. W., *Talks on Pedagogics,* New York, Kellogg, 1894.

Pestalozzi, J. H., *Letters on Early Education,* Boston, Heath, 1898.

Preyer, W., *Mental Development in Children,* New York, Appleton, 1894.

Report of the U. S. Commissioner of Education 1870-1910, Washington, G.P.O., 1910.

Spencer, H., *Education, Intellectual, Moral, and Physical,* New York, Appleton, 1878.

PRIMARY PERIODICALS

Colorado School Journal.

Columbia University Contributions to Philosophy, Psychology, and Education.

Education.

The Educational Review.

Elementary School Journal.

The Elementary School Teacher.
Journal of Education.
Kindergarten News.
Michigan School Moderator.
National Parent Teachers Magazine.
New England Journal of Education.
The Normal Instructor.
Pedagogical Seminary.
The Progressive Teacher.
The School Review.
Virginia School Journal.

Index

Bernard Wishy is Director of Medical and Administrative Systems at the Roosevelt Hospital in New York and a member of the Department of History at Brooklyn College. He is the author of *The Western World in the Twentieth Century* and *A History of the American People* (with H. J. Carman and H. C. Syrett), editor of *Prefaces to Liberty: Selected Writings of John Stuart Mill* and other works, and a contributor of articles and reviews to such periodicals as *Political Science Quarterly, The American Historical Review, Commentary, The New Leader,* and *The Journal of Higher Education.*